Jürgen Beyerer, Marco Huber (Eds.)

AF238956

Proceedings of the 2009 Joint Workshop of Fraunhofer IOSB and Institute for Anthropomatics, Vision and Fusion Laboratory

Held in La Bresse, France, on August 02–06, 2009

Karlsruher Schriften zur Anthropomatik
Band 4
Herausgeber: Prof. Dr.-Ing. Jürgen Beyerer

Lehrstuhl für Interaktive Echtzeitsysteme
Karlsruher Institut für Technologie

Fraunhofer-Institut für Optronik, Systemtechnik und
Bildauswertung IOSB Karlsruhe

Proceedings of the 2009 Joint Workshop of Fraunhofer IOSB and Institute for Anthropomatics, Vision and Fusion Laboratory

Held in La Bresse, France, on August 02–06, 2009

Edited by
Jürgen Beyerer
Marco Huber

Impressum

Karlsruher Institut für Technologie (KIT)
KIT Scientific Publishing
Straße am Forum 2
D-76131 Karlsruhe
www.uvka.de

KIT – Universität des Landes Baden-Württemberg und nationales
Forschungszentrum in der Helmholtz-Gemeinschaft

KIT Scientific Publishing 2010
Print on Demand

ISSN: 1863-6489
ISBN: 978-3-86644-469-0

Preface

The joint workshop of the Fraunhofer Institute of Optronics, System Technologies and Image Exploitation IOSB and the Vision and Fusion Laboratory (Institute for Anthropomatics, Karlsruhe Institute of Technology (KIT)), is organized annually since 2005 with the aim to report on the latest research and development findings of the doctoral students of both institutions. The workshop provides a forum for scientific discussion and debate on the presented results. Furthermore, the personal exchange of the doctoral students affords the opportunity of identifying new perspectives, future research directions, and cooperations between the students. The 2009 joint workshop was held in La Bresse, France, on August 02–06. This book provides a collection of technical reports on the research results presented on the 2009 workshop.

The editors would like to thank all the organizers of the workshop for their efforts that led in a pleasant and rewarding stay in France. The editors would also like to thank the doctoral students for writing and reviewing the technical reports and for responding to comments and suggestions of their colleagues. It is hoped that this collection of technical reports forms a valuable addition to the scientific and developmental knowledge in the main research fields of the Vision and Fusion Laboratory and Fraunhofer IOSB, which are image processing, pattern recognition, system technologies, and information fusion.

Prof. Dr.-Ing. Jürgen Beyerer
Dr.-Ing. Marco Huber

Contents

Convex Optimization Approaches to Long-Term Sensor Scheduling

Marco F. Huber

Variable Image Acquisition and Processing Research Group (VBV)
Fraunhofer Institute of Optronics, System Technologies and
Image Exploitation IOSB
marco.huber@ieee.org

Technical Report IES-2009-01

Abstract: The optimization over long time horizons in order to consider long-term effects is of paramount importance for effective sensor scheduling in multi-sensor systems like sensor arrays or sensor networks. Determining the optimal sensor schedule, however, is equivalent to solving a binary integer program, which is computationally demanding for long time horizons and many sensors. For linear Gaussian models, two efficient long-term sensor scheduling approaches are proposed in this report. The first approach determines approximate but close to optimal sensor schedules via convex optimization. The second approach combines convex optimization with a branch-and-bound search for efficiently determining the optimal sensor schedule. Both approaches are compared by means of numerical simulations.

Notation

$x, \underline{x}$	deterministic variable/vector
$\boldsymbol{x}, \underline{\boldsymbol{x}}$	random variable/vector
$\hat{x}, \underline{\hat{x}}$	mean value of random variable/vector
$\underline{x}_k, \underline{x}_{1:k}$	vector at time step k / sequence of vectors from time step 1 to k
$\mathcal{A}$	general set
$\mathbf{A}$	general matrix
$|\mathbf{A}|$	matrix determinant
$\mathcal{N}(\underline{x}; \underline{\hat{x}}, \mathbf{C})$	multivariate Gaussian density with mean $\underline{\hat{x}}$ and covariance $\mathbf{C}$
$\underline{u}_{1:k}, \underline{u}_{1:k}^*$	sensor schedule for time step 1 to k / optimal sensor schedule
$\underline{u}_{1:k}^{\mathrm{l}}, \underline{u}_{1:k}^{\mathrm{u}}$	sensor schedule obtained via:
	convex optimization (real-valued, provides lower bound) /
	conversion (binary-valued, provides upper bound)
$J(\underline{u}_{1:k})$	objective function value of sensor schedule $\underline{u}_{1:k}$

1 Introduction

Recent developments in wireless communication and sensor technology facilitate building up and deploying sensor systems for a smart and persistent surveillance. For instance, sensor networks consisting of numerous inexpensive sensor nodes are a popular subject in research and practice for monitoring physical phenomena including, e.g., temperature and humidity distributions, biochemical concentrations, or vibrations in buildings [ASSC02]. For many of such sensor systems it is necessary to balance between maximizing the information gain and minimizing the consumption of limited resources like energy, computing power, or communication bandwidth. *Sensor scheduling*, which is also referred to as sensor selection, allows trading off these conflicting goals and forms the basis for an efficient and intelligent processing of the sensor data.

A sensor schedule specifies a time sequence of sensors to be allocated for performing future measurements. The main objective is to allocate the sensors in a most informative way, which requires making decisions involving multiple time steps ahead. In this report, sensor scheduling for linear Gaussian dynamics and sensor models is studied, where one out of a set of sensors is selected at each time instant for performing a measurement. For such models, one of the first works on long-term sensor scheduling can be found in [MPD67]. It is shown that a separation principle holds, i.e., the sensor schedule can be determined independent of the control of the observed system and independent of the measurement values. The optimal sensor schedule then results from off-line traversing a decision tree consisting of all possible sensor sequences. In order to avoid enumerating all schedules in a brute force fashion, which is of exponential complexity, optimal or suboptimal pruning techniques are employed. Optimal techniques yield the optimal sensor schedule by all means without the need of examining all schedules (see for example [LI99, HH08]). Suboptimal methods as those in [GCHM04] allow more significant savings in computational demand by abdicating the guarantee of conserving the optimal schedule. Greedy, or myopic, scheduling algorithms represent an extreme case of suboptimal search, where a series of one-step ahead solutions is calculated [Osh94, QKS07].

Alternatively to traversing the decision tree, which corresponds to solving a binary integer program, convex optimization approaches have recently been proposed for solving sensor selection problems, i.e., problems of selecting the best n-element subset from a set of sensors (see [CMPS07, JB09]). These approaches can significantly improve the efficiency of determining informative sensor schedules, but they are so far not appropriate for *optimal long-term* sensor scheduling for *arbitrary* linear Gaussian dynamics and sensor models.

Both long-term sensor scheduling approaches proposed in this report overcome these restrictions. At first a general sensor scheduling problem for linear Gaussian models is formulated in Section 2. In Section 3 it is shown that this sensor scheduling problem is a convex optimization problem when employing continuous relaxation of the decision variables. The first approach directly solves the resulting convex program, which leads to suboptimal but valuable sensor schedules without demanding many computations and memory. In order to provide the optimal sensor sequence, the second approach described in Section 4 utilizes branch-and-bound search for traversing a decision tree. To exclude complete subtrees containing suboptimal sensor schedules as early as possible, the solution of the convex optimization is used for calculating tight lower and upper bounds to the subtrees' values. The performance of the proposed approaches is demonstrated by means of simulations in Section 5, while in Section 4 conclusions and an outlook to future work are given.

2   Problem Formulation

In this report, the sensor scheduling problem for discrete-time linear Gaussian models is examined. The dynamics model of the observed system is given by

$$\underline{x}_{k+1} = \mathbf{A}_k \cdot \underline{x}_k + \underline{w}_k . \tag{2.1}$$

A finite set $\mathcal{S}$ of sensors is considered for performing measurements, where measurement $\underline{z}_k^i$ from sensor $i \in \mathcal{S} = \{1, \ldots, S\}$ is related to the system state $\underline{x}_k$ via the measurement model

$$\underline{z}_k^i = \mathbf{H}_k^i \cdot \underline{x}_k + \underline{v}_k^i .$$

Both $\mathbf{A}_k$ and $\mathbf{H}_k^i$ are time-variant matrices. The noise terms $\underline{w}_k$ and $\underline{v}_k^i$ are zero-mean white Gaussian with covariance matrices $\mathbf{C}_k^w$ and $\mathbf{C}_k^{v,i}$, respectively. A measurement value $\hat{\underline{z}}_k^i$ of sensor $i \in \mathcal{S}$ is a realization of $\underline{z}_k^i$. The initial system state $\underline{x}_0 \sim \mathcal{N}(\underline{x}_0; \hat{\underline{x}}_0, \mathbf{C}_0^x)$ at time step $k = 0$ is Gaussian with mean $\hat{\underline{x}}_0$ and covariance $\mathbf{C}_0^x$.

The aim of long-term sensor scheduling is to minimize the covariance $\mathbf{C}_k^x$ of the state $\underline{x}_k$ and thus, to minimize the uncertainty of the state estimate under the consideration of the future behavior of the observed dynamical system and long-term sensing costs. For this purpose, the optimal sensor schedule $\underline{u}_{1:N}^* = \left[(\underline{u}_1^*)^{\mathrm{T}}, \ldots, (\underline{u}_N^*)^{\mathrm{T}}\right]^{\mathrm{T}} \in \{0, 1\}^{S \cdot N}$ is determined over a finite N-step time horizon. Here, $\underline{u}_k^* = \left[u_{k,1}, \ldots, u_{k,S}\right]^{\mathrm{T}}$ encodes the index of the sensor scheduled for measurement at time step k, i.e., if sensor i is scheduled at time step k then $u_{k,i} = 1$ and $u_{k,j} = 0$ for all $j \neq i$.

For determining the optimal sensor schedule $\underline{u}^*_{1:N}$, the constraint optimization problem

$$\underline{u}^*_{1:N} = \arg \min_{\underline{u}_{1:N}} J(\underline{u}_{1:N}) \tag{2.2}$$

$$\text{subject to} \sum_{k=1}^{N} \underline{c}^T_k \cdot \underline{u}_k \le C , \tag{2.3}$$

$$\underline{1}^T \cdot \underline{u}_k = 1 , \quad k = 1, \dots, N , \tag{2.4}$$

$$\underline{u}_k \in \{0,1\}^S , \quad k = 1, \dots, N \tag{2.5}$$

is formulated, where $J(\underline{u}_{1:N}) = \sum_{k=1}^{N} g_k(\underline{u}_{1:k})$ is the cumulative *objective function* to be minimized. In (2.3), $\underline{c}_k = [c_{k,1}, \dots, c_{k,S}]^T$ contains the sensor costs $c_{k,i}$, e.g., energy or communication, of selecting sensor i at time step k. With this constraint it is guaranteed that a feasible sensor schedule does not exceed a maximum cost C. The scalar functions $g_k(\,\cdot\,)$, i.e., the summands of $J(\underline{u}_{1:N})$, quantify the uncertainty subsumed in $\mathbf{C}^x_k(\underline{u}_{1:k})$. They can be

- the trace operator $\text{trace}(\mathbf{C}^x_k(\underline{u}_{1:k}))$, whose minimization corresponds (graphically spoken) to minimizing the perimeter of the rectangular region enclosing the covariance ellipsoid,

- the root-determinant $\sqrt{|\mathbf{C}^x_k(\underline{u}_{1:k})|}$, which leads to the minimization of the volume of the covariance ellipsoid, or

- the maximum eigenvalue $\lambda_{\max}(\mathbf{C}^x_k(\underline{u}_{1:k}))$, whose minimization corresponds to minimizing the largest principal axis of the covariance ellipsoid.

The covariance itself is given by the information form of the Kalman filter covariance recursion (see for example [KSH00])

$$\mathbf{C}^x_k(\underline{u}_{1:k}) = \left(\left(\mathbf{A}_{k-1} \cdot \mathbf{C}^x_{k-1}(\underline{u}_{1:k-1}) \cdot \mathbf{A}^T_{k-1} + \mathbf{C}^w_{k-1} \right)^{-1} \right.$$
$$\left. + \sum_{i=1}^{S} u_{k,i} \cdot \left(\mathbf{H}^i_k\right)^T \cdot \left(\mathbf{C}^{v,i}_k\right)^{-1} \cdot \mathbf{H}^i_k \right)^{-1} , \tag{2.6}$$

commencing from $\mathbf{C}^x_0$.

The constraints in (2.4) and (2.5) together ensure that one sensor per time step is selected for measurement. This restriction is made for brevity and clarity reasons. The extension to selecting multiple sensors per time step can be achieved by replacing the right hand side of (2.4) with the desired number of sensors. Alternatively, by modifying (2.2) and (2.3), is is also possible to minimize the sensor costs regarding a maximum allowed value of $J(\,\cdot\,)$, i.e., a maximum allowed uncertainty.

3 Convex Relaxation

The optimization problem in (2.2)–(2.5) is a so-called *binary integer program*. Problems of this type are known to be NP-hard (see [Kar72]) and thus, obtaining the optimal solution for large N and/or large S is computationally prohibitive in general. However, by replacing the binary non-convex constraints in (2.5) with the linear constraints $\underline{u}_k \in [0,1]^S$ for $k = 1, \ldots, N$, a convex relaxation of the original problem (2.2) is obtained. To see this, it is important to note that the constraints (2.3) and (2.4) are already convex. Furthermore, as shown in the following theorem, the sum to be minimized in (2.2) is now convex as well.

Theorem 1 (Convex Objective Function) *The objective function $J(\underline{u}_{1:N})$ in (2.2) is convex in terms of $\underline{u}_{1:N} \in [0,1]^{S \cdot N}$.*

PROOF. To prove the convexity of $g_k(\underline{u}_{1:k})$ and thus of $J(\underline{u}_{1:N})$, it must be shown that (see for example [BV08])

$$g_k(\lambda \cdot \underline{u}_{1:k} + (1-\lambda) \cdot \tilde{\underline{u}}_{1:k}) \leq \lambda \cdot g_k(\underline{u}_{1:k}) + (1-\lambda) \cdot g_k(\tilde{\underline{u}}_{1:k}) \qquad (3.1)$$

for $k = 1, \ldots, N$, $\forall \underline{u}_{1:k}, \tilde{\underline{u}}_{1:k} \in [0,1]^{k \cdot S}$, and $\forall \lambda \in [0,1]$.

At first, it is proven by induction that the covariance recursion (2.6) is a convex function of $\underline{u}_{1:k}$. The induction starts with $\mathbf{C}_1^x(\underline{u}_1)$. Defining $\mathbf{M}_k^i := \left(\mathbf{H}_k^i\right)^{\mathrm{T}} \cdot \left(\mathbf{C}_k^{v,i}\right)^{-1} \cdot \mathbf{H}_k^i$ and $\mathbf{P}_1(\underline{u}_1) := \left(\mathbf{A}_0 \cdot \mathbf{C}_0^x \cdot \mathbf{A}_0^{\mathrm{T}} + \mathbf{C}_0^w\right)^{-1} + \sum_i u_{1,i} \cdot \mathbf{M}_1^i$ and utilizing the results in [Kra36] on matrix convex functions, it follows from the matrix convexity property of the matrix inversion that

$$\mathbf{C}_1^x(\lambda \cdot \underline{u}_1 + (1-\lambda) \cdot \tilde{\underline{u}}_1) = (\lambda \cdot \mathbf{P}_1(\underline{u}_1) + (1-\lambda) \cdot \mathbf{P}_1(\tilde{\underline{u}}_1))^{-1}$$
$$\leq \lambda \cdot \underbrace{\mathbf{P}_1^{-1}(\underline{u}_1)}_{=\mathbf{C}_1^x(\underline{u}_1)} + (1-\lambda) \cdot \underbrace{\mathbf{P}_1^{-1}(\tilde{\underline{u}}_1)}_{=\mathbf{C}_1^x(\tilde{\underline{u}}_1)}$$

$\forall \underline{u}_1, \tilde{\underline{u}}_1 \in [0,1]^S$ and $\forall \lambda \in [0,1]$. Defining the predicted covariance $\mathbf{C}_k^p(\underline{u}_{1:k-1}) := \mathbf{A}_{k-1} \cdot \mathbf{C}_{k-1}^x(\underline{u}_{1:k-1}) \cdot \mathbf{A}_{k-1}^{\mathrm{T}} + \mathbf{C}_{k-1}^w$, it generally holds that

$$\mathbf{C}_k^x(\lambda \cdot \underline{u}_{1:k} + (1-\lambda) \cdot \tilde{\underline{u}}_{1:k})$$

$$= \left(\mathbf{C}_k^p(\lambda \cdot \underline{u}_{1:k-1} + (1-\lambda) \cdot \tilde{\underline{u}}_{1:k-1})^{-1} + \sum_{i=1}^{S} (\lambda \cdot u_{k,i} + (1-\lambda) \cdot \tilde{u}_{k,i}) \cdot \mathbf{M}_k^i\right)^{-1}$$

$$\overset{(a)}{\leq} \left(\lambda \cdot \left(\mathbf{C}_k^p(\underline{u}_{1:k-1})^{-1} + \sum_{i=1}^{S} u_{k,i} \cdot \mathbf{M}_k^i\right)\right.$$
$$\left. + (1-\lambda) \cdot \left(\mathbf{C}_k^p(\tilde{\underline{u}}_{1:k-1})^{-1} + \sum_{i=1}^{S} \tilde{u}_{k,i} \cdot \mathbf{M}_k^i\right)\right)^{-1}$$

$$\overset{(b)}{\leq} \lambda \cdot \mathbf{C}_k^x(\underline{u}_{1:k}) + (1-\lambda) \cdot \mathbf{C}_k^x(\tilde{\underline{u}}_{1:k}) \tag{3.2}$$

for $k = 2, \dots, N$, $\forall \underline{u}_{1:k}, \tilde{\underline{u}}_{1:k} \in [0,1]^{k \cdot S}$, and $\forall \lambda \in [0,1]$. Here, (a) results from the induction hypothesis that $\mathbf{C}_{k-1}^x(\underline{u}_{1:k-1})$ is convex in $\underline{u}_{1:k-1}$, from the convexity of the matrix inversion, and from rearranging terms; (b) is the result of a repeated application of the convexity of the matrix inversion.

As the trace is a linear matrix function and the root-determinant as well as the maximum eigenvalue are convex matrix functions (see for example [BV08]), the inequality in (3.1) holds if these three functions are applied on (3.2). Thus, $g_k(\underline{u}_{1:k})$ is convex and the nonnegative sum $J(\underline{u}_{1:N}) = \sum_{k=1}^{N} g_k(\underline{u}_{1:k})$ is convex as well, which concludes the proof. $\qquad\square$

It is important to note that the sensor scheduling problem formulated by (2.2)–(2.5) and its convex relaxation proven in Theorem 1 extends existing convex approaches [CMPS07, JB09] in many ways. Instead of one-step time horizons, i.e., myopic/greedy scheduling, arbitrarily long time horizons are possible. Furthermore, the dynamics model in (2.1) need not to be restricted to regular system matrices $\mathbf{A}_k$ and to system noise covariances $\mathbf{C}_k^w = \mathbf{0}$. Especially the latter is of paramount importance for realistic sensor scheduling problems. Finally, there is no restriction to a specific scalar function $g_k(\cdot)$ as in [CMPS07]. Instead, various functions for evaluating the quality of a sensor schedule are considered here.

3.1   Solving the Relaxed Problem

The computational complexity of optimally solving the original binary integer program is in $\mathcal{O}(S^N)$. Various methods are available for efficiently solving the convex relaxation of the sensor scheduling problem, e.g., interior-point methods [BV08]. These methods typically require only a few tens of iterations for calculating the optimal solution even for large problem sizes, e.g., length of time horizon and number of sensors beyond 10. The computational complexity of one iteration is polynomial in the number of variables in $\underline{u}_{1:N}$, which is $S \cdot N$. The derivation of the gradient of $J(\underline{u}_{1:N})$ necessary for interior-point methods is shown in Appendix A.

The solution $\underline{u}_{1:N}^1$ of the convex problem, however, only approximates the optimal solution $\underline{u}_{1:n}^*$ of the original scheduling problem. More specifically, $\underline{u}_{1:N}^1$ is no longer binary and the objective function value $J^1 := J(\underline{u}_{1:N}^1)$ is a *lower bound* of the optimal value $J(\underline{u}_{1:N}^*)$. The latter finding follows directly from the convexity of the relaxed problem and from the fact that the relaxed solution set $[0,1]^{S \cdot N}$ contains the binary set of the original problem.

3.2 Conversion into Binary Solution

In order to allow selecting sensors for measurement, $\underline{u}^l_{1:N}$ has to be converted into a binary vector by employing an appropriate conversion or rounding method. The value $J^u := J(\underline{u}^u_{1:N})$ of the resulting (binary) sensor schedule $\underline{u}^u_{1:N}$ has to be as close as possible to the optimal one in order to provide informative sensor measurements. In the following, two appropriate conversion methods are introduced. Independent of the chosen conversion method, the value J^u of the converted sensor schedule provides an *upper bound* to the optimal value $J(\underline{u}^*_{1:N})$.

3.2.1 Sampling

Each component $\underline{u}^l_k$ of $\underline{u}^l_{1:N}$ can be interpreted as a discrete probability distribution over the set of sensor indices $\mathcal{S}$. This is due to the constraint in (2.4), whereby the elements $u^l_{k,i}, i = 1, \ldots, S$ of $\underline{u}^l_k$ are within the interval $[0, 1]$ and sum up to one. Hence, a sensor i corresponding to an element $u^l_{k,i}$ with a large value can be considered as being more likely in the optimal sensor schedule than sensors with small values.

To convert $\underline{u}^l_{1:N}$ into a feasible binary vector, for each $k = 1, \ldots, N$ a (single) sensor is randomly selected according to the distribution $\underline{u}^l_k$. For being *feasible*, the resulting converted schedule $\underline{u}^u_{1:k}$ has to satisfy the cost constraint (2.3). Otherwise, the schedule is discarded. This procedure is repeated multiple times, where only the currently best feasible schedule, i.e., the schedule that satisfies (2.3) *and* provides the currently smallest objective function value J^u is stored. The sampling-based conversion method can be terminated for example after a predefined number of trials or when the currently best value J^u remains unchanged for a predefined number of trials.

3.2.2 Swapping

To improve a converted schedule $\underline{u}^u_{1:N}$, the swapping method proposed in [JB09] can be adapted. A modified sensor schedule is derived from $\underline{u}^u_{1:N}$ by swapping a scheduled sensor with one of the unselected sensors for each time step. The choice of an unselected sensor at time step k is *deterministically* guided according to the probabilities represented by $\underline{u}^l_k$, i.e., the sensors are selected in descending order of the values in $\underline{u}^l_k$. If the modified schedule is feasible and improves the objective function value J^u, it is used for initializing the next swapping trial.

In order to start the swapping method with a feasible schedule, the sensor schedule that selects at each time step k the sensor $i = \arg\min_j c_{k,j}$ with the smallest cost is chosen initially. The method must terminate because there is only a finite but very large number of swapping possibilities. To bound the computational demand, the number of swapping trials is limited by means of a predefined value.

4   Optimal Scheduling

Determining the optimal sensor schedule and thus, directly solving the binary integer program given by (2.2)–(2.5) can be considered as searching a decision tree with depth N and branching factor S. The problem here is that the optimal solution often can be found at an early stage when employing appropriate search methods, while the proof of its optimality requires evaluating most of the suboptimal sensor schedules, which is infeasible for large problem sizes. In this section, the previously introduced convex optimization approach is combined with efficient search methods for decision trees for early eliminating (pruning) suboptimal schedules.

4.1   Branch-and-Bound

A search technique common for classical decision problems like traveling-salesman or knapsack is branch-and-bound (BB) search. The basic idea of BB is to assign lower and upper bounds of the achievable objective function value to any visited node. Based on these bounds, nodes and thus complete subtrees can be pruned under the guarantee that the pruned node is not part of the optimal sensor schedule.

For a particular node that was reached during the search by employing the sensor schedule $\underline{u}_{1:k} \in \{0, 1\}^{k \cdot S}$, the objective function can be written according to

$$J(\underline{u}_{1:N}) = \underbrace{J(\underline{u}_{1:k})}_{\text{known}} + \underbrace{J(\underline{u}_{k+1:N})}_{\text{unkown}} , \qquad (4.1)$$

where only the value of the first summand is already evaluated and thus known. While the value of the second summand is not calculated yet, a lower and upper bound can be easily assigned to it by exploiting the results of Section 3.1 and Section 3.2. The value of the optimal solution $\underline{u}^{l}_{k+1:N}$ of the convex relaxation for minimizing $J(\underline{u}_{k+1:N})$ serves as lower bound and the conversion of $\underline{u}^{l}_{k+1:N}$ into a binary-valued vector $\underline{u}^{u}_{k+1:N}$ provides an upper bound. Hence, the inequality

$$J(\underline{u}_{1:k}) + J(\underline{u}^{l}_{k+1:N}) \leq J(\underline{u}_{1:N}) \leq J(\underline{u}_{1:k}) + J(\underline{u}^{u}_{k+1:N})$$

holds for the objective function value in (4.1).

Algorithm 4.1 Initially $J_{\min} = \infty$. For a given sensor schedule $\underline{u}_{1:k}$ do:

1: **if** leaf node, i.e., $k = N$ **then**
2: $\quad J_{\min} \leftarrow J(\underline{u}_{1:N})$ $\quad\quad$ // Global bound of currently best schedule $\underline{u}_{0:N-1}$
3: **else**
4: $\quad \mathcal{U} \leftarrow \emptyset$ $\quad\quad\quad\quad\quad\quad\quad\quad\quad\quad$ // List of sensors to expand
5: $\quad$ **for all** sensors $i \in \{1, \ldots, S\}$ **do** $\quad\quad$ // $\underline{u}_{1:k}$ and $u_{k+1,i} = 1$ fixed
6: $\quad\quad$ **if** $\text{cost}_i \leq C$ and $J_i \leq J_{\min}$ **then**
7: $\quad\quad\quad J_i^{\text{l}} \leftarrow$ Solve convex optimization problem
8: $\quad\quad\quad J_i^{\text{u}} \leftarrow$ Calculate upper bound via conversion
9: $\quad\quad\quad \mathcal{U} \leftarrow \mathcal{U} \cup \{i\}$
10: $\quad\quad$ **end if**
11: $\quad$ **end for**
12: $\quad \mathcal{U} \leftarrow \text{sort}(\mathcal{U})$ $\quad\quad\quad\quad\quad\quad\quad\quad$ // Sort sensors based on J_i^{l}
13: $\quad$ **for all** sensors $i \in \mathcal{U}$ **do**
14: $\quad\quad$ **if** $J_i^{\text{l}} \leq J_{\min}$ and $\forall j \in \mathcal{U} : J_i^{\text{l}} \leq J_j^{\text{u}}$ **then**
15: $\quad\quad\quad$ Expand i $\quad\quad\quad\quad\quad$ // Set $u_{k+1,i} = 1$, call Algorithm 4.1
16: $\quad\quad$ **end if**
17: $\quad$ **end for**
18: **end if**

It is worth mentioning that a valuable upper bound, i.e., a tight one, normally cannot be provided for branch-and-bound for sensor scheduling tasks (see for example [CMPS06, Hub09]). Here, the solution of the convex relaxation allows calculating tight upper bounds in a straightforward fashion. These further reduce the size of the search space.

4.2 Search Algorithm

The combination of BB search with convex optimization is illustrated in Algorithm 4.1, which basically employs a depth-first search. For a given sensor schedule $\underline{u}_{1:k}$ it is checked, which child nodes should be expanded, i.e., it is checked whether an element $u_{k+1,i}$, $i \in \mathcal{S}$ of $\underline{u}_{k+1}$ could be set to one or not. Therefore, for each child node $i \in \mathcal{S}$ the minimum cost possible is computed as

$$\text{cost}_i := \sum_{n=1}^{k} \underline{c}_n \cdot \underline{u}_n + c_{k+1,i} + \sum_{n=k+2}^{N} \min_j c_{n,j} \, .$$

Furthermore, the value $J_i := J(\underline{u}_{1:k+1})$ and the bounds $J_i^{\text{l}} := J_i + J(\underline{u}_{k+2:N}^{\text{l}})$, $J_i^{\text{u}} := J_i + J(\underline{u}_{k+2:N}^{\text{u}})$ are calculated, where $u_{k+1,i} = 1$ and $u_{k+1,j} = 0$ for all $j \neq i$. Based on these values, a node i is expanded only if following four requirements are fulfilled:

1. The cost constraint can be met, i.e., a feasible solution exists (line 6).

2. The value J_i of the node is below the value $J_{\min}$ of the currently best sensor schedule (line 6).

3. The lower bound J_i^l is below $J_{\min}$ (line 14).

4. The lower bound is below the upper bounds of all neighboring nodes $j \neq i$ (line 14).

Obviously, the third requirement implies the second one. But in order to avoid an unnecessary calculation of the lower and upper bound, the second requirement is checked separately together with the first requirement (line 6–10). To further accelerate the search, the remaining sensors in $\mathcal{U}$ are sorted in descending order according of their lower bounds (line 12)[1]. In doing so, the search is continued with the most promising sensor first in order to force a stronger reduction of the currently best value $J_{\min}$. This value is automatically reduced once a leaf node is reached (line 1–2).

5   Simulation Results

The effectiveness of the proposed sensor scheduling methods is demonstrated in the following by means of a numerical simulation from the field of target tracking. The state $\underline{x}_k = [x_k, \dot{x}_k, y_k, \dot{y}_k]^{\mathrm{T}}$ of the observed target comprises the two-dimensional position $[x_k, y_k]^{\mathrm{T}}$ and the velocities $[\dot{x}_k, \dot{y}_k]^{\mathrm{T}}$ in x and y direction. The system matrix and noise covariance matrix of $\underline{w}_k$ of the dynamics model (2.1) are

$$\mathbf{A}_k = \mathbf{I}_2 \otimes \begin{bmatrix} 1 & T \\ 0 & 1 \end{bmatrix} \quad \text{and} \quad \mathbf{C}_k^w = q \cdot \mathbf{I}_2 \otimes \begin{bmatrix} \frac{T^3}{3} & \frac{T^2}{2} \\ \frac{T^2}{2} & T \end{bmatrix}, \tag{5.1}$$

respectively, where $\mathbf{I}_n$ indicates an $n \times n$ identity matrix and $\otimes$ is the Kronecker matrix product. In (5.1), $T = 1$ s is the sampling interval and $q = 0.2$ is the scalar diffusion strength. Mean and covariance of the initial state $\underline{x}_0$ are $\hat{\underline{x}}_0 = [0, 1, 0, 1]^{\mathrm{T}}$ and $\mathbf{C}_0^x = 10 \cdot \mathbf{I}_4$, respectively.

---

[1] Alternatively, $\mathcal{U}$ can be sorted in ascending order with respect to the upper bounds.

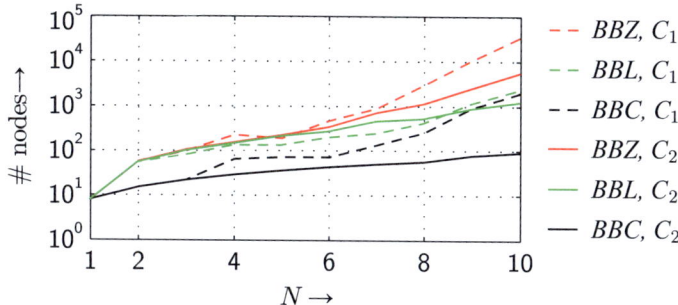

Figure 5.1: Number of nodes in the decision tree when applying the branch-and-bound-based scheduling methods *BBC* (black lines), *BBL* (green), and *BBZ* (red) for different time horizons lengths N and for two different maximum cost functions C_1 (dashed) and C_2 (solid) in log-scale.

A sensor network observes the target. It consists of six sensors with measurement matrices

$$\mathbf{H}_k^1 = \mathbf{H}_k^3 = \begin{bmatrix} 1 & 0 & 0 & 0 \end{bmatrix} , \ \mathbf{H}_k^2 = \mathbf{H}_k^5 = \begin{bmatrix} 0 & 0 & 1 & 0 \end{bmatrix} ,$$
$$\mathbf{H}_k^4 = \begin{bmatrix} 0 & 0 & 0 & 1 \end{bmatrix} , \ \mathbf{H}_k^6 = \begin{bmatrix} 0 & 1 & 0 & 0 \end{bmatrix} ,$$

noise variances $C_k^{v,1} = 0.2$, $C_k^{v,2} = C_k^{v,3} = C_k^{v,4} = 0.1$, $C_k^{v,5} = C_k^{v,6} = 0.05$, and costs $\underline{c}_k = [1, 1, 2, 1, 2, 2]^\mathrm{T}$ for each k. Furthermore, it is also possible to omit a measurement. This option can be considered as having a seventh sensor with infinite noise variance. Performing no measurement is free of cost, i.e., $c_{k,7} = 0$. Altogether, the set $\mathcal{S}$ comprises $S = 7$ sensors. The scalar functions $g_k(\cdot)$ are set to the root-determinant for each k.

For comparison, five different scheduling methods are considered: (1, denoted in the following by *CONVEX*) The approach described in Section 3, which directly solves the convex optimization problem and employs the swapping method for conversion. (2, *BBC*) The BB approach described in Section 4. For determining the upper bounds via conversion, the swapping method is employed. (3, *BBL*) Like *BBC* but without utilizing upper bounds for pruning. (4, *BBZ*) BB search that employs no upper bounds and bounds the second summand in (4.1) from below with zero. (5, *GREEDY*) The sensors are scheduled in a greedy (one-step looka-head) fashion (see for example [KG05]). For *CONVEX* and *BBC*, the number of swapping trials is set to $S \cdot N$.

In Figure 5.1, the search performance of the three BB methods is compared. For this purpose, two different maximum costs $C_1(N) = \mathrm{round}\left(\frac{3}{4} \cdot N\right)$ and $C_2(N) =$

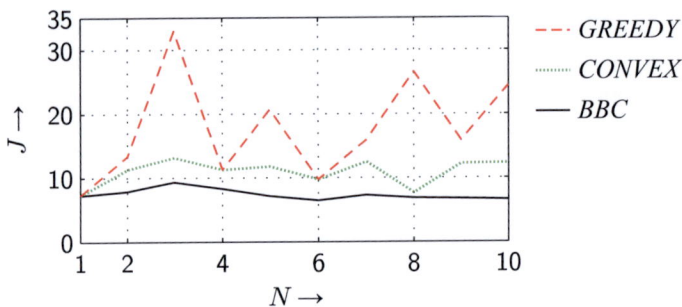

Figure 5.2: Objective function values J of the scheduling methods *BBC* (black, solid), *CONVEX* (green, dotted), and *GREEDY* (red, dashed) for maximum cost function C_1.

$2 \cdot N$ are considered, which depend on the change of the time horizon length $N = 1, \ldots, 10$. The maximum cost function $C_2(N)$ allows sensor scheduling without omitting a measurement. With the proposed optimal scheduling method *BBC*, the number of nodes in the decision tree can be kept on a low level. Here, the search performance clearly benefits from the tight lower and upper bounds provided by the convex optimization and the conversion, respectively. This can be seen in particular for C_2, where *BBC* only visits at most 92 nodes, while the complete decision tree contains $\sum_{k=1}^{N} 7^k < 3.3 \cdot 10^8$ nodes. The higher number of visited nodes for cost function C_1 compared to C_2 results from the effect that the more restrictive cost constraint provided by C_1 leads to looser bounds.

Without considering upper bounds for pruning as it is the case for *BBL*, the number of visited nodes increases significantly. But still, the search performance of *BBL* is much better than *BBZ* as the lower bound provided by the solution of the convex optimization is closer to the true values of the subtrees.

Since calculating lower and upper bounds by means of convex relaxation is computationally more demanding than calculating the simple bound used for *BBZ*, the runtime of *BBZ* is lower for short time horizons even if *BBZ* leads to larger decisions trees. But with increasing length of the time horizon, the difference in runtime between *BBZ* and the other BB methods becomes smaller and at some point, both methods outperform *BBZ*. For example, with the current, barely optimized implementation based on MATLAB version 7.9, *BBC* outperforms *BBZ* from horizon length $N = 9$ on for cost function C_1. It is expected that employing an optimized implementation, outperforming *BBZ* occurs for significantly shorter time horizons.

In Figure 5.2, the objective function values of *BBC* are compared with *GREEDY* and *CONVEX* for the costs $C_1(N)$. The *GREEDY* method is the computationally cheapest one, but provides highly suboptimal results. Due to the myopic planning, *GREEDY* is not able to anticipate the long-term effect of early selecting costly sensors. In this simulation example, *GREEDY* omits measurements at the last time steps of the horizon and not in between in order to meet the maximum cost constraint. The proposed suboptimal *CONVEX* method provides sensor schedules close to the optimal ones, whereas the computational demand is significantly smaller compared to *BBC*, especially for very long time horizons. *CONVEX* trades scheduling quality off against scheduling complexity, which is desirable for computationally constrained sensor systems.

6   Conclusions and Future Work

Employing convex optimization for determining long-term sensor schedules is a promising approach. In this report, a general sensor scheduling problem for linear Gaussian models was formulated and the convexity of its relaxation was proven. Based on this result, two scheduling methods utilizing convex optimization have been proposed. The first approach directly solves the relaxed sensor scheduling problem in order to provide suboptimal but computationally cheap solutions. The second approach provides the optimal sensor schedule, where convex optimization is utilized for eliminating suboptimal sensor schedules at an early stage of branch-and-bound search. Compared to existing approaches on sensor scheduling via convex optimization, general linear Gaussian sensor scheduling problems are covered. Furthermore, both proposed scheduling methods are appropriate for long time horizons and many sensors, where choosing the better suited approach for a given scheduling problem depends on the requirements on estimation quality and computational capabilities.

Future work is mainly devoted to three aspects: improving search speed for branch-and-bound search, incorporation of nonlinear dynamics and sensor models, and applying model-predictive/moving horizon control. Further improving search speed can for example be achieved by incorporating so-called *Gomory's cuts*, i.e., additional inequality constraints that reduce the size of the search space [SM99]. By this means the proposed branch-and-bound search would be extended into a branch-and-cut search. A completely different way of solving the sensor scheduling problem would be to employ so-called *outer approximation* [FL94]. Here, the convex relaxation of the sensor scheduling problem is transformed into a series of linear programs that finally leads to the optimal (binary) sensor schedule.

A comparison of branch-and-cut search and outer approximation with respect to computational demand would by of particular interest.

The incorporation of nonlinear models can be achieved by employing a conversion of the nonlinear models into linear ones via linearization, e.g., first-order Taylor series expansion or statistical linearization as in [Hub09]. This linearization can be combined with model-predictive control in order to facilitate sensor scheduling for very long or even infinite time horizons.

Appendix

A Analytical Expression of the Gradient

Since interior-point methods employ Newton's method, the computation time of solving the relaxed sensor scheduling problem can be significantly reduced by providing an analytical expression of the gradient of the objective function $J(\underline{u}_{1:N})$. The gradient is given by

$$\nabla J(\underline{u}_{1:n}) = \frac{\partial J(\underline{u}_{1:N})}{\partial \underline{u}_{1:N}} = \sum_{k=1}^{N} \frac{\partial g(\underline{u}_{1:k})}{\partial \underline{u}_{1:N}} \,,$$

which boils down to calculating the derivatives

$$\frac{\partial g(\underline{u}_{1:k})}{\partial \underline{u}_{1:N}} = \left[\underbrace{\left(\frac{\partial g(\underline{u}_{1:k})}{\partial \underline{u}_{1:k}} \right)^{\mathrm{T}}}_{1:k}, \underbrace{\underline{0}^{\mathrm{T}}}_{k+1:N} \right]^{\mathrm{T}} \tag{A.1}$$

for $k = 1, \ldots, N$.

The partial derivative $\frac{\partial g(\underline{u}_{1:k})}{\partial \underline{u}_{1:k}}$ in (A.1) requires determining the derivative $\frac{\partial \mathbf{C}_k^x}{\partial \underline{u}_{1:k}}$ with $\mathbf{C}_k^x$ according to (2.6).[2] With the differential identity (see [PP08])

$$\partial \mathbf{X}^{-1} = -\mathbf{X}^{-1} \cdot \partial \mathbf{X} \cdot \mathbf{X}^{-1} \,, \quad \mathbf{X} \in \mathbb{R}^{n \times n} \tag{A.2}$$

and defining

$$\mathbf{C}_k^p := \mathbf{A}_{k-1} \cdot \mathbf{C}_{k-1}^x \cdot \mathbf{A}_{k-1}^{\mathrm{T}} + \mathbf{C}_{k-1}^w \,,$$

$$\mathbf{M}_k^i := \left(\mathbf{H}_k^i \right)^{\mathrm{T}} \cdot \left(\mathbf{C}_k^{v,i} \right)^{-1} \cdot \mathbf{H}_k^i \,,$$

$$\mathbf{P}_k := \left(\mathbf{C}_k^x \right)^{-1} = \left(\mathbf{C}_k^p \right)^{-1} + \sum_i u_{k,i} \cdot \mathbf{M}_k^i \,,$$

---

[2]The argument $\underline{u}_{1:k}$ is omitted in the following for clarity.

the desired derivative of $\mathbf{C}_k^x$ accords to

$$\frac{\partial \mathbf{C}_k^x}{\partial \underline{u}_{1:k}} = \frac{\partial \mathbf{P}_k^{-1}}{\partial \underline{u}_{1:k}} \overset{(A.2)}{=} -\mathbf{C}_k^x \cdot \frac{\partial \mathbf{P}_k}{\partial \underline{u}_{1:k}} \cdot \mathbf{C}_k^x$$

$$\overset{(A.2)}{=} \begin{bmatrix} \mathbf{C}_k^x \cdot (\mathbf{C}_k^p)^{-1} \cdot \frac{\partial \mathbf{C}_k^p}{\partial \underline{u}_{1:k-1}} \cdot (\mathbf{C}_k^p)^{-1} \cdot \mathbf{C}_k^x \\ \mathbf{C}_k^x \cdot \left(\frac{\partial}{\partial \underline{u}_k} \sum_i u_{k,i} \cdot \mathbf{M}_k^i \right) \cdot \mathbf{C}_k^x \end{bmatrix} . \tag{A.3}$$

The first row in (A.3) can be written in recursive form as

$$\mathbf{C}_k^x \cdot (\mathbf{C}_k^p)^{-1} \cdot \frac{\partial \mathbf{C}_k^p}{\partial \underline{u}_{1:k-1}} \cdot (\mathbf{C}_k^p)^{-1} \cdot \mathbf{C}_k^x =$$

$$\mathbf{C}_k^x \cdot (\mathbf{C}_k^p)^{-1} \cdot \mathbf{A}_{k-1} \cdot \frac{\partial \mathbf{C}_{k-1}^x}{\partial \underline{u}_{1:k-1}} \cdot \mathbf{A}_{k-1}^{\mathrm{T}} \cdot (\mathbf{C}_k^p)^{-1} \cdot \mathbf{C}_k^x$$

commencing from $\frac{\partial \mathbf{C}_1^x}{\partial u_{1,i}} = -\mathbf{C}_1^x \cdot \mathbf{M}_1^i \cdot \mathbf{C}_1^x$ for $i = 1, \ldots, S$. For each element $i = 1, \ldots, S$ of the second row in (A.3) holds $\frac{\partial}{\partial u_{k,i}} \sum_i u_{k,i} \cdot \mathbf{M}_k^i = \mathbf{M}_k^i$.

As the function $g(\cdot)$ can be the trace, root-determinant, or the maximum eigenvalue (see Section 2), the identities

$$\partial \operatorname{trace}(\mathbf{X}) = \operatorname{trace}(\partial \mathbf{X}) , \tag{A.4}$$

$$\partial \sqrt{|\mathbf{X}|} = \tfrac{1}{2} \sqrt{|\mathbf{X}|} \cdot \operatorname{trace}\left(\mathbf{X}^{-1} \cdot \partial \mathbf{X} \right) , \tag{A.5}$$

$$\partial \lambda_i(\mathbf{X}) = \underline{v}_i^{\mathrm{T}} \cdot \partial \mathbf{X} \cdot \underline{v}_i \tag{A.6}$$

from matrix calculus in differential form have to be applied *to each* partial derivative $\frac{\partial g(\underline{u}_{1:k})}{\partial u_{k,i}}$ for concluding the derivation of $\frac{\partial g(\underline{u}_{1:k})}{\partial \underline{u}_{1:k}}$. In (A.4)–(A.6), $\mathbf{X} \in \mathbb{R}^{n \times n}$ has to be replaced by $\mathbf{C}_k^x$. (A.4) and (A.5) can be found in [PP08]. In (A.6), λ_i is the i-the eigenvalue of $\mathbf{X}$ and $\underline{v}_i$ is the corresponding i-th normalized eigenvector, with $\lambda_1 \leq \lambda_2 \leq \ldots \leq \lambda_n$ (see [OW95]).

Bibliography

[ASSC02] Ian F. Akyildiz, Weilian Su, Yogesh Sankarasubramaniam, and Erdal Cayirci. Wireless sensor networks: a survey. *Computer Networks*, 38:393–422, January 2002.

[BV08] Stephen Boyd and Lieven Vandenberghe. *Convex Optimization*. Cambridge University Press, 2008.

[CMPS06] Amit S. Chhetri, Darryl Morrell, and Antonia Papandreou-Suppappola. Nonmyopic Sensor Scheduling and its Efficient Implementation for Target Tracking Applications. *EURASIP Journal on Applied Signal Processing*, 2006:1–18, 2006.

[CMPS07]   Amit S. Chhetri, Darryl Morrell, and Antonia Papandreou-Suppappola. On the Use of Binary Programming for Sensor Scheduling. *IEEE Transactions on Signal Processing*, 55(6):2826–2839, June 2007.

[FL94]   Roger Fletcher and Sven Leyffer. Solving mixed integer nonlinear programs by outer approximation. *Mathematical Programming*, 66(1):327–349, August 1994.

[GCHM04]   Vijay Gupta, Timothy H. Chung, Babak Hassibi, and Richard M. Murray. Sensor Scheduling Algorithms Requiring Limited Computations. In *Proceedings of the IEEE International Conference on Acoustics, Speech, and Signal Processing (ICASSP)*, pages 825–828, Montreal, Quebec, Canada, 2004.

[HH08]   Marco F. Huber and Uwe D. Hanebeck. Priority List Sensor Scheduling using Optimal Pruning. In *Proceedings of the 11th International Conference on Information Fusion (Fusion)*, Cologne, Germany, July 2008.

[Hub09]   Marco Huber. *Probabilistic Framework for Sensor Management*. PhD thesis, Universität Karlsruhe (TH), 2009.

[JB09]   Siddharth Joshi and Stephen Boyd. Sensor Selection via Convex Optimization. *IEEE Transactions on Signal Processing*, 57(2):451–462, February 2009.

[Kar72]   Richard M. Karp. Reducibility Among Combinatorial Problems. In R. E. Miller and J. W. Thatcher, editors, *Complexity of Computer Computations*, pages 85–104. New York: Plenum, 1972.

[KG05]   Andreas Krause and Carlos Guestrin. Near-optimal Nonmyopic Value of Information in Graphical Models. In *Proceedings of the Twenty-First Annual Conference on Uncertainty in Artificial Intelligence*, pages 324–33, Edinburgh, Scotland, July 2005.

[Kra36]   Fritz Kraus. Über konvexe Matrixfunktionen. *Mathematische Zeitschrift*, 41(1):18–42, December 1936.

[KSH00]   Thomas Kailath, Ali H. Sayed, and Babak Hassibi. *Linear Estimation*. Prentice Hall, 2nd edition, 2000.

[LI99]   Andrew Logothetis and Alf Isaksson. On sensor scheduling via information theoretic criteria. In *Proceedings of the 1999 American Control Conference (ACC)*, volume 4, pages 2402–2406, San Diego, CA, 1999.

[MPD67]   Lewis Meier, John Peschon, and Robert M. Dressler. Optimal Control of Measurement Subsystems. *IEEE Transactions on Automatic Control*, AC-12(5):528–536, October 1967.

[Osh94]   Yaakov Oshman. Optimal Sensor Selection Strategy for Discrete-Time State Estimators. *IEEE Transactions on Aerospace and Electronic Systems*, 30(2):307–314, April 1994.

[OW95]   Michael L. Overton and Robert S. Womersley. Second Derivatives for Optimizing Eigenvalues of Symmetric Matrices. *SIAM Journal on Matrix Analysis and Applications*, 16(3):697–718, July 1995.

[PP08]   Kaare Brandt Petersen and Michael Syskind Pedersen. The Matrix Cookbook. Online: http://www.imm.dtu.dk/pubdb/views/edoc_download.php/3274/pdf/imm3274.pdf, November 2008.

[QKS07]   Zhi Quan, William J. Kaiser, and Ali H. Sayed. A Spatial Sampling Scheme Based on Innovations Diffusion in Sensor Networks. In *Proceedings of the Sixth International Conference on Information Processing in Sensor Networks (IPSN)*, pages 323–330, Cambridge, MA, April 2007.

[SM99]   Robert A. Stubbs and Sanjay Mehrotra. A branch–and–cut method for 0–1 mixed convex programming. *Mathmatical Programming*, 86(3):515–532, December 1999.

The Mumford-Shah Functional and its Applications in Image Processing: the Image Registration Case

Ioana Gheţa

Vision and Fusion Laboratory
Institute for Anthropomatics (IFA)
Karlsruhe Institute of Technology (KIT), Germany
ioana.gheta@ies.uni-karlsruhe.de

Technical Report IES-2009-02

Abstract: This contribution presents a short overview of the development of the Mumford-Shah functional (MSF) and its applications in image processing with emphasis on image registration. MSF has been primarily developed for image segmentation having the main advantage of not requiring prior information. Its main disadvantages are the ill-posedness and the need of discretization when employing the continuous formulation.

Despite these disadvantages MSF is meanwhile also employed for object detection, image registration and inpainting. The known methods for image registration of stereo series perform a pairwise registration mostly based on grey values. If the image series are combined image series (e.g., stereo and spectral image series) a registration method invariant with regard to the grey values is necessary. This contribution presents new ideas of how MSF can be used to perform an edge based registration of such combined image series.

1   Introduction

The Mumford-Shah functional (MSF) has been developed by D. Mumford and J. Shah and first published in a short article in 1985 [MS85]. This has been followed by a circumstantial contribution in 1989, which also discusses optimal approximations [MS89]. The functional can be considered as one of the most powerful methods for image segmentation, its main advantage being that no prior information is necessary. The main disadvantage is that the functional in its standard form is ill-posed.

As a result the subsequent scientific researches have been following two directions:

- The first direction is being given by those who employ the functional in image processing applications trying to regularize it, or by using a discrete formulation.

- The second direction is being mainly followed by mathematicians, who research and prove properties of the functional and possible regularizations mostly for the n dimensional case; see Section 3.

Following, the problem formulation is presented in its continuous form for the two dimensional case. The main goal is to segment an image (defined as a function):

$$g : \Omega \to \mathbb{R}, \quad \Omega \subseteq \mathbb{R}^2$$

such that the resulting image can be written as:

$$s : \Omega \to \mathbb{R}, \quad \text{with } \Omega = \Omega_1 \cup \Omega_2 \cup \ldots \cup \Omega_N \cup \Gamma.$$

The domain Ω of the original image g is segmented in more regions Ω_i, and Γ, which is a closed set of C^1 curves [MS85, MS89].

The image segmentation is obtained by minimizing MSF:

$$E(s, \Gamma) := \mu E_d(s, \Gamma) + E_s(s, \Gamma) + \nu E_l(\Gamma). \tag{1.1}$$

Thus the minimization of the functional imposes with its terms the following conditions on the result:

- $E_d(s, \Gamma)$ ensures that the segmented image is as similar as possible to the original image.

- $E_s(s, \Gamma)$ demands the smoothness of the result.

- $E_l(\Gamma)$ demands that the sum of the lengths of the curves is minimal.

μ and ν are weights for scale and contrast. μ influences the dimensions of the segmented regions and ν influences the contrast between them.

For the discrete case a more common and simpler formulation for describing images using matrices (unlike in [MS85, MS89] where the notion of latices [Her67] is employed) is chosen. In this case, the image to be segmented is represented using a matrix B. The segmented image is a partitioning of the initial image. This means, the resulting image can be represented using distinct submatrices S_i of B, such that all S_i put together form B. Γ remains a closed set of C^1 curves describing the partitioning; see Figure 1.1. The structure of the functional is the same as in Eq. (1.1).

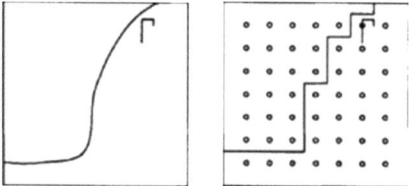

Figure 1.1: Examples for the set of curves Γ for the continuous and discrete case [MS85, MS89].

The present contribution gives first in Section 2 an overview of the developed models of the Mumford-Shah functional, followed by some of its main properties in Section 3. Further on, a parallel between the discrete and continuous models is discussed in Section 4. An overview of the applications of MSF in image processing is given in Section 5. The emphasis is on possibilities to use MSF for the registration of combined stereo and spectral series.

2   Models of the Mumford-Shah Functional

The most simple model is the Ising model [Mum94]:

$$E(s,\Gamma)_{\text{Ising}} := \mu E_{\text{d}}(s,\Gamma) + \nu E_{\text{l}}(s,\Gamma)$$
$$= \mu \iint_{\Omega} (s(\boldsymbol{u}) - g(\boldsymbol{u}))^2 \mathrm{d}\boldsymbol{u} + \nu \mathcal{H}^1(\Gamma) .$$

It only consists of two terms, renouncing on the demand of the smoothness of the result, at the cost of only being able to segment grey value images, by which foreground and background "obviously" differ [Mum94]. The first term measures the similarity between the original image g and the segmented one s. The second term gives the length of the curve by means of the 1D Hausdorff measure [CS05]. The Ising model has the advantage of being superior to the simple threshold based segmentation, by a better handling of outliers.

The second model is called the Cartoon model and it is the standard model of MSF:

$$E(s,\Gamma) := \mu \iint_{\Omega} (s(\boldsymbol{u}) - g(\boldsymbol{u}))^2 \mathrm{d}\boldsymbol{u} + \iint_{\Omega \backslash \Gamma} \|\nabla s(\boldsymbol{u})\|^2 \mathrm{d}\boldsymbol{u} + \nu \mathcal{H}^1(\Gamma) . \quad (2.1)$$

The second additional term $E_{\text{s}}(s,\Gamma)$ with regard to the Ising model assures the smoothness of the result on the entire domain Ω without Γ.

The discrete formulation is similar to the continuous one [MS85, MS89]:

$$E(\Gamma)_{\text{discrete}} := \mu \sum_k (s_k - g_k)^2 + \sum_{\substack{(k,l) \\ (k,l) \in \mathcal{N}}} (s_k - s_l)^2 + \nu \|\Gamma\|.$$

s_k and g_k are elements of the resulting S and original B matrices, respectively (i.e., s_k and g_k are image pixels). $\mathcal{N}$ is a set containing the indexes of neighbouring matrix elements (i.e., neighbouring pixels in the image) and $\|\Gamma\|$ describes the length of the curves (generally, $\|\Gamma\|$ is a measure for volume).

The only assumption made for the segmentation by means of MSF is that the regions to be segmented are separated by sharp curves. The disadvantage of the model is its tendency to approximate the curves with minimal surfaces [Oss97], see also Section 3.

This disadvantage is compensated by the Theater-Wing model, which takes into consideration, that the objects in the image occlude each other. Therefore the curves describing the boundaries of the objects can be treated separately and the problem of minimal surfaces is avoided [Mum94].

Another model is the Spectrogramm model, which is able to segment textured surfaces by using their local spectral signature in the image [Mum94]. The next sections of this contribution concentrate on the properties and applications of the Cartoon model (Eq. (2.1)), as this is the most reviewed and analyzed model in the literature.

3   Properties of the Mumford-Shah Functional

One of the most important properties of the MSF is its tendency to perform the segmentation such that the obtained curves are minimal surfaces. The property of minimal surfaces is that they intersect only three at a time with 120° angles between them [Oss97, Dav05]. This property also known as the Mumford-Shah conjecture results from the definition of Γ as a finite union of C^1 curves [Dav05] and holds for the two dimensional case.

Further, the set Γ of curves does not contain isolated (short) curves or dispersed curves [LS94] . These properties prove the superiority of the MSF with regard to other image segmentation algorithms, which strongly depend on image features (e.g., corners and edges).

Another property of MSF is that it is well-posed only in its discrete formulation. The continuous formulation is ill-posed [Mum94]. [KKB+07] proposes an equivalent convex formulation (i.e., if a minimum of the functional is found, then it is the

Figure 3.1: Example of two different optimal segmentation results of the left image using MSF [Dav05].

global minimum). Some other proposed regularization are presented in Sections 4 and 5.

The segmentation problem by means of MSF always has a result, i.e., the existence of the result has been proven in [LS94], but the uniqueness is not provided. A clear example is given in Figure 3.1. The left image in Figure 3.1 can be optimal segmented in the two ways shown in the two right images.

4   Discrete vs. Continuous Models

One of the common approaches to use MSF in its continuous formulation (see Eq. (2.1)) is by approximating Γ with level sets [CV01]. More exactly, Γ is the zero level set of a Lipschitz continuous function ϕ segmenting two regions of an image [Osh03]:

$$\phi : \Omega \to \mathbb{R}, \quad \Gamma := \{u \in \Omega | \phi(u) = 0\}.$$

The two segmented regions of the image are given by the sets:

$$\omega := \{u \in \Omega | \phi(u) > 0\}$$
$$\Omega \setminus \omega^\circ := \{u \in \Omega | \phi(u) < 0\},$$

with ω° as the interior of the set ω. It is important to mention that none of the sets ω or $\Omega \setminus \omega^\circ$ must be connected. Therefore it is straightforward that Γ is, in this case, defined as the set of pixels u describing the boundary $\partial \omega$ of the set ω.

The MSF functional is then defined as [CV01]:

$$E(b_1, b_2, \phi) := \iint_\Omega (g(\boldsymbol{u}) - b_1)^2 H(\phi(\boldsymbol{u})) \mathrm{d}\boldsymbol{u}$$

$$+ \iint_\Omega (g(\boldsymbol{u}) - b_2)^2 (1 - H(\phi(\boldsymbol{u}))) \mathrm{d}\boldsymbol{u} \qquad (4.1)$$

$$+ \nu \iint_\Omega \delta(\phi(\boldsymbol{u})) \|\nabla \phi(\boldsymbol{u})\| \mathrm{d}\boldsymbol{u} \,.$$

b_1 and b_2 are the mean grey values in the two segmented regions ω and $\Omega \setminus \omega^\circ$. $H(\phi)$ is the Heaviside function and $\delta(\phi(\boldsymbol{u})) := D^1 H(\phi(\boldsymbol{u}))$ is the generalized derivative of the Heaviside function [Osh03]. ∇ represents the divergence.

The first two terms of the formulation of MSF using level sets in Eq. (4.1) approximate the first term $E_\mathrm{d}(s, \Gamma)$ in Eq. (2.1), by supposing that the regions to be segmented are homogeneous. Therefore, it is only necessary to measure the difference between the grey values of the original image and the mean grey values (i.e., b_1 for the interior and b_2 for the exterior of the set ω, respectively) of the segmented images. The sum of the first two terms is then minimal, if the zero level set of ϕ best approximates the boundaries of objects [CV01]. The last term of Eq. (4.1) is a surface integral and computes in the two dimensional case the length of the curves represented by the zero level set of ϕ. The result of the segmentation is obtained by minimizing the functional in Eq. (4.1) e.g., by using finite difference method [CV01].

The advantage of combining MSF with level sets like in Eq. (4.1) is that the smoothness assumption acts regularizing. The disadvantages of the model in Eq. (4.1) are that it can only segment foreground from background and that the results depend on the initialization of the curve and the approximations of $H(\phi)$ and $\delta(\phi)$ [CV01].

Another possibility of segmenting images by means of MSF is using a discrete formulation similar to the continuous one [EXSE07]:

$$E(b_1, b_2, \Gamma) := \sum_{\boldsymbol{u}} (g(\boldsymbol{u}) - b_1)^2 \varpi_{\boldsymbol{u}} + \sum_{\boldsymbol{u}} (g(\boldsymbol{u}) - b_2)^2 (1 - \varpi_{\boldsymbol{u}}) \qquad (4.2)$$

$$+ \nu \sum_{\boldsymbol{u}^k} \sum_{\boldsymbol{u}_i^l \in \mathcal{N}(\boldsymbol{u}^k)} w_i \left(\varpi_{\boldsymbol{u}^k}(1 - \varpi_{\boldsymbol{u}_i^l}) + \varpi_{\boldsymbol{u}_i^l}(1 - \varpi_{\boldsymbol{u}^k}) \right) ,$$

where ϖ_u is a binary variable:

$$\varpi_u := \begin{cases} 1, & \phi(u) > 0 \\ 0, & \text{else}. \end{cases}$$

The first two terms of the functional in Eq. (4.2) are similar to the first two terms of Eq. (4.1) and have the same functionality. The third term measures the length of the curves of Γ by means of the Cauchy-Crofton formula [BK03], i.e., if the curves Γ lie between two neighbouring pixels u^l and u^k, then a weight w_i is added, depending on which neighbor of u_k the pixel u_i^l is (e.g., left or right neighbor).

The minimization of the functional in Eq. (4.2) is done using the graph cuts algorithm [BK03, EXSE07], which searches for the maximum flow cut in a graph having as nodes the pixels in the image and as costs on the edges the values of the respective terms of Eq. (4.2) [BK03].

The advantage of the use of the discrete formulation of MSF minimized by means of graph cuts (besides the well-posedness) is that the result is independent of initializations. Moreover, graph cuts guarantee to converge to a "good" minimum; i.e., a boundary is given in [Vek99]. The disadvantage of being able to only segment foreground from background remains.

5 Applications in Image Processing: the image registration case

The only application of MSF mentioned until now was image segmentation. In this section more applications and modalities to employ MSF in image processing are presented.

Besides the usual segmentation of an image in foreground and background, the detection of objects in images is an important topic in image processing. There are two contributions employing MSF for object detection to be mentioned:

- The first one proposes a method to expand the continuous formulation of MSF by another term, which contains prior information about Γ (e.g., the form of the curves) [CTWS02]. This term acts regularizing, such that the objects can be correctly detected and segmented in the images, even if they are partially occluded.

- The second contribution provides the connection between snakes, geodesics and MSF by proving that the minimization of MSF is equivalent to the minimization of the geodesic snake functional [BEV$^+$05].

Another important domain where MSF is useful is image registration. The main purpose here is to find a transformation $f : \Omega_{g_i} \to \mathbb{R}^2$ between two images $g_i :$ $\Omega_{g_i} \to \Omega_{g_j}$ and $g_j : \Omega_{g_j} \to \mathbb{R}^2$ such that:

$$d(g_j, g_i \circ f) \to \min,$$

with d being an arbitrary distance function, which measures the differences between two images. The registration by means of MSF is an edge based registration; i.e., the only functionality of f is to warp the curves of Γ from one image into the other; see Eq. (5.1).

The functional for registering two images comprises therefore, among other terms, the segmentation terms of the standard MSF (Eq. (2.1)) for both images:

$$E(s_i, s_j, \Gamma, f) := \mu \left(\iint\limits_{\Omega_{g_i}} (s_i(\boldsymbol{u}) - g_i(\boldsymbol{u}))^2 \mathrm{d}\boldsymbol{u} + \iint\limits_{\Omega_{g_j}} (s_j(\boldsymbol{u}) - g_j(\boldsymbol{u}))^2 \mathrm{d}\boldsymbol{u} \right) +$$
$$\iint\limits_{\Omega_{g_i} \backslash \Gamma} \|\nabla s_i(\boldsymbol{u})\|^2 \mathrm{d}\boldsymbol{u} + \iint\limits_{\Omega_{g_j} \backslash f(\Gamma)} \|\nabla s_j(\boldsymbol{u})\|^2 \mathrm{d}\boldsymbol{u} + \nu \mathcal{H}^1(\Gamma).$$

$$(5.1)$$

The results are two segmented images s_i and s_j along with the transformation function f and one set of curves Γ, which best segment both images g_i and g_j. Therefore, the first two terms measuring the difference between the original and the segmented images are alike. The third and fourth terms ensure the smoothness of the resulted segmented images, such that the smoothness of the second segmented image g_j is demanded on its support Ω_{g_j} without the transformed set of curves $f(\Gamma)$. As there is only one set of curves for both images, only one term is necessary to measure their length.

Figure 5.1: The tiger grabbed in the image series in Figure 5.2.

As a regularization approach, [Dro05] proposes the Dirichlet boundary condition, which is formulated as an additional term to the functional in Eq. (5.1). [Dro05] registers pairs of positron density (PD) and magnetic resonance (MR) images.

This contribution proposes another possibility of extending MSF for simultaneously pairwise registration of stereo image series (i.e., more than two images).

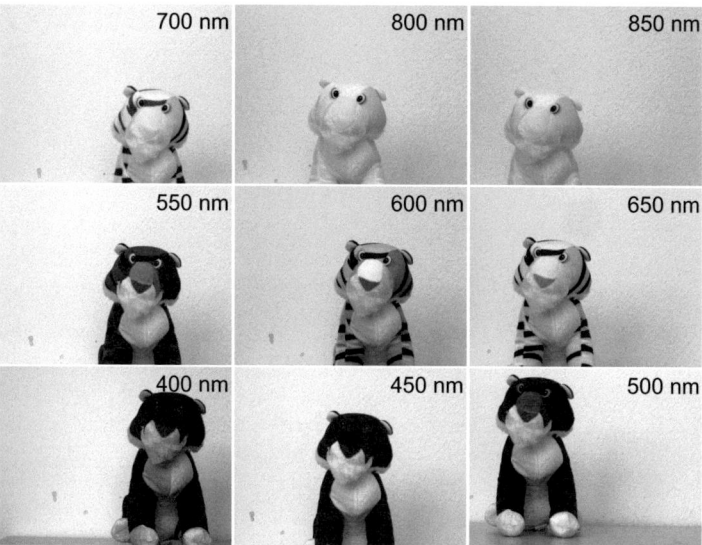

Figure 5.2: Stereo and spectral image series of the scene in Figure 5.1 acquired with a camera array. The cameras were equipped with different spectral filters. The middle transmission wavelength of the spectral acquisition filters is written in the upper right corner of each image.

Particularly for combined stereo and spectral image series, where standard stereo registration algorithms can not be applied, could such an extension be very useful. Due to the spectral component, the images in the combined stereo and spectral series have different grey values for the same object point; see Figure 5.2. In Figure 5.1 the original acquired scene (an orange tiger with black and white stripes) is presented.

There are two possibilities of registering such combined image series by means of MSF:

- The first one is to built a functional having the terms of MSF from Eq. (2.1) for each image and additionally a term that measures the dissimilarity between the segmentations:

$$E(s_1, \ldots, s_n, \Gamma_1, \ldots \Gamma_n) :=$$

$$\sum_{i=1}^{n} \left(\mu \iint_{\Omega_{g_i}} (s_i(\boldsymbol{u}) - g_i(\boldsymbol{u}))^2 \mathrm{d}\boldsymbol{u} + \iint_{\Omega_{g_i} \setminus \Gamma_i} \|\nabla s_i(\boldsymbol{u})\|^2 \mathrm{d}\boldsymbol{u} + \nu \mathcal{H}^1(\Gamma_i) \right)$$

$$+\alpha \sum_{(i \neq j)} \left(\iint_{\Gamma_i} h \left(\min_{\boldsymbol{\xi} \in \Gamma_j} d_e(\boldsymbol{u}, \boldsymbol{\xi}) \right) \mathrm{d}\boldsymbol{u} + \iint_{\Gamma_j} h \left(\min_{\boldsymbol{\xi} \in \Gamma_i} d_e(\boldsymbol{u}, \boldsymbol{\xi}) \right) \mathrm{d}\boldsymbol{u} \right),$$

$$(5.2)$$

with d_e as a distance measure taking in consideration the disparity (i.e., the difference between the position of corresponding pixels in the images, which is inversely proportional to depth) and h a function which ensures robustness. α is a weight for the dissimilarity term. The result consists in the segmented images $s_1, \ldots, s_n$ and the sets of curves $\Gamma_1, \ldots, \Gamma_n$.

- The second possibility is to extend Eq. (5.1). For this a labeling function $z : \Omega_z \to \mathcal{L}$ is defined on the set of all pixels $\Omega_z := \Omega_{g_1} \cup \ldots \cup \Omega_{g_n}$ in the images of the series. The labels are disparities between the pixels of a chosen image pair of the series [GHB08]. z is consequently a function describing corresponding pixels in the images.

$$E(s_1, \ldots s_n, \Gamma, z) :=$$

$$\sum_i \left(\mu \iint_{\Omega_{g_i}} (s_i(\boldsymbol{u}) - g_i(\boldsymbol{u}))^2 \mathrm{d}\boldsymbol{u} + \sum_i \iint_{\Omega_{g_i} \setminus \Gamma_i} \|\nabla s_i(\boldsymbol{u})\|^2 \mathrm{d}\boldsymbol{u} \right) + \nu \mathcal{H}^1(\Gamma),$$

$$(5.3)$$

whereas Γ is the determined set of curves in one selected image. Γ_i is computed by image warping using the function z [FL04]. In this case, the results comprise besides the segmented images only one set of curves Γ, which should best segment all images of the series and the function z, which describes the registration.

The advantage of the first formulation in Eq. (5.2) is that for images that are very different (e.g., spectral images, by which the contrast between neighbouring image regions differs from image to image, see Figure 5.2) a segmentation of each image is found, even if these are different; see Figure 5.3. In the second case of Eq. (5.3) the solution is forced to one set of curves, which in some cases might fail to work (i.e., such that no set of curves Γ is found). As an example, the segmented images

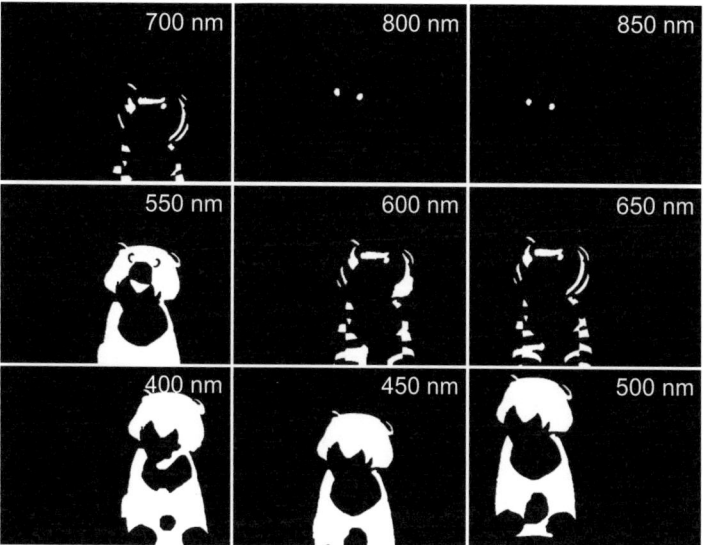

Figure 5.3: Segmented images from Figure 5.2 using MSF from Eq. (4.2).

in the lower row of Figure 5.3 are completely different from the segmented images in the upper row.

Even though the segmentation results with MSF are very promising, further experiments are necessary to prove its superiority with regard to the methods employed until now to register combined image series [GMHB08, GHB08], i.e., the images were segmented using the watershed transformation [GW08] and then registered by comparing the features of the obtained regions. The main problem of this approach was that the segmentations of the images were very different (see Figure 5.4), which has been making the feature based registration difficult.

Summing up, the advantages of using MSF for segmenting combined image series are:

- The segmentation results for the images are similar, at least for images acquired in neighbouring spectral bands; see Figure 5.3.

- The segmentation and registration steps are performed simultaneously.

- No prior information or parametrization (e.g., for the segmentation) is required.

The disadvantages that could be established until now are:

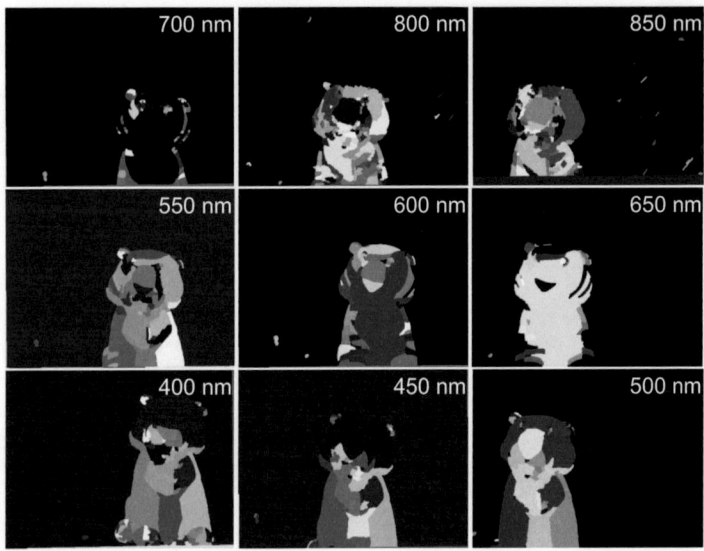

Figure 5.4: Segmented images from Figure 5.2 using the watershed transformation.

- Opposite to the watershed transformation, which gives a detailed segmentation of each image (see Figure 5.4), MSF segments only foreground from background. This means that only some edges (those of the segmented region) can be used for registration. The computed transformation might therefore be not representative for all pixels in the image. As an example, the segmented regions in Figure 5.3 in the images acquired at 800 and 850 nm may at most be representative for the face of the tiger, but not for its legs; i.e., the depth values of the respective scene planes are different. A possible solution is a sequential segmentation and registration by masking the regions previously registered.

- In the case of combined stereo and spectral images, it is difficult to find a common segmentation for all images.

For completeness, some other applications of MSF in image processing worth mentioning are: inpainting [ES02] and dynamic texture segmentation [DCFS03].

6   Conclusions and Future Work

This contribution presented a short overview of the Mumford-Shah functional and its applications in image processing. It has been observed that mainly one of the four models given by [Mum94], namely the Cartoon model, is being employed in image processing. Since MSF is ill-posed regularizations are needed. These can be achieved either by adding an additional term to the functional (e.g., describing boundary conditions) or by assuming that the regions to be segmented are homogeneous.

One important image processing application for which MSF can be employed is image registration. This contribution presented some new ideas for registering combined stereo and spectral image series by means of MSF. Even though the first enquires are very promising, a more detailed analysis and tests are required. The results will be published in future contributions.

Bibliography

[BEV+05]   X. Bresson, S. Esedoḡluy, P. Vandergheynst, J.P. Thiran, and S. Osher. Global Minimizers of the Active Contour/Snake Model. Technical report, Swiss Federal Institute of Technology (EPFL), University of California, 2005.

[BK03]   Yuri Boykov and Vladimir Kolmogorov. Computing Geodesics and Minimal Surfaces via Graph Cuts. In *Proceedings of the Ninth IEEE International Conference on Computer Vision (ICCV'03)*, 2003.

[CS05]   Tony F. Chan and Jianhong Shen. *Image Processing and Analysis: Variational, PDE, Wavelet, and Stochastic Methods*. Society for Industrial and Applied Mathematics, 2005.

[CTWS02]   Daniel Cremers, Florian Tischäuser, Joachim Weickert, and Christoph Schnörr. Diffusion Snakes: Introducing Statistical Shape Knowledge into the Mumford-Shah Functional. *International Journal of Computer Vision*, 50(3):295–313, 2002.

[CV01]   Tony F. Chan and Luminita A. Vese. Active Contours Without Edges. *IEEE Transactions on Image Processing*, 10(2):266–277, 2001.

[Dav05]   Guy David. *Singular Sets of Minimizers for the Mumford-Shah Functional*. Birkhäuser Verlag, 2005.

[DCFS03]   Gianfranco Doretto, Daniel Cremers, Paolo Favaro, and Stefano Soatto. Dynamic Texture Segmentation. In *Proceedings of IEEE International Conference on Computer Vision*, pages 1236–1242, 2003.

[Dro05]   Marc Droske. *On Variational Problems and Gradient Flows in Image Processing*. Gerhard-Mercator-Universität Duisburg, 2005.

[ES02]   Selim Esedoglu and Jianhong Shen. Digital Inpainting Based on the Mumford-Shah-Euler Image Model. *European Journal of Applied Mathematics*, 13:353–370, 2002.

[EXSE07]   Noha El-Zehiry, Steve Xu, Prasanna Sahoo, and Adel Elmaghraby. Graph Cut Optimiza-
           tion for the Mumford-Shah Model. In *Proceedings of the Seventh IASTED International
           Conference visualization, imaging and image processing*, number 182–187, 2007.

[FL04]   Olivier Faugeras and Quang-Tuan Luong. *The Geometry of Multiple Images*. MIT Press,
           2004.

[GHB08]   Ioana Gheţa, Michael Heizmann, and Jürgen Beyerer. Bayesian Fusion of Multivariate
           Image Series to Obtain Depth Information. In *Proceedings of Fusion 2008*, pages 1731–
           1737, 2008.

[GMHB08]   Ioana Gheţa, Markus Mathias, Michael Heizmann, and Jürgen Beyerer. Fusion of Com-
           bined Stereo and Spectral Series for Obtaining 3D Information. In *Multisensor, Multi-
           source Information Fusion: Architectures, Algorithms, and Applications, Proceedings of
           SPIE 6974*, 2008.

[GW08]   Rafael C. Gonzalez and Richard E. Woods. *Digital Image Processing*. Prentice Hall,
           2008.

[Her67]   Hans Hermes. *Einführung in die Verbandstheorie*. Springer-Verlag Berlin, 1967.

[KKB+07]   Kalin Kolev, Maria Klodt, Thomas Brox, Selim Esedoglu, and Daniel Cremers. Con-
           tinuous Global Optimization in Multiview 3D Reconstruction. In *Energy Minimization
           Methods in Computer Vision and Pattern Recognition*, 2007.

[LS94]   Antonio Leaci and Sergio Solimini. *Geometry-Driven Diffusion in Computer Vision*,
           chapter Variational Problems with a Free Discontinuity Set, pages 147–154. Kluwer
           Academic Publischers, 1994.

[MS85]   David Mumford and Jayant Shah. Boundary Detection by Minimizing Functionals, I. In
           Proc. IEEE Conference on Computer Vision and Pattern Recognition, 1985.

[MS89]   David Mumford and Jayant Shah. Optimal Approximations by Piecewise Smooth Func-
           tions and Associated Variational Problems. *Communications on Pure and Applied
           Mathematics*, XLII:577–685, 1989.

[Mum94]   David Mumford. *Geometry-Driven Diffusion in Computer Vision*, chapter Bayesian Ra-
           tionale for the Variational Formulation, pages 135–146. Kluwer Academic Publischers,
           1994.

[Osh03]   Stanley Osher. *Level Set Methods and Dynamic Implicit Surfaces*. Springer-Verlag New
           York, 2003.

[Oss97]   R. Osserman, editor. *Minimal Surfaces*, volume Geometry V. Springer-Verlag Berlin,
           1997.

[Vek99]   Olga Veksler. *Efficient Graph-Based Energy Minimization Methods in Compute Vision*.
           PhD thesis, Faculty of the Graduate School of Cornell University, 1999.

Further Investigation of Focussed Bayesian Fusion

Jennifer Sander

Vision and Fusion Laboratory
Institute for Anthropomatics
Karlsruhe Institute of Technology (KIT), Germany
jennifer.sander@kit.edu

Technical Report IES-2009-03

Abstract: Local Bayesian fusion approaches reduce high computational costs caused by Bayesian fusion. This paper mainly deals with focussed Bayesian fusion, a special local Bayesian fusion technique, which is easily realizable in practice. An interval scheme for global probabilities is derived. Using concepts from information theory and decision theory, other new results concerning the global meaning of focussed Bayesian fusion and its consistency with Bayesian decision theory are presented.

1 Introduction

To automate the combination of information from several information sources, an adequate fusion methodology is needed. The Bayesian fusion methodology fulfills all essential requirements on a reasonable fusion methodology [BSW07]. It is mathematically funded and has theoreticly a comprehensive range of application. Information is represented by probability distributions in the sense of the Degree of Belief interpretation. By this, the Bayesian fusion methodology accounts for every kind of uncertainty in an adequate manner [Lin87]. However, its practical application in real world examples is often critical due to high storage and computational costs.

By the use of local Bayesian fusion approaches, high costs caused by Bayesian fusion can get circumvented. At local Bayesian fusion, the complete calculation of the posterior distribution for all possible values of the Properties of Interest (PoI) is avoided. For this, ideally all task specific information, i.e., prior knowledge and source specific information, is pre-evaluated. The aim is the detection of values of the PoI that have a higher potential to be the true value than others have.

Probabilistic statements are then made with respect to modifications of the usual Bayesian model.

Restricting the space Z that specifies the possible values of the PoI delivers a straightforward fusion scheme. With respect to the PoI, the actual Bayesian fusion task gets completely restricted on $U \subset Z$, here. The set U contains the most task relevant part of Z. All other possible values of the PoI, i.e., the elements of $Z \setminus U$, are completely ignored. Because of its theoretic similarity to the focussing mechanism of the Bayesian fusion methodology [BHSG08], this technique has been termed focussed Bayesian fusion in [SHGB09].

1.1 Contributions

Focussed Bayesian fusion has been already considered in particular in [SB08] and [SHGB09]. The aim of the present paper is to report new results on this local Bayesian fusion technique. The main focus of the investigations is the global meaning of focussed Bayesian fusion. Additionally, questions with regard to its consistency with decision theory are addressed. Within this report, focussed Bayesian fusion is looked from different perspectives. For this, purely probabilistic, information theoretic, and decision theoretic views are adopted.

1.2 Structure

Necessary basics of Bayesian fusion are shortly reviewed in Section 2. For a more detailed introduction, the reader is referred for example to [BSW07, Bey99, BS04]. In Section 3, a purely probabilistic view is adopted to derive an interval scheme for global probabilities. Provided that the global prior relevance of the local context U is known, this interval scheme is computable within a focussed Bayesian model. Therefore, it is described in Section 3.1 what knowledge about global probabilities is obtainable if only their focussed equivalents are known. These results are also generally useful for probabilistic modelling in cases in that it is unknown if the domains are chosen comprehensive enough. Possible negative consequences of the closed world assumption of Bayesian modelling, which usually makes quantitative Degree of Belief statements possible, become clear. Facts concerning a meaningful construction of focussed Bayesian models are used in Section 3.2 for the derivation of lower bounds for global probabilities, which are computable if the prior relevance of the local context is ratable. These bounds complement known upper bounds, which are reviewed in Section 3.1. The resulting probability interval scheme is analyzed in Section 3.3. As shown in [SHGB09], an information theoretic quality indicator for local Bayesian fusion makes sense on the basis of both, the Minimum Information Principle (MIP) [Wil80] and Walkers minimization rule for Bayesian inference [Wal06]. The information theoretic quality indicator also serves as a construction rule for meaningful focussed Bayesian models. In Section 4.1, the meaning of Walkers minimization rule for local Bayesian fusion is further clarified without taking recourse to the theoreticly more complex MIP. In Section 4.2, the value of the knowledge of the global prior and global posterior relevance, respectively, of the local context is rated information theoreticly. Therefore, an information measure, which is the basis of the analysis in Section 4.1, is used. In Section 5, local Bayesian fusion is considered in the context of decision theory. Bayesian theory distinguishes itself by its consistency with decision theory [Bey99]. Bayesian inference is even a special form of a decision problem [BS04]. The consistency of focussed Bayesian fusion with decision theory is demonstrated in Section 5.1. A way to solve a decision problem on the basis of a focussed Bayesian model by the use of the derived probability interval scheme is discussed in Section 5.2. Finally, Section 6 is a short conclusion.

1.3   Remarks

By the transformation of all information into a probabilistic representation, fusion tasks, which may involve most diverse kinds of information, get methodically unified. For the comprehensive validity of the results about local Bayesian fusion, their development is based on the assumption that the pre-evaluation is done after performing the transformation.

In case of statistical conditional independence of the information contributions, the individual transformation of each of them in a probabilistic representation by a source specific Likelihood is sufficient to realize exact Bayesian fusion, see Section 2. Here, the Likelihood with respect to all information contributions results from the multiplication of the source specific ones. For mathematical simplicity, the presented results are based on the consideration of the Likelihood with respect to all information contributions. However, their special adaption for source specific Likelihoods is straightforward—at least if the statistical conditional independence of the information contributions holds.

2   Bayesian Fusion

By $z = (z_1, \ldots, z_N) \in Z = Z_1 \times \ldots \times Z_N$, $N \in \mathbb{N}$, the PoI are denoted. We assume that the quantity z adopts a certain, but not directly observable true value. Let $d_s \in D_s$ denote the information contribution of the information source

$s \in \{1, \dots, S\}$, $S \in \mathbb{N}$, and $d = (d_1, \dots, d_s)$ summarize all source specific information.

At Bayesian fusion, prior knowledge with respect to the PoI is represented probabilistically by[1] the prior distribution $p(z)$ and source specific information specifies the Likelihood $p(d|z)$. Bayesian inference on the basis of the Bayesian theorem delivers the posterior distribution $p(z|d)$:

$$p(z|d) = \frac{p(d|z)\,p(z)}{p(d)} \propto p(d|z)\,p(z)\,, \quad z \in Z\,.$$

If the information contributions are statistically independent given z, which can be assumed for example if heterogenous information sources have to be fused, a sequential inference scheme is mathematically exact:

$$p(z|d) \propto \prod_{s=1}^{S} p(d_s|z)\,p(z)\,, \quad z \in Z\,.$$

The computational complexity for the calculation of the posterior distribution is[2] $O(\prod_{n=1}^{N} |Z_n|) = O(\zeta^N)$ where $\zeta = \sqrt[N]{\prod_{n=1}^{N} |Z_n|}$ denotes the geometric mean value. To obtain meaningful estimates for the true value of z, decision theoretic concepts have to be used. Because they have to applied on $p(z|d)$, Bayesian fusion demands considerable computational resources regardless of wether the whole posterior distribution or wether a simple estimate for the true value is demanded as final result. It gets clear that the complete calculation of $p(z|d)$ for all $z \in Z$ has to be avoided to reduce the computational complexity of Bayesian fusion. Local Bayesian fusion approaches realize this objective.

3 Probability Bounds

3.1 Meaning of Restricted Probability Statements

The restriction of Z on U mathematically corresponds to a conditioning on the local context U, see [SHGB09]. The focussed posterior distribution $p_U(z|d)$ is

---

[1]The components of d and z are discrete or continuous depending on the fusion task. The term distribution is used for a density distribution in the case of continuous quantities and for a discrete distribution in the case of discrete quantities.

[2]By $|Z_n|$, the cardinality of a discrete subspace Z_n and the Lebesgue measure (length, area, or volume) of a continuous subspace Z_n is denoted.

given by

$$p_U(z|d) = p(z|d, U) = \begin{cases} \frac{p(z|d)}{P(U|d)}, & z \in U, \\ 0, & z \in Z \setminus U. \end{cases} \tag{3.1}$$

In the focussed Bayesian model, events[3] $E \subseteq Z \setminus U$ are assumed to be impossible. Because of the normalization requirement on a probability distribution, the global posterior probability mass[4] $P(Z \setminus U|d) = \int_{Z \setminus U} p(z|d) \, \mathrm{d}z$ of $Z \setminus U$ is redistributed on U. This is done for $z \in U$ by the division of the global posterior distribution $p(z|d)$ by the global posterior probability mass $P(U|d) = \int_U p(z|d) \, \mathrm{d}z$ of the local context U. By this, the global posterior probability $P(E|d) = \int_E p(z|d) \, \mathrm{d}z$ of events $E \subseteq U$ gets increased by the distortion factor $\frac{1}{P(U|d)}$. Hence, within the local context U, local posterior probability statements $P_U(\cdot|d)$ represent upper bounds for their global equivalents:

$$P(E|d) \leq P_U(E|d), \quad E \subseteq U. \tag{3.2}$$

There are two influence factors that affect the degree by that the absolute value of the posterior probability of an event $E \subseteq U$ is distorted by the focussing. The lesser the global posterior relevance $P(U|d)$ of the local context U, the more global posterior probability statements are overestimated by the use of the focussed posterior distribution, i.e., for two different local contexts $U_1, U_2 \subseteq Z$ and an event $E \subseteq U_1 \cap U_2$, it holds

$$P(U_1|d) < P(U_2|d) \Rightarrow P_{U_2}(E|d) < P_{U_1}(E|d).$$

The lesser the global probability $P(E|d)$ of an event $E \subseteq U$, the lesser its absolute value gets increased by the focussing: for $E_1, E_2 \subseteq U$, one has

$$P(E_1|d) < P(E_2|d) \Rightarrow P_U(E_1|d) - P(E_1|d) < P_U(E_2|d) - P(E_2|d). \tag{3.3}$$

It should be remarked that certain conclusions on the basis of a focussed Bayesian model are globally fully meaningful. These are comparisons of posterior probability statements for events $E \subseteq U$ by the use of probability ratios [SB08]. In particular, the focussed posterior distribution introduces with respect to events $E \subseteq U$ the same preference ordering as the global posterior distribution does.

3.2 Special Knowledge at Focussing

If the pre-evaluation is performed with respect to the probabilistic information representations, see Section 1.3, U is defined to contain these elements z of Z

---

[3]Events are sets to that a probability is assigned.

[4]The notation $\int_Z \ldots \mathrm{d}z$ stands for integration with respect to continuous subspaces and for summation with respect to discrete subspaces of Z.

for that $p(d|z)$ or $p(z)$ is high enough[5]. The introduction of a threshold δ for the value of the Likelihood with respect to z is critical because there is no normalization requirement for the Likelihood with respect to z. As consequence, δ has to depend on parameters that give it a relative nature. E.g., the dependency $\delta = \delta(\max_{z \in Z} p(d|z))$ makes sense [SB08]. Another kind of dependency is described in Section 4.1.

The results of Section 3.1 hold in an analogous manner for prior probability statements. The global prior probability $P(U) = \int_U p(z) \, \mathrm{d}z$ rates the global prior relevance of the local context U. By the focussing, the prior relevance of U gets modified to one. However, in many focussed Bayesian fusion tasks, the value of $P(U)$ is at least approximately ratable.

Assuming $P(U)$ to be known, the inequality $p(d|z) \le \delta$ for $z \in Z \setminus U$ delivers a lower bound for the global posterior relevance $P(U|d)$ of U:

$$
\begin{aligned}
P(U|d) &= \frac{\int_U p(d|z)\,p(z)\,\mathrm{d}z}{p(d)} \\[2mm]
&= \frac{\int_U p(d|z)\,p(z)\,\mathrm{d}z}{\int_U p(d|z)\,p(z)\,\mathrm{d}z + \int_{Z \setminus U} p(d|z)\,p(z)\,\mathrm{d}z} \\[2mm]
&\ge \frac{\int_U p(d|z)\,p(z)\,\mathrm{d}z}{\int_U p(d|z)\,p(z)\,\mathrm{d}z + \delta \int_{Z \setminus U} p(z)\,\mathrm{d}z} \qquad (3.4)\\[2mm]
&= \frac{\int_U p(d|z)\,p(z)\,\mathrm{d}z}{\int_U p(d|z)\,p(z)\,\mathrm{d}z + \delta\,(1 - P(U))} \\[2mm]
&= \frac{\int_U p(d|z)\,p_U(z)\,\mathrm{d}z}{\int_U p(d|z)\,p_U(z)\,\mathrm{d}z + \delta\left(\frac{1}{P(U)} - 1\right)} =: \beta \,.
\end{aligned}
$$

The focussed prior distribution $p_U(z)$ is related to the global prior distribution $p(z)$ by the identity $p_U(z) = \frac{p(z)}{P(U)}$. The Likelihood of the focussed Bayesian model is exactly an extract of the Likelihood of the global Bayesian model. To make these connections clear, the general inference scheme for focussed Bayesian fusion [SB08] is cited:

$$
p_U(z|d) \propto p(d|z)\,p_U(z)\,, \quad z \in U \,.
$$

From these considerations, it becomes clear how β is computable within the focussed Bayesian model.

---

[5]If an interpretation of the prior knowledge as an additional information contribution is possible, the analysis can be unified [SB08]. However, this possibility is not used, here.

By the application of the lower bound for $P(U|d)$, the factor by that a focussed probability statement with respect to an event $E \subseteq U$ is distorted relative to its global equivalent can be bounded from above:

$$\frac{P_U(E|d)}{P(E|d)} = \frac{1}{P(U|d)} \leq \frac{1}{\beta} , \quad E \subseteq U . \tag{3.5}$$

By the use of (3.5), lower bounds for global posterior probability statements can get calculated within the focussed Bayesian model:

$$P(E|d) \geq \beta P_U(E|d) , \quad E \subseteq U . \tag{3.6}$$

3.3 Probability Interval Scheme

An interval scheme for global posterior probability statements is delivered by (3.2) and (3.6): it holds

$$P(E|d) \in [\beta P_U(E|d), P_U(E|d)] , \quad E \subseteq U .$$

These probability intervals are calculable within a focussed Bayesian model if δ is known and if the global prior relevance $P(U)$ of the local context U is ratable.

The interval scheme can get easily extended to events $E \subseteq Z \setminus U$ because by the use of (3.4), one obtains

$$P(E|d) \leq 1 - P(U|d) \leq 1 - \beta , \quad E \subseteq Z \setminus U .$$

Hence, we have

$$P(E|d) \in [l(E), r(E)] := \begin{cases} [\beta P_U(E|d), P_U(E|d)] , & E \subseteq U , \\ [0, 1 - \beta] , & E \subseteq Z \setminus U . \end{cases} \tag{3.7}$$

In an experimental evaluation, it has been demonstrated that β is a qualitatively good bound for the global posterior relevance $P(U|d)$ of the local context U at focussed Bayesian fusion. It becomes shaper with increasing concentration of the Likelihood on U. There are cases in that the knowledge of the probability interval scheme (3.7) is sufficient to identify the maximum a posteriori estimate of a discrete global posterior distribution.

In [SHGB09], the small world formalism has been used to explain the consistency of local Bayesian fusion approaches with Bayesian theory in a demonstrative manner. Here, the basic essentials of the argumentation will be reviewed and further expanded.

For the mathematical solution of a fusion task, an adequate modelling is needed. It is not possible to model the real world completely. A global Bayesian model $(Z \times D, p(z, d))$ corresponds to a so called model world. It contains at least that part of the real world that is meaningful for the fusion task. At local Bayesian fusion approaches, the actual fusion task is solved only with respect to a so called local world, which is a real subset[6] of the model world. By construction, the local world has a high chance to be task relevant. At focussed Bayesian fusion, the local world corresponds to the focussed Bayesian model[7] $(U \times D, p_U(z, d))$.

Focussing makes events $E \subseteq U$ more probable than they globally are. By the knowledge of the bound β for the global posterior relevance $P(U|d)$ of the local context U, this overestimation is reversible in principle. However, this reversion is to strong and as consequence, it makes events $E \subseteq U$ less probable than they globally are.

By the additional introduction of a reference world that lies between real world and model world, all derived probability bounds can get included in the small world formalism. The reference world has the form $(R \times D, p_R(z, d))$ with $Z \subseteq R$. Thereby, the probability distribution $p_R(z, d)$ is not known completely. Taking into account (3.7), one obtains for the corresponding posterior distribution:

$$p_R(z|d) = \begin{cases} = \beta\, p_U(z|d)\,, & z \in U\,, \\ \leq 1 - \beta\,, & z \in Z \setminus U\,, \\ = ?\,, & z \in R \setminus Z\,. \end{cases} \tag{3.8}$$

At focussed Bayesian fusion, the local world also represents a focussing of such a reference world. The exact values of reference posterior probability statements $P_R(E|d)$ are known for events $E \subseteq U$. They are equal to the bounds $l(E)$ of the probability intervals in (3.7). For events $E \subseteq U$, the upper bounds in (3.7) are the focussed probability statements. Hence, for events $E \subseteq U$, the length $d(E) := r(E) - l(E)$ of the probability intervals is identical to the absolute value of the distortion that results from the focussing of the reference world on the local world. The distortion factor at this transition is $\frac{1}{\beta}$.

By the application of the previous results, conclusions concerning $d(E)$ can be easily derived. The larger β, the lesser $d(E)$ is for all $E \subseteq U$. Because of (3.4), a large value of β indicates that the global posterior relevance $P(U|d)$ of the local context U is large. Hence, large values of $P(U|d)$ generally correspond to small

---

[6]All kinds of subset relations within the small world formalism are task specific, see [SHGB09].

[7] Strictly speaking, in a focussed Bayesian model of the kind $(U \times D, p_U(z, d))$, the probability of events $E \not\subseteq U$ is not defined. To demonstrate the connection between global and local Bayesian models explicitly, such probability values nevertheless have been introduced in (3.1) and been declared to be zero.

probability intervals for events $E \subseteq U$. It is directly clear from (3.7) that this connection also holds for events $E \subseteq Z \setminus U$. For events $E_1, E_2 \subseteq Z \setminus U$, it holds that $d(E_1) = d(E_2) = 1 - \beta$, i.e., the probability intervals of such events all have the same length. In contrast, the length $d(E)$ of an probability interval for an event $E \subseteq U$ depends of the global posterior probability of E. More precisely, for $E_1, E_2 \subseteq U$, it holds

$$P(E_1|d) < P(E_2|d) \Rightarrow d(E_1) < d(E_2) . \tag{3.9}$$

The proof of (3.9) bases on (3.3). Because of (3.3), its clear that the reference posterior probability $P_R(E|d)$ influences the length of the probability interval: the lesser $P_R(E|d)$, the lesser $d(E)$ is. Combining (3.1) and (3.8), one obtains for $E \subseteq U$ the identity $P_R(E|d) = \frac{\beta \, p(E|d)}{P(U|d)}$. Due to the fact that β and $P(U|d)$ do not depend on the choice of E, (3.9) gets clear from this identity.

A comprehensive analysis about the best use of the probability interval scheme may be an important topic in further research. In this regard, it should be stressed out that by the use of probability intervals, uncertainty is not described purely probabilistically. However, we generally hold the view that the probabilistic calculus in the Bayesian sense is completely sufficient to handle every kind of uncertainty.

4 Information Theoretic Analysis

4.1 Meaning of Walkers Minimization Rule

Walkers minimization rule bases on Zellners investigation of the information theoretic optimality of Bayesian inference, see for example [Zel02]. He demonstrated that a distribution $r(z)$ embodies given information in the form of prior knowledge and source specific information in an optimal manner if it minimizes the functional

$$F(r(z)) := - \int_{z \in Z} r(z) \log p(d|z) \, dz + \mathrm{KD}[r(z), p(z)] . \tag{4.1}$$

In (4.1), KD denotes the Kullback-Leibler distance. The domain of F is the set of all probability distributions $r(z)$ on Z with $\mathrm{KD}[r(z), p(z)] < \infty$.

This minimization rule is structurally different to the minimization rule that underlies the MIP. At the application of the MIP to Bayesian inference, a functional over probability distributions on $Z \times D$ is minimized in the strict sense.

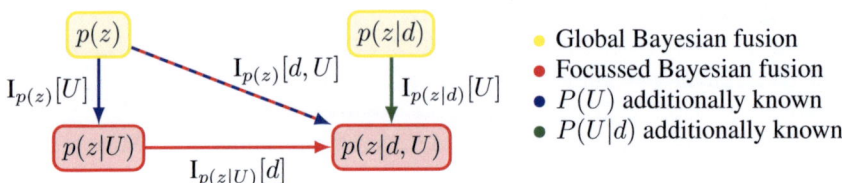

Figure 4.1: Schematic illustration of the information theoretic value of additionally knowing $P(U)$ and $P(U|d)$, respectively, at focussed Bayesian fusion.

At Bayesian inference, the amount of information about the quantity of interest y that is provided by the given data x is usually[8] defined to be

$$\mathrm{I}_{p(y)}[x] := \mathrm{KD}[p(y|x), p(y)] \ . \tag{4.2}$$

Because of the identity $F(p(z|d, U)) - F(p(z|d)) = \mathrm{I}_{p(z|d)}[U]$, the difference $F(p(z|d, U)) - F(p(z|d))$ measures the amount of information that is additionally delivered about z by the assumption "$z \in U$", which underlies focussed Bayesian fusion. Clearly, the local context U should be chosen such that the value of this quantity is low.

As explained in [SHGB09], from the identity $\mathrm{I}_{p(z|d)}[U] = -\log P(U|d)$ it follows that at focussing, one should ignore preferably these $z \in Z$ for that both, $p(d|z)$ and $p(z)$, adopt low values. Thereby, the additional requirement that $\mathrm{KD}[p(z|U, d), p(z|d)]$ has to be hold low enough gives the thresholds for $p(z)$ and $p(d|z)$ a relative nature.

4.2 Knowledge of the Relevance of Local Contexts

The knowledge of the global prior relevance $P(U)$ of the local context U is indispensable for the calculation of the derived lower bounds of global posterior probability statements on the basis of a focussed Bayesian model, see Section 3.2. Here, the value of the knowledge of the global prior and global posterior relevance, respectively, of the local context U is also rated in the context of information theory.

---

[8]This common definition is for example given by Bernardo [BS04]. Lindley introduced another definition, see [Lin56]. The difference between the two definitions is often overseen because the expected value of the amount of information about y provided on average by data that are distributed according to $p(x)$, i.e., the mutual information between x and y, is the same with respect to both of them. Bernardos definition seems to make more sense, here, because it corresponds to a real posterior analysis.

In Figure 4.1, it is graphically shown which connections between a global and a focussed Bayesian model are information theoreticly quantifiable by the use of the information measure that has been defined in (4.2). It is marked to what extent the knowledge of $P(U)$ and $P(U|d)$, respectively, is needed for this.

If the focussed Bayesian fusion has been performed, the amount of information about z that is locally provided by d, i.e., $I_{p(z|U)}[d]$, can get calculated. If the global prior relevance $P(U)$ of the local context U is known, the amount of information that is delivered about z solely by the assumption "$z \in U$" is additionally calculable because we have $I_{p(z)}[U] = -\log P(U)$. Another straightforward calculation delivers the identity

$$I_{p(z|U)}[d] + I_{p(z)}[U] = I_{p(z)}[d, U] .$$

Hence, by the knowledge of the global prior relevance $P(U)$ of the local context U, the amount of information that is delivered about z by both together, d and the assumption "$z \in U$", is also quantitatively ratable.

On the other hand, by the knowledge of the global posterior relevance $P(U|d)$ of the local context U, the amount of information that is additionally to the information from d delivered about z by the assumption "$z \in U$", i.e., $I_{p(z|d)}[U]$, is exactly calculable: it holds $I_{p(z|d)}[U] = -\log P(U|d)$. In Section 4.1, this quantity has been identified as basis for a construction rule for meaningful focussed Bayesian models. It is stressed out that in Section 4.1 the knowledge of the exact value of this quantity has not been assumed.

5 Decision Theoretic Analysis

5.1 Fundamental Consistency of Focussed Bayesian Fusion

Bayesian inference aims at the probabilistic representation and further development of the state of knowledge with respect to the PoI. Bayesian decision theory also considers the consequences that result from choosing an action $a \in A$. The consequences usually depend on the true value of the PoI.

A preference ordering on the set A of available actions subject to the true value of the PoI can be specified by the determination of an utility function $u(a, z)$. An action a_Z is globally optimal if it maximizes the expected utility with respect to the global posterior distribution, i.e., if it holds

$$a_Z = \arg\max_{a \in A} \mathbf{U}[a; p(z|d)] \quad \text{with} \quad \mathbf{U}[a; p(z|d)] := \int_Z u(a, z) \, p(z|d) \, \mathrm{d}z .$$

Usually, a decision maker is termed to act *rational* within this kind of decision theoretic model if and only if he chooses a globally optimal action [RN03].

At focussed Bayesian fusion, the global posterior distribution is not known completely. The choice of an action may be based on the expected utility with respect to the focussed posterior distribution $p_U(z|d)$: an action a_U is defined to be locally optimal if it holds

$$a_U = \arg\max_{a \in A} \mathbf{U}[a; p_U(z|d)] \quad \text{with} \quad \mathbf{U}[a; p_U(z|d)] = \int_U u(a, z) \, p_U(z|d) \, \mathrm{d}z \, .$$

Obliviously, it may hold

$$\mathbf{U}[a_Z; p(z|d)] > \mathbf{U}[a_U; p(z|d)] \, ,$$

i.e., a locally optimal action is not globally optimal in general. This may call the global rationality of a decision maker who uses a focussed Bayesian model into question.

This seeming inconsistency arises if the storage and computational costs that are necessary for the solution of a decision problem are not taken into account. In this case, the decision is based on posterior expected utility considerations without reconsidering the costs that arise for the necessary calculations. At Bayesian decision theory, calculation costs in dependence of the choice of the domains of the involved quantities are usually neglected. This is because Bayesian theory generally does not address questions with respect to the task specific generation of these domains[9]. In particular, modifications of a Bayesian model with respect to Z are usually not analyzed.

To make such an analysis possible, let $\mathbf{C}[V]$ denote the costs that are caused by a Bayesian fusion scheme that is focussed on $V \subseteq Z$ and let a_V denote the respective optimal action. The effective posterior expected utility is defined by

$$\mathbf{U}_{\mathrm{eff}}[a_V; p(z|d), \mathbf{C}[V]] := \mathbf{U}[a_V; p(z|d)] - \mathbf{C}[V] \, .$$

Generally, the inequality $\mathbf{C}[U] < \mathbf{C}[Z]$ will hold for $U \subset Z$. Hence, it is possible that the effective posterior expected utility of an action that is locally optimal with respect to $U \subset Z$ may exceed the effective posterior expected utility of the globally optimal action. This means that it may hold

$$\mathbf{U}_{\mathrm{eff}}[a_Z; p(z|d), \mathbf{C}[Z]] \leq \mathbf{U}_{\mathrm{eff}}[a_U; p(z|d), \mathbf{C}[U]] \, .$$

---

[9]See for example the discussion in [BS04] about the generation of a dynamic frame of discourse.

I.e., taking into account the significant savings of storage and computational costs that can be reached by focussed Bayesian fusion, a locally optimal action may be effectively a better choice than an action that is globally optimal. Assuming that $u(a, z)$ is uniquely chosen, not negative, and bounded, the following estimation holds:

$$0 \leq \mathbf{U}[a_Z; p(z|d)] - \mathbf{U}[a_U; p(z|d)]$$
$$= \int_{z \in U} (u(a_Z, z) - u(a_U, z)) \, p(z|d) \, \mathrm{d}z$$
$$+ \int_{z \in Z \setminus U} (u(a_Z, z) - u(a_U, z)) \, p(z|d) \, \mathrm{d}z$$
$$\leq \int_{z \in Z \setminus U} (u(a_Z, z) - u(a_U, z)) \, p(z|d) \, \mathrm{d}z$$
$$\leq (1 - P(U|d)) \left(\max_{a \in A} \max_{z \in Z \setminus U} u(a, z) - \min_{a \in A} \min_{z \in Z \setminus U} u(a, z) \right)$$
$$\leq (1 - P(U|d)) \max_{a \in A} \max_{z \in Z \setminus U} u(a, z) \, .$$

This means for example that a Bayesian model that is focussed on $U \subset Z$ is preferable for the solution of a decision problem if the global posterior relevance $P(U|d)$ of the local context U is large and if the value of the utility function is low for all actions with regard to these values of z that lie in the part of Z that is ignored at focussing—in comparison to the costs that would be caused by an evaluation of this part of Z.

If rational decision making is set equally to expected utility maximization, the given justification has still a shortcoming because mathematically the effective posterior expected utility does not have the form of an expected utility.

However in reality, the described kind of expected utility maximization can not be termed always rational: strictly speaking, the calculation of an expected utility itself corresponds to an act and may not possess maximal expected utility [Sar09].

To formalize this fact, Sargent introduced in [Sar09] the concept of decision levels. By an (informal) adaption of this concept, the meaning of effective posterior expected utilities can be further explained within the decision theoretic context. The application of a global Bayesian model and the application of a Bayesian model that is focussed on $U \subset Z$ for the solution of the decision problem correspond to acts on a second decision level. Their utilities can be defined to be the respective effective posterior expected utilities. After the second level decision has been made, the actual decision problem is solved on the first level by an expected utility maximization on the basis of the Bayesian model that has been chosen on the second level. Hence on the first decision level, the choice of a locally optimal action that is not globally optimal may be fully rational.

An exact weighting of costs in the form of computational and storage costs and an abstract kind of utility may not be possible. As consequence, the exact mathematical solution of the second level decision problem will not work in general. It is stressed out, however, that the main application area of local Bayesian fusion approaches are tasks where global Bayesian fusion is not feasible due to its prohibitive complexity. In such a case, the costs of global Bayesian fusion have to exceed the expected utility of a globally optimal action. It is also clear that local Bayesian fusion approaches will deliver the best possible results if the size of the local context U is scaled accordingly to the available resources.

5.2 Use of Probability Intervals

The integration of the probability interval scheme that has been derived in Section 3.3 offers an additional approach to the handling of decision problems that are solved on the basis of a focussed Bayesian model. Exemplarily, a technique for the case of a discrete Z, which traces back to Fishburn [Fis64], will be adapted, here. To make it directly applicable, (3.7) is rewritten in the following form:

$$f(z) \leq p(z|d) := f(z) + h(z) \leq f(z) + g(z) , \quad z \in Z . \tag{5.1}$$

The functions $f(z)$ and $g(z)$ are known while $h(z)$ is unidentified. According to (3.7), we have $f(z) = 0$ for $z \in Z \setminus U$. It must hold

$$\sum_{z \in Z} h(z) = 1 - \sum_{z \in U} f(z) \quad \text{and} \quad 0 \leq h(z) \leq g(z) , \quad z \in Z . \tag{5.2}$$

On basis of (5.1), bounds for the differences of the global posterior expected utilities of actions $a_1, a_2 \in A$ are obtained:

$$\mathbf{U}[a_1; p(z|d)] - \mathbf{U}[a_2; p(z|d)]$$
$$= \sum_{z \in U} (u(a_1, z) - u(a_2, z)) \, f(z) + \sum_{z \in Z} (u(a_1, z) - u(a_2, z)) \, h(z) \tag{5.3}$$
$$\in [m(a_1, a_2), M(a_1, a_2)] .$$

The first term at the right side of the identity in (5.3) is calculable within the focussed Bayesian model even without regarding values of the utility function for $z \in Z \setminus U$. This does not hold for the second term, which contains the unknown function $h(z)$.

In the case that $m(a_1, a_2) \geq 0$ holds, a_1 definitively has a higher posterior expected utility than a_2 has. It becomes clear that a_2 is surely not globally optimal in this case. Analogously, if $M(a_1, a_2) \leq 0$, a_2 is globally preferable to a_1 and a_1 is surely not globally optimal. Additionally, if $[m(a_1, a_2), M(a_1, a_2)] \subseteq [c, d]$, it holds $\mathbf{U}[a_1; p(z|d)] \in [\mathbf{U}[a_2; p(z|d)] + c, \mathbf{U}[a_2; p(z|d)] + d]$.

Fishburn also describes a method for the identification of $[m(a_1, a_2), M(a_1, a_2)]$. Firstly, the elements of Z are ordered according to the value of their utility differences with respect to a_1 and a_2. For this, we determine a sequence $(z(i))_{i \in \{1, \ldots, |Z|\}}$ as follows:

$$z(1) := \arg \max_{z \in Z} (u(a_1, z) - u(a_2, z)) \ ,$$

$$z(i) := \arg \max_{z \in Z \setminus \{z(1), \ldots, z(i-1)\}} (u(a_1, z) - u(a_2, z)) \ , \quad i \in \{2, \ldots, |Z|\} \ .$$

(5.4)

For the identification of $M(a_1, a_2)$, this sequence is then processed in ascending order. Thereby, for each $i \in \{1, \ldots, |Z|\}$, the value of $h(z(i))$ is set to be the maximal possible one such that $h(z)$ satisfies (5.2). Inserting the resulting function $h(z)$ in the second line of (5.3) delivers $M(a_1, a_2)$. The calculation of $m(a_1, a_2)$ works mostly analogously. Therefore, the sequence (5.4) has to be processed in reversed order.

Generally, the identification of $m(a_1, a_2)$ and $M(a_1, a_2)$ is not completely locally realizable. Because of this, a further adaption of the described proceeding to local approaches could be a topic of further research.

For the rest of this section, the current problems will be exemplarily discussed with respect to the calculation of $M(a_1, a_2)$. The determination of an ordering according to (5.4) may cause problems because it has to be done for all $z \in Z$. In the resulting sequence, elements of $Z \setminus U$ may be stand on each possible position. Verifying the second condition in (5.2) for the determination of $h(z)$ is not critical. Checking the first condition in (5.2) is only locally realizable if there exists a $j \in \{1, \ldots, |Z|\}$ such that $T := \bigcup_{i=1}^{j} z(i) \subseteq U$ and $\sum_{z \in T} h(z) = 1 - \sum_{z \in U} f(z)$ holds.

6 Conclusion

An interval scheme for global probabilities, which is calculable in a focussed Bayesian model, has been presented. Thereby, the lower bounds are calculable if the prior relevance of the local context can be rated. Focussed Bayesian fusion has also been analyzed by the use of concepts from information theory and decision theory. By these considerations, new results concerning the global meaning and consistence of focussed Bayesian fusion have been obtained. It has been demonstrated that the solution of a decision problem on the basis of a focussed Bayesian model can be termed to be rational.

Bibliography

[Bey99]   Jürgen Beyerer. *Verfahren zur quantitativen statistischen Bewertung von Zusatzwissen in der Meßtechnik*. VDI-Verl., Düsseldorf, 1999.

[BHSG08]   Jürgen Beyerer, Michael Heizmann, Jennifer Sander, and Ioana Gheta. Bayesian Methods for Image Fusion. In Tania Stathaki, editor, *Image Fusion: Algorithms and Applications*, pages 157–192. Acad. Press, 2008.

[BS04]   Jóse M. Bernardo and Adrian F. M. Smith. *Bayesian Theory*. Wiley, Chichester, repr. edition, 2004.

[BSW07]   Jürgen Beyerer, Jennifer Sander, and Stefan Werling. Bayes'sche Methodik zur lokalen Fusion heterogener Informationsquellen. *tm – Technisches Messen*, 74(3):103–111, 2007.

[Fis64]   Peter C. Fishburn. *Decision and Value Theory*. Publications in Operations Research; 10. Wiley, New York [u.a.], 1964.

[Lin56]   Dennis V. Lindley. On a Measure of the Information Provided by an Experiment. *The Annals of Mathematical Statistics*, 27(4):986–1005, 1956.

[Lin87]   Dennis V. Lindley. The Probability Approach to the Treatment of Uncertainty in Artificial Intelligence and Expert Systems. *Statistical Science*, 2(2):3–44, 1987.

[RN03]   Stuart Russell and Peter Norvig. *Artificial Intelligence: A Modern Approach*. Prentice Hall, Upper Saddle River, NJ, 2. ed., internat. ed. edition, 2003.

[RW91]   Stuart Russell and Eric Wefald. *Do the Right Thing: Studies in Limited Rationality*. MIT Press, Cambridge, Mass., 1991.

[Sar09]   Mark Sargent. Answering the Bayesian Challenge. *Erkenntnis*, 70(2):237–252, 2009.

[SB08]   Jennifer Sander and Jürgen Beyerer. Decreased Complexity and Increased Problem Specificity of Bayesian Fusion by Local Approaches. In *Proceedings of 11th Conference on Information Fusion 2008 (Fusion 2008)*, pages 1035–1042. IEEE, 2008.

[SHGB09]   Jennifer Sander, Michael Heizmann, Igor Goussev, and Jürgen Beyerer. A local approach for focussed Bayesian fusion. In Belur V. Dasarathy, editor, *Multisensor, Multisource Information Fusion: Architectures, Algorithms, and Applications 2009: 16 - 17 April 2009, Orlando, Florida, United States*. SPIE, 2009.

[Wal06]   Stephen G. Walker. Bayesian Inference via a Minimization Rule. *Sankhya: The Indian Journal of Statistics*, 68(4):542–553, 2006.

[Wil80]   Peter M. Williams. Bayesian Conditionalisation and the Principle of Minimum Information. *The British Journal for the Philosophy of Science*, 31(2):131–144, 1980.

[Wol82]   Hartmut Wollenhaupt. *Rationale Entscheidungen bei unscharfen Wahrscheinlichkeiten*. Becker, Velten, 1982.

[Zel02]   Arnold Zellner. Information processing and Bayesian analysis. *Journal of Econometrics*, 107(1-2):41–50, 2002.

Semantic Interoperability of Manufacturing Execution Systems (MES)

Miriam Schleipen

Vision and Fusion Laboratory
Institute for Anthropomatics
Karlsruhe Institute of Technology (KIT), Germany
miriam.schleipen@ies.uka.de

Technical Report IES-2009-04

Abstract: Today's manufacturing plants are faced with continuous changes and enhancements. They are equipped with heterogeneous software systems for different types of tasks, both manufacturing operations and factory planning. To remain competitive, plant operators have to respond quickly to the situation and requirements of the market. Technology has to support this. Any change has to be considered, and the equipment and the information technology have to be able to adapt quickly. Technology has to support this: Efficient modifications result in an increased demand for *adaptability* or *flexibility*.

For an efficient and usable information exchange, all systems involved have to interact as seamlessly as possible in the heterogeneous environment. This is called *interoperability*, which is based on the compliance with consistent standards. Therefore, it is not only important how to communicate, but also what to communicate. Data descriptions must be examined as well as suitable communication. MES have to form a part of the integrated industrial engineering chain from mechanical engineering, PLC programming to operations. This contribution deals with some of the challenges that have to be handled to achieve interoperability.

1 Introduction

MES have to cope with different challenges to achieve interoperability. Interoperability within this context is the ability of different independent production-related systems to cooperate and exchange information efficiently. *Semantic interoperability* means that the systems also understand each other. This can also be described as seamless semantic integration. Therefore Flexibility or even mutability are necessary. Flexibility means the ability to react or the adaptability to several known issues. Ultimately, this leads to the adaptability and the ability to react to unknown issues. This is called mutability.

These topics address mainly the phase of engineering MES. In the following contribution, engineering is viewed as a creative planning process, which is done step by step in collaboration of different disciplines such as mechanical or electrical engineers. Within this process, the involved persons are searching for a solution for an individual, but not particular task. This is very complex and comprises many participants, ideas, and tools. Thus, it is expensive, time-consuming, and error-prone [Dra08].

The base of interoperability and flexibility is an integrated engineering chain also consisting of MES. Therefore, the complete engineering process of MES has to be changed and even improved. At the moment, engineering of MES takes place at the end of the plant planning or reconfiguration process and is done manually. This results in a big amount of manual effort and is cost-intensive and error-prone.

Many different groups are engaged in the improvement of the engineering process– not only in the field of MES, but also in the more general area of automation and control technology. A German example is the VDI (Verein deutscher Ingenieure) standardization committee called 'Integrated engineering of control systems' (VDI/VDE-Gesellschaft Mess- und Automatisierungstechnik (GMA): Fachausschuss 6.12 'Durchgängiges Engineering von Leitsystemen') [SLF+08], [FSM09].

In this contribution, the complex field of MES is represented by production monitoring and control systems, which are a special type of production-related IT. In this context a production monitoring and control system is a complex central or decentral IT system for collecting, aggregating/condensing and processing process signals and values in real time. It has a controlling effect on manufacturing and assembling processes, either in an automated way or by means of user interventions. In line with the definition by Polke in [Pol94], a control system is meant to support shop floor staff in managing their equipment, and in controlling and monitoring the production processes.

Challenges and possibilities for the interoperability of MES are depicted in Figure 1.1. These are: Vertical interoperability (1), horizontal interoperability (2), lifecycle interoperability (3), the interoperability interface (man-machine interoperability/interaction, 4), and an interoperability data representation (interoperability data format, 5). They all lead to new potentials and possibilities (6).

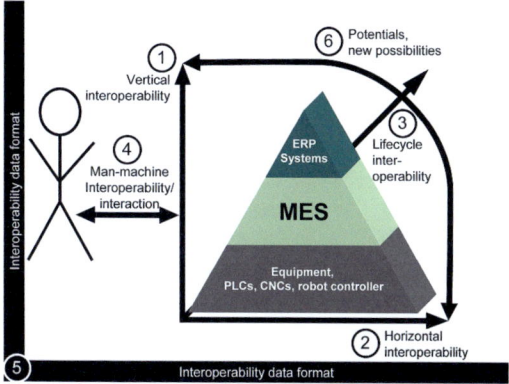

Figure 1.1: Interoperability of MES

Hereinafter, the author tries to explain how to face these challenges. Thus, different solutions, concepts, and tools are explained, which were developed in different research and development projects at the Fraunhofer IITB and the Universität Karlsruhe (TH), also in cooperation with industrial partners.

2   Challenges and Concepts Towards Semantic Interoperability of MES

2.1   Vertical MES Interoperability

Future MES will be integrated vertically with the shop floor and collaborate and interact with components of this level. Plug-and-work mechanisms support this integration. If something changes within the plant, this leads to changes within the MES. The vision is an automated integration of new components and the automated adaption of existing components.

The ProduFlexil research project [SBO+09], [EOB07], sponsored by the Federal Ministry of Education and Research, deals with adaptivity and self-configuration of manufacturing plants by developing appropriate software mechanisms and architecture patterns that allow plants and plant components to be integrated in an existing production system as efficiently as possible. In this context, the focus is on enhancing the flexibility of the plant software and on the configuration and integration of superordinated systems, e.g., a production monitoring and control system.

At the production of the 'Mercedes C-class', the production monitoring and control system is connected to 450 PLCs and administrates round about 1000 process visualization images. According to Fraunhofer IITB's experience in this field, the manual engineering effort is 30-40 percent of the total effort for such a software solution. Out of this percentage, plug-and-play could save about 80 percent.

The pre-requisite for an automated engineering is a self-description containing all information required by the production monitoring and control system from different sources [BMSE08]. These are details about the process signals, but also visualization data. Existing standards in the field of automation technology limit the amount of describable information. The vision is a plant, which can simply be linked into the process by 'plug-and-work'.

Production monitoring and control system engineering of the future will therefore require a consistent and neutral data format into which existing data formats can be integrated. It has to answer the question 'What to communicate?'–Necessary contents must be structured. At the same time, the semantic of the contents must be clear. In addition, standardized communication and processing mechanisms are necessary to answer the question 'How to communicate?'–This includes the process as well as the methods. Therefore, the IITB presents a solution, which combines two standards to form one framework for automated engineering [SE07].

The independent XML-based CAEX (Computer Aided Engineering Exchange, IEC62424) data exchange format was originally developed in process engineering. Fraunhofer IITB, however, has proved that the format is also suited for the efficient exchange of data in production engineering [SDS08]. The format takes account of the problem that the standardization of the tools available on the market only makes sense to a certain degree, if it makes sense at all. The exchange of CAE (Computer Aided Engineering) planning data between various systems is structured and organized, and it is used as a standardized data format for the automated engineering of production monitoring and control systems. It is explained in more detail below.

In this application, CAEX was complemented by OPC UA (OPC Unified Architecture, IEC62541), the service-oriented successor to the industrial OPC communication standard. OPC UA allows for data communication, synchronization and processing in the prototypical engineering framework (see [Sch08]).

The underlying idea is a consistent standard interface, standardized communication with all systems involved, service-oriented processing, investment protection in view of supplier-specific formats and ultimately the enhancement of the quality of data throughout automated processes. Combining both standards to form one framework boosts the strengths of each and opens up new potentials for the red-hot topic of "automation of automation" [Sch09b].

2.2   Horizontal MES Interoperability

MES components–even from different vendors–must be integrated horizontally. This is done by instruments and concepts as Service-Oriented Architectures (SOA), ontologies or an integrated data management. ProVis.Agent® is a production monitoring and control system and in this respect, a core component of modern MES. The underlying software agent-based communication enables our customers to integrate existing applications, which opens up new synergy potentials. ProVis.Agent® can be seen as a vacuum cleaner for data, in other words a data integration platform.

Today, MES are isolated applications. Tomorrow, they have to be interconnected to each other in SOA, for instance, based on OPC UA (OPC Unified Architecture). Each MES has its own view on the common information.

As mentioned above, OPC UA is a standard, which accomplishes to support process communication in a structured way with an underlying user-defined information model. The information model enables users to create a representation of their plant using the object-oriented model paradigm. The OPC foundation therefore provides an XML schema for describing these models. Furthermore, the foundation defined a graphical representation for OPC UA information models, which is much more intuitive for users than the XML representation.

For the information model, the Fraunhofer IITB developed a graphical editor (see Figure 2.1). It allows to model graphically 'address spaces' of OPC UA servers, which are the 'living' online representation of the underlying information model. Therefore, it provides the graphical base elements defined by the OPC Foundation and reacts as a normal painting program. The whole application is based on the Silverlight technology to enable web application.

The defined graphical model can be exported to an XML file, which is conform to the UA XML schema and can be imported into the OPC UA servers, but the UA modeller goes even further. It includes the possibility to import CAEX (see Section 2.4) data and transforms it to an OPC conform description. Thus, MES can take advantage of the capabilities of OPC-UA servers and CAEX data can be managed online.

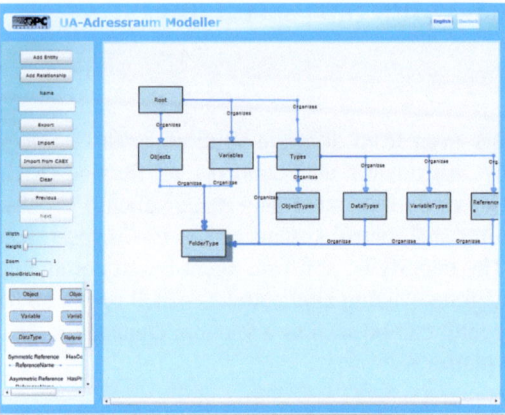

Figure 2.1: OPC UA Modeller

It is essential for horizontal integration that MES 'understand' other systems. Therefore, the IITB gets involved in standardization. Within the German association for engineers (VDI), the IITB conducts the working group 'MES-logical interfaces', which forms part of the MES standardization committee (VDI-Gesellschaft Produkt- und Prozessgestaltung (VDI-GPP): Arbeitsgruppe 'Logische Schnittstellen MES-Maschinenebene' des Fachausschusses 2.5.1 'Manufacturing Execuction Systems'). The motivation of the standardization committee results from the existence of numerous standards and the lack of one unique standard. Thus, machines and plant manufacturers have to adapt to the particular standard of their customers, which results in manual effort. The goal of the standardization committee is to standardize the communication contents between production plants and MES. There, machines and plants manufacturers and operators develop together a common interface. The semantic description of the contents is done by means of an OWL (Web Ontology Language) ontology. Every user can read this description, interpret, and integrate it in his automation and IT environment. The results will be published.

2.3   Man-machine Interface for MES Interoperability

Interoperability comes along with the interaction of different systems as well as different users. Thus, the interface between man and machine is essential. Human-centered computing providing only required information to the users according to their tasks and roles has to be taken into account as well as legal effects. The modified engineering process results from the user's requirements and possibilities. Hence, the automated engineering framework consists of different tools providing the user the possibility to influence the automatically generated results. Examples for such tools are the layout manager and the process-product-resource (PPR) visualization for the engineering framework (see Section 2.1), which are described hereinafter. Furthermore, a modified engineering process resulting from the automation of automation has to be considered.

Within the engineering process, the generation of the process control images as the human-machine interface has to be considered above all. If users create process control images manually, the very same process may be depicted differently depending on the preferences of the person who has drafted them. Thus, the process control images should be as standardized as possible, while, at the same time, being as individual as necessary.

In manufacturing, an automated system for image generation will only be accepted if the user interface is user-friendly and intuitive. The special field of human engineering [Syr70] aims at adapting machinery and other technical equipment to humans to optimize their cooperation. The characteristics, potentials and requirements of human beings are taken into account, and the visualization of machinery and/or equipment is based on these conditions. In this process, visualization must be based on ergonomic guidelines.

The layout of the visualized information has to be as clear and well-arranged as possible, enabling even inexperienced users to interpret the data intuitively. In addition, appropriate algorithms have to be developed to position the existing equipment components as well as I/O signals on the process control image in line with the actual layout. Finally, users should be able to adapt the process control images to their personal requirements. The layout manager generates process images out of CAEX data. The user just has to define his preferences, the rest is done automatically [SS08]. This ensures that the visualization is consistent and always up to date.

In addition to typical resource visualization in control technology, the engineering component also visualizes products and processes involved in the production process [Sch09a]. Products stand for all products and product components, processes include all kinds of activities, and resources comprise equipment, staff, software, etc. This classification brings about additional semantic meaning for the system elements, such as 'I am a product', 'I am a resource' or 'I am a process'. The individual types of elements can be linked with each other, with resources being the central component in this model as resources execute processes and resources process products. The movement of produced products and changes in

ongoing processes (activities) are visualized on the basis of dynamically updated
CAEX data. The structure of elements, equipment, and products contained in the
images is created dynamically. The allocation of products and processes to a resource (equipment) is equally performed dynamically. It is not necessary to update
processes and product positions in real-time for control technology. The process
signals, by contrast, continue to be visualized in real-time.

2.4   Data Representation for MES Interoperability

Improving efficiency in MES engineering and achieving interoperability requires
an integrated data representation–an interoperability data format.

CAEX is one possible example for such a format. It was developed in cooperation
between the Department of Process Control Engineering of the RWTH Aachen
and the ABB Research Center in Ladenburg. The definition of CAEX has been
taken down in the standard IEC62424. CAEX is a semi-formal description language, which is based on XML. It contains an XML-meta model for describing
the setup and structure of plant data. First and foremost, the format supports library concepts and object-oriented approaches. It is possible to integrate libraries
from users and suppliers as well as project libraries. In addition, both a top-down
and a bottom-up system design is supported. The technical innovation of this approach is the syntactic and semantic unification of the data. This allows decoupling
of the required configuration algorithms from the data sources. As mentioned in
Section 2.1, CAEX is used as a data format within the engineering framework
[SDS08]. To work with CAEX data Fraunhofer IITB developed an intelligent
CAEX-Editor. It hides the XML specific syntax and enables the user to compre-
hend the data structure at a glance. Hence, it is intuitionally usable and helps to
understand CAEX.

One 'other' interoperability data representation to meet these challenges is the
Automation Markup Language (AutomationML, http://www.automationml.org),
which is a superset of CAEX. AutomationML is an XML based data format for the
exchange of plant engineering information. It is defined by the AutomationML Or-
ganization. Members are the companies Daimler, ABB, KUKA, Siemens, Phoenix
contact, NetAllied, and Zühlke as well as the Fraunhofer IITB and the Universi-
ties of Karlsruhe and Magdeburg. The standardization committee 'DKE K941.0.2
AutomationML' (Deutschen Kommission Elektrotechnik Elektronik Information-
stechnik (DKE): Gremium 'DKE K941.0.2 AutomationML') works on the standardization of the format. The vision is a seamless integration of production monitoring and control systems into the virtual startup and a digital production release.
This allows plants to be evaluated and optimized within the Digital Factory by

software systems used during real-world operation. The mission is to intercon-
nect engineering tools of different disciplines and to reduce in consequence the
work-intensive engineering process. Therefore, it integrates different standards
and consolidates them 'under one umbrella'. Hence, the AutomationML architecture consists of many differnt formats. As top-level and semantic-integrating data
format, CAEX was chosen. This is supplemented by Collada (http://collada.org/)
for geometry and kinematics and PLCOpen XML (http://www.plcopen.org/) for
behavior and sequencing. The integration of further standard formats is possible
(see [DLPH08]). The author estimates that AutomationML will become the 'glue
for seamless automation engineering'.

From the semantic point of view ontologies are also an adequate instrument to
model manufacturing and process plants. CAEX and AutomationML therefore
adapt several concepts and mechanisms from ontologies and can be seen as domain
specific specialism.

2.5   Concept of Automated Engineering

Figure 2.2 depicts the overall concept for automated MES engineering. Its goal
is to provide maximum assistance to the user. Therefore, system-specific CAEX
is created by the CAEX importer out of the existing XML export of the users'
tools. This CAEX data is unified with CAEX data from other tools. To this end,
a mapping consisting of transformation as well as fusion operations is necessary.
After extracting a MES view on these data, a reverse generator extracts system-
specific XML data out of this CAEX data. The whole processing is based on OPC
UA and is completed by a GUI-based interface as Man-machine-interface. The
following aspects cover specific parts of the concept, which are depicted within
the corresponding figures.

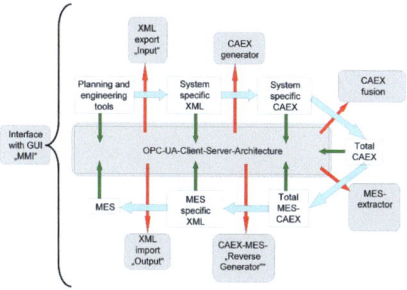

Figure 2.2: Overall concept for automated MES engineering

Almost every production planning tool posseses an XML export. The CAEX importer shown in Figure 2.3 and developed for semantic import takes advantage of this circumstance and utilizes XML technology. Its purpose is to transform a system-specific XML file into a system-specific CAEX file. In this process, it support the user and reduces manual work. At the same time, it provides the user the possibility to integrate his implicit knowledge and helps to explicitly model this knowledge.

Semantic is in this process incorporated by turning the specific XML tags and structures into standardized CAEX structures. To achieve this, several steps have to be processed. First, the user specifies one or more connections between elements from the CAEX XML schema and elements within his XML export file. This can be assisted by an interactive CAEX explanation describing the four base structures: Interfaces (logical, technical, and mechanical interfaces), SystemUnits (types), InternalElements (instances), and Roles (semantic identifier/name). After having defined all possible relations, the user starts the 'AutoImport'. Within this step, the XML and XPath technology is used to create multiple connection between elements out of the starting elments. After a review of the automatically created connections by the user, the original XML can be transformed into a 'raw CAEX'. This means that elements of specific CAEX types already exist, but no semantic connections between them. This is done in the next step. Roles of an existing CAEX role library (either standardized, i.e., by AutomationML or user-defined) are assigned to the generated elements. This interlinking must be done by the user as the CAEX importer cannot imagine or invent the meaning of an element, but it's possible to apply learning mechanisms to include and extend this in the future. Further development focus certainly on the expansion of the user assistance.

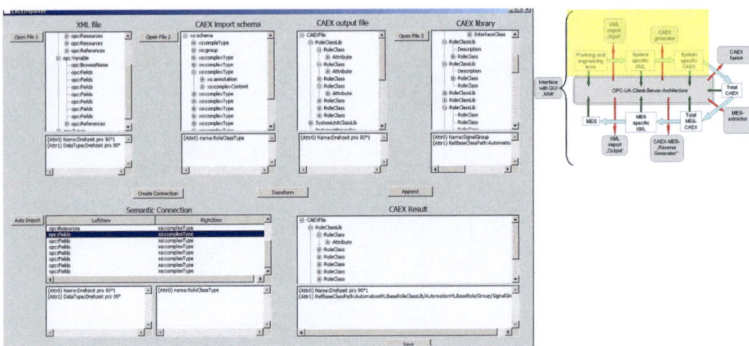

Figure 2.3: Semantic CAEX importer

After having a system-specific CAEX file, the next goal is to unify the heterogeneous landscape of system-specific data by integrating it into one CAEX 'world'. This is called semantic MES Mapping (SMM). It consists of transformation of the existing files as well as fusion of them. One basic tool for this is depicted in Figure 2.4. It serves as platform for the integration of different mapping mechanisms, which can be applied. These are for instance name or structural equivalence.

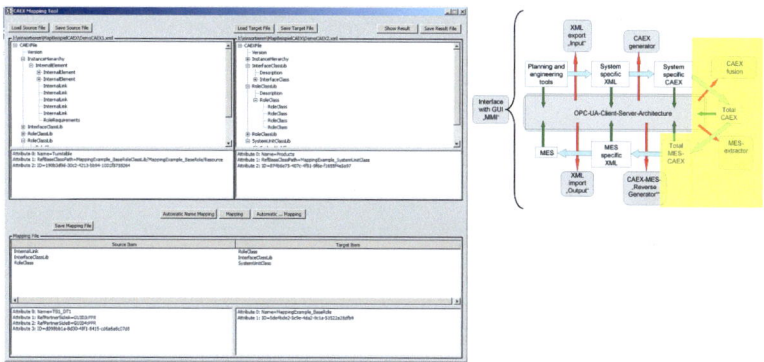

Figure 2.4: CAEX mapping

For completing the implementation of the concept for the Provis-Production-Suite. A prototypical engineering framework (see Section 2.1 and Figure 2.5) exists, which processes data in the standardized format CAEX describing plants. By means of this CAEX information, the engineering of ProVis.Agent® and the generation of images for ProVis.Visu® can be done. The whole framework is based on OPC UA. It serves as one possible prototype for an automated MES engineering.

2.6   MES Interoperability Along the Lifecycle

Future MES have to be completely connected to the Digital Factory following the objective of permanent planning. This means that in the case of a change, every system involved will be adapted immediately. This takes place during the whole lifecycle where MES are supported by online simulation within the Digital Factory.

Today, the engineering of MES takes place at the end of the plant planning process. In most cases, the plant already exists at that time and recognized errors are very time and cost-intensive. However, this engineering effort can be shifted into earlier phases. MES can be connected to and evaluated against the Digital Factory. In doing so, the full range of features of those systems is available at that time. This helps to reduce startup time and to improve the engineering process and results.

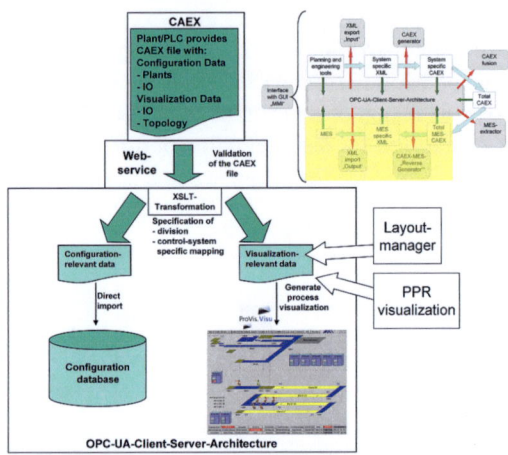

Figure 2.5: Automated engineering framework for MES

From planning to start-up and operation, tools and methods of the Digital factory are applied. Depending on the development status, as much as possible real systems are introduced. It is important that real control programs are used as early as possible for controlling the model [Mew09]. At an early time virtual equipment and virtual controller (Figure 2.6, 1) can be linked to the MES. This results in an absolute simulation below the MES. In the course of evolution, virtual controllers can be changed to real controllers (2). This is the so-called hardware-in-the-loop simulation. If the equipment with the corresponding controllers is assembled (3), the MES can be connected to it and operate on it. In this way, engineering, evaluation, and optimization can be done step by step.

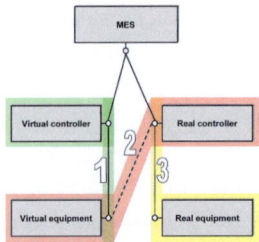

Figure 2.6: System combinations

Thus, MES close the loop between operation and planning. Examples for such a virtual startup of MES are given in [SSB+09]. In this domain the IITB manages the standardization committee 'Digital factory operation' (VDI-Gesellschaft Fördertechnik Materialfluss Logistik (FML): Arbeitsgruppe 'Digitaler Fabrikbetrieb' des Fachausschusses 'Digitale Fabrik'). This group of industrial and research partners deals with the development of a VDI recommendation concerning the main goals of Digital factory operation, possible domains of application and the application in different phases of the lifecycle. The recommendation will be published as VDI recommendation 4499 part 2.

3 Application Examples, Conclusion and Potentials

To evaluate the developed tools and methods, various application examples have been created. For one thing, there are various conveyor systems at hand to validate engineering and the generation of simple visualization. They include conveyor belts and turntables as well as a test station or welding cell.

For another, a hierarchical example (Figure 3.1, left) was developed to test the layout manager, which consists of different hierarchical levels, different equipment aggregates including conveyors, turntables, and test stations.

To allow for the overall visualization of resources, processes, and products, one of the conveyor belt examples was complemented by processes and products (Figure 3.1, right). To this end, a three-view modeling concept was developed, which is a prime example for interlinked engineering data.

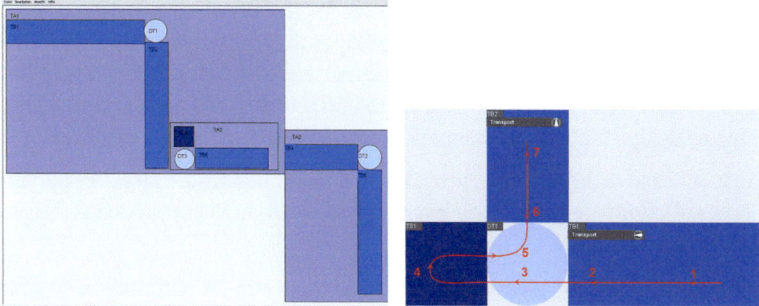

Figure 3.1: Hierarchy-based sample application (left) and basic image of the sample application for resources, products, and processes (right)

Furthermore, two application examples of process industry were modelled to show that the developed concepts are also applicable there. The three-view concept was also applied there, the underlying data format is AutomationML, which was described in Section 2.4. In the first example (see Figure 3.2), a filling and closing line for baby food was modelled. The second example consists of a Tetra filling plant, which is situated within the liquid filling production hall. The example is described in detail in [SD09].

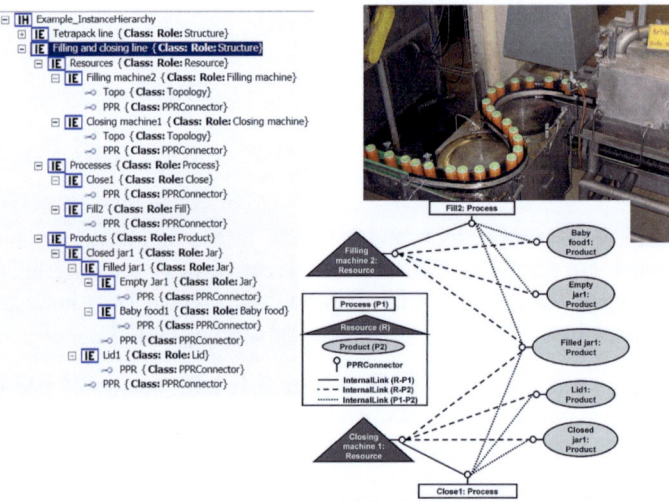

Figure 3.2: Application example of process industry (1) (plant image source: Nestlé Deutschland AG)

Semantic interoperability between facilities and superordinate IT-systems inside the factory becomes the major prerequisite for the future of adaptive manufacturing. Open questions are: how will a corresponding standard would look like, will there be lots of 'standards', e.g., standards related to different branches of industry, company internal standards or will the manufacturing and automation community be able to design a common standard for various branches and equipment?

The aspects and examples pointed out in this paper illustrate that interoperability of MES is not completely realized, but possible. The shown approaches are possible steps towards this goal.

Moreover, new potentials evolve. Some of them are an automatically generated documentation and order lists, the calculation of the energy consumption of a plant by integration of additional slots within the data representation or online simulation to support decisions concerning unexpected changes on the shop floor.

Bibliography

[BMSE08] Thomas Bär, Sven Mandel, Olaf Sauer, and Miriam Ebel. Durchgängiges Datenman-agement durch plug-and-work zur virtuellen Linieninbetriebnahme. In *Proceedings of Karlsruher Leittechnisches Kolloquium (KLK)*, pages 105–121, Karlsruhe, May 2008.

[DLPH08] Rainer Drath, Arndt Lueder, Jörg Peschke, and Lorenz Hundt. AutomationML – the glue for seamless Automation Engineering. In *Proceedings of IEEE International Conference on Emerging Technologies and Factory Automation (ETFA)*, Hamburg, September 2008.

[Dra08]   Rainer Drath. Die Zukunft des Engineering – Herausforderungen an das Engineer-ing von fertigungs- und verfahrenstechnischen Anlagen. In *Proceedings of Karlsruher Leittechnisches Kolloquium (KLK)*, pages 33–40, Karlsruhe, May 2008.

[EOB07]   Miriam Ebel, Michael Okon, and Michael Baumann. ProduFlexil Flexible Produktion mit SOA-Architektur und Plug-and-Work-Mechanismus. In *Proceedings of Stuttgarter Softwaretechnik Forum (Science meets business)*, pages 65–74, Stuttgart, December 2007.

[FSM09]   Alexander Fay, Miriam Schleipen, and Mathias Mühlhause. Wie kann man den Engineering-Prozess systematisch verbessern? *atp – Automatisierungstechnische Praxis*, (01.-02.2009):80–85, 2009.

[Mew09]   Jürgen Mewes. Inbetriebnahme von Förderanlagen mit Feldbusemulation und Materi-alflusssimulation am Beispiel einer SKID-Anlage. In *Proceedings of Automation 2009*, Baden-Baden, June 2009.

[Pol94]   Martin Polke. *Prozeßleittechnik*. Oldenbourg Verlag, München, 1994.

[SBO+09] Miriam Schleipen, Michael Baumann, Michael Okon, Martin Neukäufer, Christian Fedrowitz, Martin Feike, Natalya Popova, Markus Nick, Sören Schneickert, and Martin Wessner. Design and engineering processes in highly adaptive plants with ambient intel-ligence techniques. In *Proceedings of CIRP International Conference on Manufacturing Systems (ICMS)*, Grenoble, June 2009.

[Sch08]   Miriam Schleipen. OPC UA supporting the automated engineering of production moni-toring and control systems. In *Proceedings of IEEE International Conference on Emerg-ing Technologies and Factory Automation (ETFA)*, pages 640–647, Hamburg, September 2008.

[Sch09a] Miriam Schleipen. Usage of dynamic product and process information in a production monitoring and control system by means of CAEX and OPC-UA. In *Proceedings of CIRP International Conference on Changeable, Agile, Reconfigurable and Virtual Production (CARV)*, München, October 2009.

[Sch09b] Stefan Schmitz. Automation of Automation – Definition, Components and Challenges. In *Proceedings of IEEE International Conference on Emerging Technologies and Factory Automation (ETFA)*, Palma, September 2009.

[SD09]   Miriam Schleipen and Rainer Drath. Three-View-Concept for modeling process or man-ufacturing plants with AutomationML. In *Proceedings of IEEE International Conference on Emerging Technologies and Factory Automation (ETFA)*, Palma, September 2009.

[SDS08]   Miriam Schleipen, Rainer Drath, and Olaf Sauer. The system-independent data exchange format CAEX for supporting an automatic configuration of a production monitoring and control system. In *Proceedings of IEEE International Symposium on Industrial Electronics (ISIE)*, pages 1786–1791, June 2008.

[SE07]   Olaf Sauer and Miriam Ebel. Engineering of production monitoring & control systems. In *Proceedings of 52nd IWK – Computer science meets automation*, pages 237–244, Illmenau, September 2007.

[SLF+08]   Andreas Schertl, Ulrich Löwen, Alexander Fay, Rainer Drath, Georg Gutermuth, Mathias Mühlhause, and Miriam Ebel. Systematische Beurteilung und Verbesserung des Engineerings von automatisierten Anlagen. In *Proceedings of Automation 2008*, Baden-Baden, June 2008.

[SS08]   Miriam Schleipen and Klaus Schick. Self-configuring visualization of a production monitoring and control system. In *Proceedings of CIRP International Conference on Intelligent Computation in Manufacturing Engineering (ICME)*, July 2008.

[SSB+09]   Miriam Schleipen, Olaf Sauer, Lisa Braun, Kamran Shakerian, and Nicole Frieß. Production monitoring and control systems within the Digital Factory. In *Proceedings of CIRP International Conference on Digital Enterprise Technology (DET)*, Hong Kong, December 2009.

[Syr70]   Max Syrbe. Anthropotechnik, eine Disziplin der Anlagenplanung. *Elektrotechnische Zeitschrift*, Volume A:692–697, 1970.

An Inverse Illumination Technique for Automated Visual Inspection

Robin Gruna

Vision and Fusion Laboratory
Institute for Anthropomatics
Karlsruhe Institute of Technology (KIT), Germany
robin.gruna@kit.edu

Technical Report IES-2009-05

Abstract: In many machine vision applications for automated inspection the illumination design is crucial to the robustness and speed of the inspection process. Therefore, there is need to investigate and experimentally evaluate new illumination designs and techniques. We briefly review a representative selection of illumination techniques that aim to minimize the effort of defect detection by adapting the illuminating light field to the nominal state of the inspection task. Based on this principle we propose an illumination technique using a projector-camera system which provides inspection images that directly display differences in reflectance between two scenes.

1 Introduction

The choice of an appropriate illumination design is one of the most important steps in creating successful machine vision systems for automated inspection tasks. Since in image acquisition all information about a scene is encoded in its exitant light field, the incident light field provided by the illumination must be able to reveal information relevant to the inspection task about the test object. Moreover, in real-time machine vision applications where time is a major constraint, appropriate illumination can greatly simplify digital image processing tasks and improve their processing time and reliability. For instance, via an illumination that results in images with high contrast between object and background, simple image thresholding may suffice for object segmentation and more sophisticated and time consuming algorithms can be avoided.

While there are well-founded design rules for choosing the imaging optics for a machine vision system [BH85], rules for illumination design are less elaborated.

However, one general design objective is to provide an illumination that accentuates the features of interest, such as surface defects of a faulty test object, while it minimizes distracting features, e.g., flawless object regions. Some popular illumination techniques like dark-field illumination [Gre04] and techniques based on polarized light [SUW07] explicitly take care of this demand. In dark-field illumination, a directional illumination is used to enhance the visibility of surface features like scratches or indentations on an otherwise smooth surface. In the presence of a perfectly smooth surface, which is assumed to be the desired nominal state of the inspection task, all incident light is reflected away from the camera's lens and the captured image is dark. Imperfections on the surface scatter light into the lens and appear as bright image features. Similarly, in an illumination setup where a polarized illumination (*polarizer*) is used in combination with a crossed polarizing light filter in front of the camera (*analyzer*), object features with polarizing properties can be highlighted. Viewing the test object in its desired nominal state where it is assumed that no change in polarisation occurs, the light received by the camera is almost completely attenuated by the analyzer and thus a dark inspection image is captured. However, object features that cause a rotation in the angle of polarization, like unwanted refractive index variations or stress in transparent objects, are captured as bright image features. The principle behind both illumination techniques is to generate inspection images that highlight deviations from a predefined desired nominal state with high contrast.

Recently, some novel inspection methods have been proposed that take the aforementioned principle a step further by employing more sophisticated illumination techniques. Techniques like inverse fringe projection [LBOK04][CS07], inverse patterns for deflectometric inspection [WB07a] and comparative digital holography [BOKJ] are able to directly highlight differences in the shape of two objects. Defect detection by comparing the actual state of a test object with the desired nominal state of a master object is a standard task in industrial inspection. In the case of fringe projection and deflectometry, the shape information of a preceding measurement is used to computed an inverse structured light pattern of the master object which is then used to evaluate a test object. If master and test object are identical, a predefined undistorted pattern is obtained. Otherwise, shape differences are directly highlighted by local geometric distortions in the projected pattern. In the case of holography techniques for object comparison, the coherent optical wave field of the master object is obtained by digital holography. By illuminating the test object with the coherent mask of the master object, differences in the shape between the two objects are directly displayed in the inspection image.

All the described inspection techniques have in common that the illuminating light field is adapted to the desired nominal state of the inspection task. Hence, the captured inspection images directly highlight deviations from the nominal state and therefore reduce the effort of defect detection through digital image or signal processing. This means that feature extraction for defect detection partly takes place in the optical domain, that is, during image formation. We believe that this illumination principle is a promising technique for fast and robust industrial inspection tasks and is worth to be investigated in more detail.

In this technical report, we apply this principle to propose an illumination technique that is designed to highlight the difference in reflectance and shape of two objects or scenes. Our goal is to provide a spatially adapted illumination pattern that results in a featureless flat-gray inspection image if the illuminated test object is identical to the master object. However, differences in reflectance of the two objects, e.g., caused by defects, should result in detectable image features that highlight the faulty areas. This goal is archived by utilizing a digital light projector as light source and a technique referred to as *radiometric compensation* in the literature [NPGB03].

In the following sections, we describe the setup of a projector-camera system that is able to generate such illumination patterns and explain the radiometric compensation methods used in our experiments. Moreover, experimental results are presented and the advantages of the proposed illumination technique compared to conventional techniques for deviation detection are discussed. In the following, the adapted illumination pattern that results in a flat-gray camera image is referred to as the *inverse illumination mask* of a scene or object.

2 Inspection Image Formation by Means of Radiometric Compensation

In recent years, digital video projectors gained great interest in the computer vision and graphics community due to enormous technological advancements such as higher spatial resolution and dynamic range [BIWG08][RLW00][GTLL06]. Since the radiance of each projector pixel can be controlled separately, they are ideally suited as experimental platforms for evaluating new illumination techniques. In combination with a light sensing device such as a camera, systems that utilize digital video projectors as controllable illumination are referred to as *projector-camera systems* in the literature. Projector-camera systems allow to project arbitrary complex illumination patterns onto a scene and to capture the corresponding images. These optically coded images allow computing information about the scene which is not possible to be retrieved with standard illumination techniques.

Computing the inverse illumination mask of a scene is closely related to the problem of radiometric compensation, which has been widely discussed in the field of

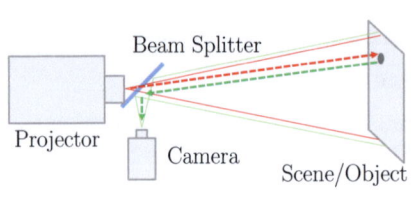
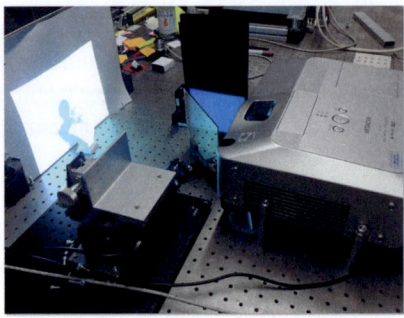

(a) Schematic of a coaxial projector-   (b) Prototype system
camera system

Figure 2.1: A coaxial projector-camera system.

projector-camera systems [NPGB03][WB07b][AOSS06]. Radiometric compensation deals with the problem of displaying projected images on arbitrary surfaces with varying color, reflectance and geometry. When an image is projected onto such a non-cooperative surface, the appearance of the image is modulated by the spatially varying reflectance and distorted by geometric variations. To be able to preserve the original intended appearance of the projected image, a camera serves as a proxy for the human viewer and provides information on how the projected image has to be compensated prior to projection in order to account for the aforementioned perturbations. For our purposes, radiometric compensation is used to compute the compensated flat-gray image for a given test scene. Then, the compensated image is exactly the inverse illumination mask that has to be project onto the scene in order to capture a flat-gray inspection image.

2.1   Projector-Camera Correspondence

For radiometric compensation a precise mapping between camera and projector pixels has to be established. To avoid parallax errors, a coaxial projector-camera setup, as proposed in [FGN05], is chosen. As shown in Figure 2.1, a beam-splitter is put in front of both the camera and the projector optics. In addition, the camera is attached to an assembly of mechanical positioners, which allows a precise linear and angular positioning of the camera. By a manual calibration procedure, both centers of field of view are aligned so that a scene-independent geometry is yielded.

However, a pixel-wise alignment cannot not be established in a purely optical manner. Hence, a geometrical mapping between points $\mathbf{x}_p = (u_p, v_p)$ in the projected image and points $\mathbf{x}_c = (u_c, v_c)$ in the captured camera image is introduced. For this purpose, piecewise second-order polynomials for modeling this mapping are used as proposed in [NPGB03]. The polynomial model for each piece of the image domain can be written as

$$\mathbf{x}_p = \mathbf{A}\hat{\mathbf{x}}_c, \quad \text{where} \quad \hat{\mathbf{x}}_c = (u_c^2, v_c^2, u_c v_c, u_c, v_c, 1)^T, \tag{2.1}$$

where the matrix $\mathbf{A} \in \mathbb{R}^{2 \times 6}$ contains the unknown coefficients for the mapping. These coefficient are computed by the least-squares-error fitting method using corresponding points from camera and projector images. Corresponding point pairs are obtained by projecting and capturing a sequence of binary coded markers, which are then extracted by image thresholding and connected component analysis.

With (2.1), for each camera pixel the corresponding projector pixel can be determined. However, the calculated pixel positions usually do not fall into the integer grid of the input image of the projector. Hence, the value of each projector pixel has to be determined by interpolation, taking neighboring pixel values into account. Due to the well know problems of geometric forward image transformations [Wol94], backward transformation is used to geometric transform and resample the image prior to projection. The needed inverse geometric mapping is obtained by swapping input and output points and fitting the polynomial model as described above. When the geometric backward transformation is applied to an input image, the projected image appears undistorted to the camera and the captured image matches with the original image in an almost pixel-wise manner (see Figure 2.2).

2.2 Physics-Based Modelling for Radiometric Compensation

Most approaches to radiometric compensation found in the literature are based on the inversion of a radiometric model that describes the image formation in a projector-camera system via a projection screen with spatially varying reflectance [NPGB03][GPNB04][BEK05a][AOSS06]. The model parameters for a static scene are computed by projecting and capturing a set of calibration images. This allows to compensate arbitrary images before projection onto the same static scene. However, whenever the scene changes, all model parameters have to be recomputed.

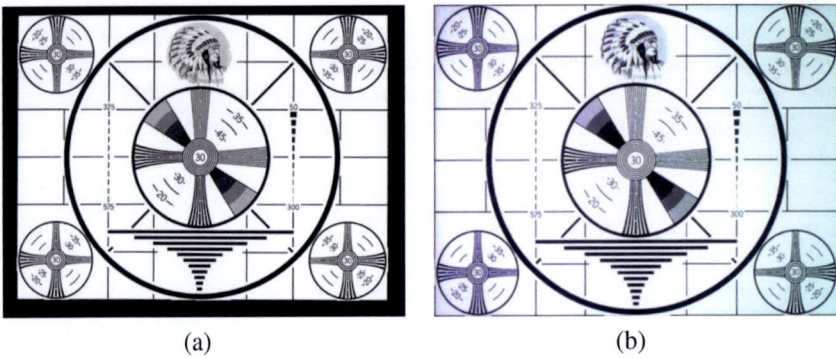

(a) (b)

Figure 2.2: Geometric transformation of a test projector image (a) and the corresponding captured camera image (b). The geometric transformation of the input image accommodates for geometric distortions that may be caused by a misalignment of projector and camera.

Figure 2.3 illustrates the information flow of our projector-camera system and introduces the relevant photometric quantities. Note that the illustrated model applies only to a single scene point and projector and camera are restricted to a single spectral channel. However, the model can be applied to any scene point and all combinations of projector and camera channels.

Let $K \in \{R, G, B\}$ be a color channel of the projector with spectral response $w_K(\lambda)$ where λ denotes wavelengths. The scalar pixel value I_K in the projector input image is mapped by the projector intensity transfer function p_K by the electronics of the projector to a projector brightness

$$P_K = p_K(I_K) .$$

The function p_K is assumed to be non-linear and monotonic. In addition, it is assumed to be spatially invariant but different for each color channel. By modulation of the projector brightness P_K with the spectral response w_k, the irradiance

$$E_K(\lambda) = P_K w_K(\lambda)$$

is produced and illuminates the scene point with spectral reflectance $s(\lambda)$ in the viewing direction of the camera. Then the radiance of the scene point in direction of the camera is

$$L_J(\lambda) = P_K w_K(\lambda) s(\lambda) ,$$

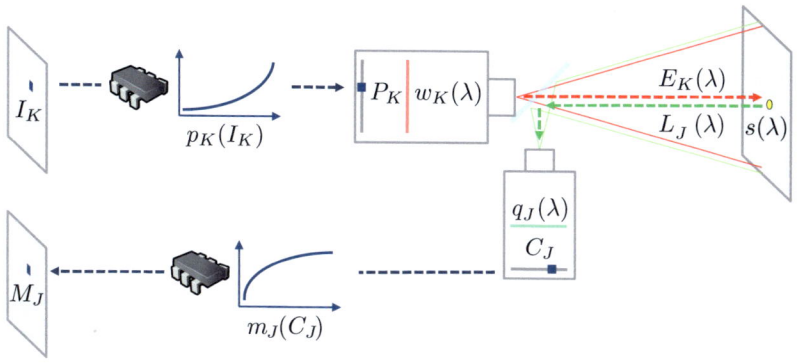

Figure 2.3: Information flow and radiometric quantities for a projector-camera system.

which is measured by the camera channel $J \in \{R, G, B\}$ with spectral response function $q_J(\lambda)$. The irradiance detected by the camera's sensor is then

$$C_J = P_K \int w_K(\lambda) s(\lambda) q_J(\lambda) \, \mathrm{d}\lambda \,,$$

which is further processed by the electronics of the camera to produce the scalar pixel value

$$M_J = m_J(C_J).$$

The function m_J which relates sensor irradiances to image pixel values is referred to as *camera transfer function* and is assumed to be non-linear and monotonic. Furthermore, it is assumed to be spatially invariant but different for each channel. With the physical model for a single channel, the model can be extended to three color channels for projector and camera, i.e., $J, K \in \{R, G, B\}$. In matrix notation this yields

$$\mathbf{C} = \mathbf{V}\mathbf{P}, \tag{2.2}$$

where

$$\mathbf{C} = \begin{pmatrix} C_R \\ C_G \\ C_B \end{pmatrix}, \mathbf{V} = \begin{pmatrix} V_{RR} & V_{RG} & V_{RB} \\ V_{GR} & V_{GG} & V_{GB} \\ V_{BR} & V_{BG} & V_{BB} \end{pmatrix}, \mathbf{P} = \begin{pmatrix} P_R \\ P_G \\ P_B \end{pmatrix}$$

and

$$V_{KJ} = \int w_K(\lambda)s(\lambda)q_J(\lambda)\,\mathrm{d}\lambda\,.$$

This is the linear part of the radiometric model which describes the spectral couplings between the projector and the camera channels and their interactions with the spectral reflectance of the scene. Note that the spectral responses of projector and camera are unknown but are typically broad and overlapping and thus, they mutually interfere with each other.

The nonlinear part of the model is expressed by the projector intensity transfer function

$$\mathbf{p}(\mathbf{I}) = \mathbf{P},$$

where $\mathbf{p}(\mathbf{I}) = (p_R(I_R), p_G(I_G), p_B(I_B))^T$, and camera transfer function

$$\mathbf{m}(\mathbf{C}) = \mathbf{M},$$

where $\mathbf{m}(\mathbf{C}) = (m_R(C_R), m_G(C_G), m_B(C_B))^T$. The camera transfer function is required by all computer vision tasks that need to measure scene radiance, e.g., photometric stereo or shape from shading, and its recovery is therefore a well studied problem [GN03]. In our work, the approach described in [MN99] is applied where images of a static scene are captured with different exposures and samples of the camera transfer function are implicitly collected. Then, this discrete function is inverted to obtain discrete samples of the inverse camera transfer function

$$\mathbf{m}^{-1}(\mathbf{M}) = \mathbf{C}\,, \tag{2.3}$$

which is needed to map measured camera pixel values to scene radiances.

The intensity transfer function of the projector can normally be obtained by a spectroradiometer, but this device was not available for our experiments. However, the off-line calibration procedure described in [NPGB03] allows computing the model parameters $\mathbf{V}$ without any prior knowledge regarding the projector intensity transfer function, provided that the transfer function of the camera is known. The calibration procedure is based on two steps as follows: In the first step, the model parameters in matrix $\mathbf{V}$ are computed for each pixel. For this means, the diagonal entries V_{KK} are treated separately by defining the diagonal matrix $\mathbf{D} = \mathrm{diag}(V_{RR}, V_{GG}, V_{BB})$. Then the matrix $\hat{\mathbf{V}} = \mathbf{VD}^{-1}$ is defined so that $\hat{V}_{KK} = 1$, which models only the mixing between unlike color channels. To determine the 6 model parameters in $\hat{\mathbf{V}}$, 4 images with constant color have to be projected and captured. For more details on this procedure see [GPNB04].

In the second step, the non-linear projector intensity transfer function is estimated for each pixel. Substituting $\mathbf{V} = \hat{\mathbf{V}}\mathbf{D}$ in equation (2.2) and multiplying with $\hat{\mathbf{V}}^{-1}$ from left yields

$$\underbrace{\hat{\mathbf{V}}^{-1}\mathbf{C}}_{=:\hat{\mathbf{C}}} = \mathbf{DP} \,. \tag{2.4}$$

Then, since $\hat{\mathbf{C}}$ and $\mathbf{P}$ are vectors and $\mathbf{D}$ is diagonal, (2.4) can be written element-wise as

$$\hat{C}_K = V_{KK} \cdot p_K(I_K) \,, \tag{2.5}$$

for each channel $K \in \{R, G, B\}$. Equation (2.5) shows that $\hat{C}_K$ only depends on the input pixel values I_K of channel K and is independent of the other channels. By defining $p'_K(I_K) := V_{KK} \cdot p_K(I_K)$ the unknown scaling factors V_{KK} are included in the unknown camera transfer function p'_K and equation (2.5) can be written as

$$\hat{C}_K = p'_K(I_K) \,.$$

This means, the function p'_K can be sampled by projecting constant images for each projector pixel value $I_K = 1, \ldots, 255$, capturing the corresponding images M_K and determining $\hat{C}_K$ via equation (2.3) and (2.4). The samples are then inverted in order to obtain the inverse projector intensity transfer function $\mathbf{p}'^{-1}$ (see [NPGB03] for a detailed explanation on this procedure). A similar method for recovering the inverse intensity transfer function is presented in [GPNB04], but there only two calibration images instead of 260 are required.

Once all model parameters have been determined off-line for a static scene by the calibration procedure, a compensation image can be computed on-line for any desired camera image. For each desired camera pixel value $\mathbf{M} = (M_R, M_G, M_B)^T$, the corresponding projector pixel value $\mathbf{I} = (I_R, I_G, I_B)^T$ can be computed according to

$$\mathbf{I} = \mathbf{p}'^{-1}(\hat{\mathbf{V}}^{-1}\mathbf{m}^{-1}(\mathbf{M})) \,.$$

Note, since the radiometric model is only valid as long as the scene remains static, the calibration procedure must be repeated making this method inefficiently when experimenting with different scenes and objects. Furthermore, problems in recovering the projector non-linearity introduced by the intensity transfer function were encountered in our experiments. Both calibration methods proposed in [GPNB04] and [NPGB03] were attempted to determine the relationship between camera irradiance and projector input, but with limited success. Both approaches yielded samples of the intensity transfer function, but however, which were inappropriate for inversion due to strong noise.

2.3   Error-Feedback Approach To Radiometric Compensation

In [FGN05] and [NPGB03], a method for radiometric compensation using the error between the desired and measured appearance of the projected image is proposed. The appearance of the projected image is continually measured by the camera and the computed error is used to adapt the projected image to meet the desired appearance. Let $\mathbf{I}$ be the desired original image and $\mathbf{M}(t)$ the corresponding measured image when $\tilde{\mathbf{I}}(t)$ is projected. At $t = 0$, the algorithm starts by projecting $\tilde{\mathbf{I}}(0) = \mathbf{I}$. Then the adapted compensation image for time $t + 1$ can be computed as

$$\tilde{\mathbf{I}}(t + 1) = \tilde{\mathbf{I}}(t) + \alpha(\mathbf{M}(t) - \mathbf{I}),$$

where $\alpha \in (0, 1)$ is a gain factor and addition is defined component-wise for each color channel separately. By setting $\mathbf{I}$ to a flat-gray image and let the error-feedback algorithm converge to a small constant error, $\tilde{\mathbf{I}}$ becomes the inverse illumination mask. Typically, the algorithm converges after a few iterations (see Figure 3.1(d)) and is therefore ideally suited for dynamic scenes.

3   Experimental Results

Due to the aforementioned problems associated with the model-based approach, the error-feedback method presented in Section 2.3 is utilized to compute the inverse illumination mask of a test scene. Figure 3.1 summarizes the results obtained for a scene that consists of a flat colored background and a gypsum bust in the foreground. Figure 3.1(a) shows the measured camera image when a flat-gray image is projected. This resembles a coaxial bright-field illumination of the scene. Figure 3.1(b) shows the inverse illumination mask obtained by the feedback algorithm after 15 iterations. By projecting this image onto the scene, the camera measures a nearly constant gray image (see Figure 3.1(c)). Figure 3.1(d) illustrates the *root mean square* (RMS) error [GW08] between desired flat-gray and actual measured camera image for each iteration. As clearly can be seen, the RMS error decreases rapidly and after approximately five iterations no further decrease of the RMS error is observable.

To evaluate the feasibility of the inverse illumination method for inspection tasks, the test scene is modified by small paper patches to simulate deviations from the desired nominal state of our scene. Then, the actual (modified) scene is illuminated by the inverse illumination mask of the nominal scene and an image is captured. The results are summarized in Figure 3.2. As expected, deviations from the nominal scene, which are simulated by colored paper patches, are clearly highlighted

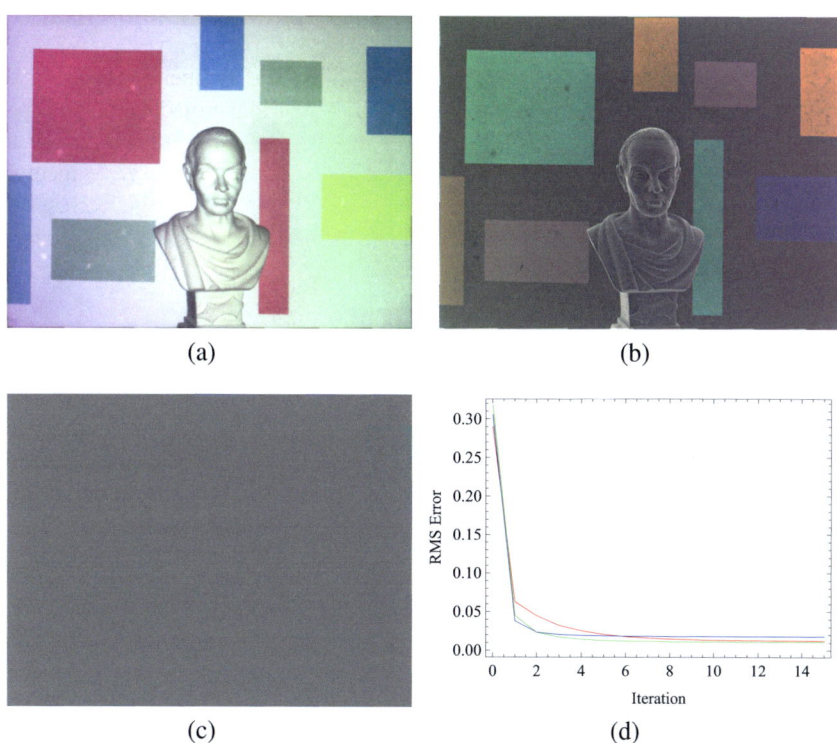

(a)   (b)

(c)   (d)

Figure 3.1: Experimental results of the error-feedback algorithm. (a) Image of scene when a flat-gray image is projected. (b) Inverse illumination mask computed by the error-feedback algorithm. (c) Measured camera image when the inverse illumination mask is projected onto the scene. (d) RMS error between desired flat-gray image and actual measured camera image for each iteration of the error-feedback algorithm (red, green and blue indicate the error for each color channel).

by the inverse illumination mask. Since deviations in reflectance and shape are directly displayed in the captured inspection image, the effort to detect these can be reduced. For instance, conventional image segmentation techniques based on color thresholding [GW08] may be used to identify the faulty regions in the inspection image (compare Figures 3.3(a) and 3.3(b)).

Obviously, similar result like in Figure 3.1(d) can be obtained by capturing images from the nominal and actual (modified) scene under conventional bright-filed illumination and by subtracting the images from each another to get a difference

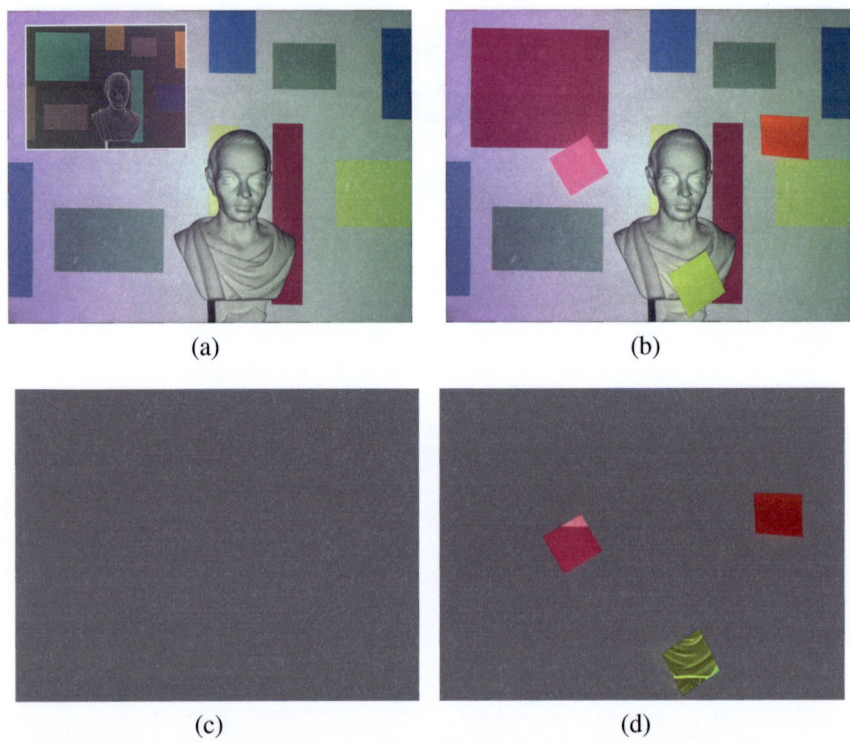

(a)   (b)

(c)   (d)

Figure 3.2: Inverse illumination to highlight deviations from the desired nominal state of a test scene. (a) Nominal state of the scene with its inverse illumination mask shown as inset. (b) Modified scene by paper patches. (c) Original scene and (d) modified scene illuminated with the inverse illumination mask of the nominal state of the test scene.

image. However, since the usable dynamic range of digital cameras used in machine vision is much smaller than the dynamic range associated with most technical scenes, saturation and underexposures in images are common. Consequently, by controlling the exposure of the camera so that the brightest scene point is captured without saturation, image regions corresponding to low radiance are captured with low *signal-to-noise ratio* (SNR).

By illuminating a scene with its inverse illumination mask, the exposure of each pixel on the camera sensor is adapted independently. The notion of spatially varying pixel exposures was first introduced in [NM00] at the cost of

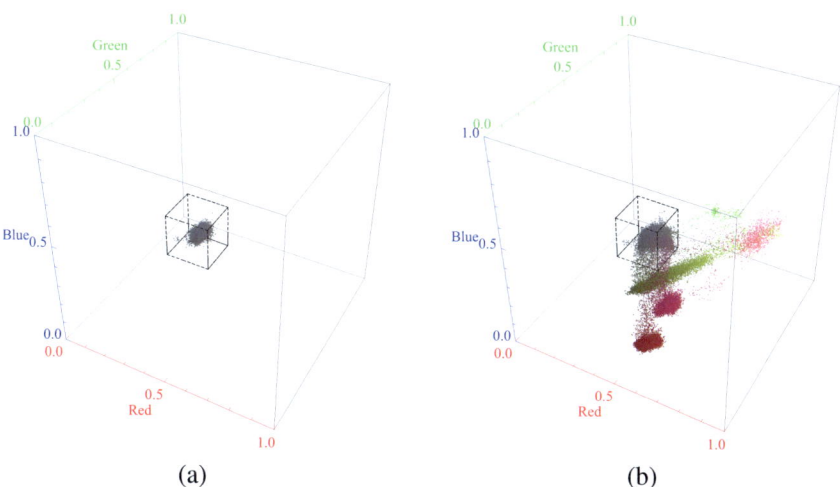

(a)   (b)

Figure 3.3: Segmentation in RGB color space by enclosing data regions. (a) Color distribution of the image pixels in Figure 3.2(c). Each image pixel corresponds to a vector in the RGB color space. The pixels are densely clustered and are enclosed by a bounding box which is centered on the color gray. (b) Color distribution of the image pixels in Figure 3.2(d). Points outside the bounding box belong to image regions that mark deviations from the nominal state of the scene.

reduced spacial resolution. Some novel approaches have been introduced in [NB03][NBB04][MSM+07] where different optical attenuators like liquid crystals are used to control the incident irradiance of each camera pixel. In our approach, the exposure of each camera pixel is controlled indirectly by changing the irradiance of the corresponding scene point, with the result that all scene radiance values are brought to the same predefined measurable camera pixel value. Consequently, an inspection image with spatially constant SNR is acquired. Furthermore, by computing the inverse illumination mask that corresponds to an optimally exposed flat-gray inspection image just below saturation, deviation detection is performed in the image signal region with highest SNR.

4 Summary

An illumination technique that directly highlights deviations in reflectance between two scenes is proposed. This is achieved by generating an inverse illumination mask of the desired nominal state of the scene which "neutralizes" the appearance of the nominal state to a flat-gray image. By this means, inspection images with high and constant SNR are obtained that can render the subsequent digital image processing tasks for defect detection more efficient and reliable. In future works, we shall investigate the common principle and possible advantages of scene adapted illumination techniques more formally and attempt to apply this principle to develop novel illumination techniques. Furthermore, projector-camera systems in general will be utilized and investigated as programmable light sources for machine vision applications.

Bibliography

[AOSS06] Marc Ashdown, Takahiro Okabe, Imari Sato, and Yoichi Sato. Robust Content-Dependent Photometric Projector Compensation. In *Conference on Computer Vision and Pattern Recognition Workshop*, 2006.

[BEK05a] Oliver Bimber, Andreas Emmerling, and Thomas Klemmer. Embedded Entertainment with Smart Projectors. *Computer*, 38(1):48–55, 2005.

[BH85] Bruce G. Batchelor and D. A. Hill. *Automated Visual Inspection*. Elsevier Science Publishing Company, April 1985.

[BIWG08] Oliver Bimber, Daisuke Iwai, Gordon Wetzstein, and Anselm Grundhöfer. The Visual Computing of Projector-Camera Systems. *Computer Graphics Forum*, 27(8):2219–2245, 2008.

[BOKJ] Torsten Baumbach, Wolfgang Osten, Christoph von Kopylow, and Werner Jüptner. Remote Metrology by Comparative Digital Holography. *Applied Optics*, 45(5).

[CS07] Yuanyuan Cai and Xianyu Su. Inverse Projected-Fringe Technique Based on Multi Projectors. *Optics and Lasers in Engineering*, 45(10):1028–1034, October 2007.

[FGN05] Kensaku Fujii, Michael D. Grossberg, and Shree K. Nayar. A Projector-Camera System with Real-Time Photometric Adaptation for Dynamic Environments. In *IEEE Computer Society Conference on Computer Vision and Pattern Recognition*, volume 1, pages 814–821 vol. 1, 2005.

[GN03] Michael D. Grossberg and Shree K. Nayar. Determining the Camera Response from Images: What Is Knowable? *IEEE Transactions on Pattern Analysis and Machine Intelligence*, 25(11):1455–1467, 2003.

[GPNB04] Michael D. Grossberg, Harish Peri, Shree K. Nayar, and Peter N. Belhumeur. Making One Object Look Like Another: Controlling Appearance Asing a Projector-Camera System. In *Proceedings of the IEEE Computer Society Conference on Computer Vision and Pattern Recognition*, volume 1, pages I–452–I–459 Vol.1, 2004.

[Gre04] John E. Greivenkamp. *Field Guide to Geometrical Optics*. SPIE Society of Photo-Optical Instrumentation Engineers, illustrated edition edition, 2004.

[GTLL06] Gaurav Garg, Eino-Ville Talvala, Marc Levoy, and Hendrik P. A. Lensch. Symmetric Photography: Exploiting Data-Sparseness in Reflectance Fields. *Rendering Techniques*, pages 251–262, 2006.

[GW08] Rafael C. Gonzalez and Richard E. Woods. *Digital Image Processing*. Prentice Hall International, 3rd international edition. edition, August 2008.

[LBOK04]   Wangsong Li, Thorsten Bothe, Wolfgang Osten, and Michael K. Kalms. Object Adapted Pattern Projection — Part I: Generation of Inverse Patterns. *Optics and Lasers in Engineering*, 41(1):31–50, 2004.

[MN99]   Tomoo Mitsunaga and Shree K. Nayar. Radiometric Self Calibration. In *IEEE Computer Society Conference on Computer Vision and Pattern Recognition*, volume 1, page 1374, Los Alamitos, CA, USA, 1999. IEEE Computer Society.

[MSM$^+$07] Hidetoshi Mannami, Ryusuke Sagawa, Yasuhiro Mukaigawa, Tomio Echigo, and Yasushi Yagi. Adaptive Dynamic Range Camera with Reflective Liquid Crystal. *Journal of Visual Communication and Image Representation*, 18(5):359–365, October 2007.

[NB03]   Shree K. Nayar and Vlad Branzoi. Adaptive Dynamic Range Imaging: Optical Control of Pixel Exposures Over Space and Time. In *Ninth IEEE International Conference on Computer Vision*, pages 1168–1175 vol.2, 2003.

[NBB04]   Shree K. Nayar, Vlad Branzoi, and Terry E. Boult. Programmable Imaging using a Digital Micromirror Array. In *IEEE Conference on Computer Vision and Pattern Recognition (CVPR)*, volume I, pages 436–443, June 2004.

[NM00]   Shree K. Nayar and Tomoo Mitsunaga. High Dynamic Range Imaging: Spatially Varying Pixel Exposures. In *IEEE Conference on Computer Vision and Pattern Recognition*, volume 1, pages 472–479 vol.1, 2000.

[NPGB03]   Shree K. Nayar, Harish Peri, Michael D. Grossberg, and Peter N. Belhumeur. A Projection System with Radiometric Compensation for Screen Imperfections. In *First IEEE International Workshop on Projector-Camera Systems (PROCAMS-2003)*, 2003.

[RLW00]   Ramesh Raskar, Kok Low, and Greg Welch. Shader Lamps: Animating Real Objects with Image-Based Illumination. Technical report, University of North Carolina at Chapel Hill, 2000.

[SUW07]   Carsten Steger, Markus Ulrich, and Christian Wiedemann. *Machine Vision Algorithms and Applications*. Wiley-Vch, 1., auflage edition, October 2007.

[WB07a]   Stefan Werling and Jürgen Beyerer. Inspection of Specular Surfaces with Inverse Patterns. *tm-Technisches Messen*, 74(4):217–223, 2007.

[WB07b]   Gordon Wetzstein and Oliver Bimber. Radiometric Compensation Through Inverse Light Transport. In *Proceedings of the 15th Pacific Conference on Computer Graphics and Applications*, pages 391–399, 2007.

[Wol94]   George Wolberg. *Digital Image Warping*. IEEE Computer Society Press, Los Alamitos, CA, USA, 1994.

A Framework for Analyzing Natural Gaze Behavior in Dynamic Environments

Thomas Bader

Vision and Fusion Laboratory
Institute for Anthropomatics
Karlsruhe Institute of Technology (KIT), Germany
bader@ies.uni-karlsruhe.de

Technical Report IES-2009-06

Abstract: Gaze data contains valuable information about user's cognitive processes during execution of a task. In order to use this information, e.g., for studying user's strategies or for designing new gaze-based interaction techniques for HCI, gaze data needs to be aligned with the task executed by the user.

In this paper we propose a novel framework based on the theory of Markov Decision Processes for putting gaze data into context, allowing for automated interpretation of gaze position and movement with respect to the task performed by the user. The model can be used for offline analysis of gaze data, e.g., for studying gaze behavior, as well as for online interpretation for realizing new interaction techniques. We evaluate the proposed model with an indirect object manipulation task and demonstrate how it can be used for intention recognition and/or detection of a mismatch between the mental model build by the user and the real system.

1   Introduction

Visual perception is an important information channel during manipulation of real or virtual objects (e.g., icons on a graphical user interface). It allows for perceiving the current state of manipulated objects and/or for visuomotoric control of manipulators like our hands or a computer mouse. During manipulation tasks, our gaze behavior is mainly controlled top-down and subconsciously by cognitive processes which are responsible for task execution. Therefore, natural gaze behavior provides a window into the human mind and allows a conclusion to be drawn about user's intentions and cognitive processes. This information could be very valuable for future adaptive and proactive human-computer interfaces (HCIs).

However, natural gaze behavior is very complex and is influenced by a vast amount of factors. Therefore, in order to allow for integration of natural gaze as an additional modality into HCIs the following steps need to be undertaken:

1. A thorough understanding of natural gaze behavior in dynamic environments needs to be established.
2. Methods for automated online analysis of gaze data in the context of dynamic environments need to be developed.
3. New multimodal gaze-supported HCIs need to be designed, implemented, and evaluated.

All of the three points above have been already covered by a large body of research. *Natural gaze behavior* has been studied in different natural environments (e.g., during block-copying [PHL01], basic object manipulation [JWBF01], driving [LL94], and playing cricket [LM00]) as well as during human-computer interaction (e.g., [SHAZ00]) and on the field of psychology and physiology (e.g., [GBOF08, FJ03]). However, the results of these studies in the form of different gaze behavior observed during task execution mostly are reported in an informal way, e.g., as verbal descriptions or as plots of gaze data. Such descriptions can help to improve the principal understanding of gaze, however, a more formal description of different gaze behaviors in different contexts is required in order to make results comparable and accessible for automated interpretation.

General *methods for automated online analysis* of gaze data currently are mainly limited to fixation detection [SG00, SA01] and analysis of fixation frequency, duration, and position (e.g., [SA00]). Alignment of gaze data with the task or cognitive processes often is done manually or is restricted to static environments (e.g., [SG00, HMR03, SA01]). In order to develop new methods for interpretation of natural gaze behavior in arbitrary dynamic environments a common formal framework would be very helpful.

Most state-of-the-art *gaze-based interfaces* use gaze as an explicit pointing device, e.g., as a replacement for a mouse [Lan00]. This requires gaze to be used for manipulation (e.g., for pressing keys on a virtual keyboard [Lan00]) in addition to its natural purpose, namely visual perception. Such interaction techniques might be useful for certain applications, e.g., when hands are not available as an input modality. However, using gaze-based pointing as a general input technique for human computer interaction has many limitations (see [BVK09]). Promising examples for gaze-supported interaction techniques are presented in [HMR03] and [ZMI99]. In both approaches natural gaze behavior is analyzed and the user is not forced to diverge from that natural behavior for interaction purposes. *iDict* [HMR03] analyzes the duration of fixations while the user reads a text in a foreign language and automatically provides a translation of the fixated word if a longer fixation is detected. In the approach "Manual And Gaze Input Cascaded (MAGIC) Pointing" [ZMI99] the mouse pointer is placed close to the currently fixated object in order to eliminate a large portion of the cursor movement. Both approaches do not use gaze directly as pointing or input device, but interpret gaze data in the context of the task (reading, pointing). However, the link between gaze and cognition in none of the two approaches is made explicit, e.g., in form of a model. This limits generalization and development of a deeper understanding of the underlying principles of such techniques. The need for modeling the dependencies between gaze and the task was also already stated by other researchers (e.g., [SA00] suggest to use tools from cognitive modeling).

In this paper we propose a new framework based on the theory of Markov Decision Processes (MDPs), which can provide a common ground for all of the three above mentioned steps towards adequate interpretation of natural gaze behavior in dynamic environments and usage as additional modality in future HCIs. In particular we consider the following aspect as important to be covered by such a framework

- *Uncertainty of knowledge* of the user about the system which is interacted with seems to play an important role for explaining and interpreting natural gaze behavior [BVK09]. In contrast to traditional approaches to cognitive modeling of tasks like GOMS [Joh90] the proposed framework explicitly allows for modeling uncertain knowledge.
- *Multiple strategies* may lead to a desired goal when interacting with a system. Natural gaze behavior therefore can be influenced by more than one of those strategies and by the choice between them, respectively. In the propose framework multiple possible strategies can be explicitly modeled and/or generated automatically.
- *Simplicity* of the framework is important for keeping it applicable for the above mentioned steps. Even if important components of cognition like short-time memory are not explicitly covered by the framework, it provides a good basis for investigating and interpreting natural gaze behavior for many tasks.

The framework proposed here is an extension of the work presented in [BVK09], where fundamental causal relations between task execution and gaze behavior are discussed and modeled in a probabilistic framework.

2 Framework for alignment of gaze data

In this section we propose a formal framework for modeling the interdependencies between gaze data and the task executed by the user. We first derive the formal model, then show how gaze behavior can be classified into different categories related to the current state of task execution. Finally, we illustrate what can be further inferred from the model regarding intention recognition and detection of model mismatches.

2.1 A formal model of an interactive system and its mental representation

The human decision process during interaction with an interactive system consisting of a number of interactive objects can be modeled by the 4-tupel $(\mathcal{Q}^o, \mathcal{I}, P(Q^o_{t+1}|Q^o_t, I_t), c(\,\cdot\,)^o)$, which defines an MDP. We denote $\mathcal{Q}^o$ as the set of all possible states of an object. $\mathcal{I}$ is the set of possible inputs or actions which can be performed by the user in order to change the system state. $P(Q^o_{t+1} = \boldsymbol{q}^o_{t+1}|Q^o_t = \boldsymbol{q}^o_t, I_t = \boldsymbol{i}_t)$ denotes the probability of a state transition of object o from state $\boldsymbol{q}^o_t$ to state $\boldsymbol{q}^o_{t+1}$ if input $\boldsymbol{i}_t \in \mathcal{I}$ is performed by the user. The function c defines costs for each system state and state transition, respectively. These costs can reflect relevance of certain system states for the success of the whole task, but also cognitive or physical load induced by certain inputs. Without loss of generality, in the following we will focus on one single object and therefore omit the index o in the formulas above.

Usually, state transitions in a technical interactive system, in contrast to those in natural ones, are deterministic. Hence, the state transition probabilities P^T for most technical systems reduce to

$$P^T(Q_{t+1} = \boldsymbol{q}^i_{t+1} \mid Q_t = \boldsymbol{q}_t, I_t = \boldsymbol{i}_t) = 1 \text{ and}$$
$$P^T(Q_{t+1} \neq \boldsymbol{q}^i_{t+1} \mid Q_t = \boldsymbol{q}_t, I_t = \boldsymbol{i}_t) = 0,$$

where $\boldsymbol{q}^i_{t+1}$ denotes the state induced by input $\boldsymbol{i}_t$. However, the mental model of such a deterministic system can be incomplete and/or uncertain. Since gaze behavior is determined by this mental representation of the interactive system P^M and not by the real one (P^T) we chose to use a probabilistic framework in order to allow for modeling of effects such as a model mismatch ($P^M \neq P^T$). The different basic components of the model are illustrated in Figure 2.1.

When interacting with a system, the user mostly has a certain goal in mind. He/she wants the system to take a certain target state, which has to fulfill some requirements. We therefore model a goal as a subset of system states $\mathcal{G} \subseteq \mathcal{Q}$ with the indicator function

$$\mu_{\mathcal{G}}(\boldsymbol{q}) = \begin{cases} 1 \text{ if } \boldsymbol{q} \in \mathcal{G}, \\ 0 \text{ if } \boldsymbol{q} \notin \mathcal{G}. \end{cases}$$

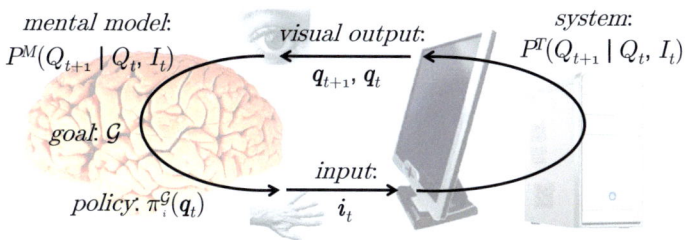

Figure 2.1: Basic components of the model.

Such a goal for example can be the selection of a set of objects or their positioning in a target area on the screen. A complete task can consist of multiple subgoals, which have to be reached subsequently.

To convey an interactive system from its initial state q^0 into a target state $q^{\mathcal{G}} \in \mathcal{G}$, the user has to execute a sequence of actions. In most tasks not only one action sequence leads to the target state, but many different "ways" can be chosen by the user. The different *policies* the user can follow are described as a set of functions

$$\pi_i^{\mathcal{G}}(q) : \mathcal{Q} \to \mathcal{I}, \quad i = 1, ..., N_\pi,$$

where the function $\pi_i^{\mathcal{G}}(q)$ specifies the action the user will choose according to policy i when the system is in state q and the goal is $\mathcal{G}$. N_π is the number of possible policies.

Given a certain task with an initial state q^0 and a goal $\mathcal{G}$ the user has to decide, which actions are to be executed in order to reach the goal. $P^M(Q_{t+1}|Q_t = q_t, I_t = i_t)$ reflects the knowledge the user has about the system, namely which effects a certain input i_t has on the state of an object and the system, respectively. If the user had perfect knowledge of the system ($P^M = P^T$), he could calculate the set of optimal policies for reaching the goal according to his internal value function c, describing costs for executing the different inputs and the amount of reward for reaching certain system states. If the user had no knowledge of the system, he could have the same value function c but would not be able to calculate any policy, since the effect of actions to the system state would be unknown. Therefore, in this case the user would have to build a mental model of the system previous or in parallel to the execution of the primary task.

2.2   Two reasons why we look where we look

In this section we analyze what kind of natural gaze behavior would be predicted by the above model. Generally, we have two reasons to draw our visual attention on a certain location in an interactive environment.

The first one is *control of input i*. If the human operator once has decided to execute a certain action in order to reach the goal, it is important to perform this input as accurate and fast as possible. Since absolute positioning of limbs by only proprioceptive feedback is not very accurate [BRS03], vision is needed as additional feedback channel for accurate position, e.g., of the hand. An input can be either controlled *directly* by observing the input device or body part, or *indirectly* by observing the system reaction.

The second reason for drawing our visual attention on a certain location is the *verification of system reactions or states*. If we had a perfect mental model of the system and complete and accurate non-visual feedback about our actions i, we could execute the task successfully with closed eyes. However, neither the first nor the second assumption is realistic. In most cases the mental model is incomplete or uncertain, and, as already mentioned above, non-visual feedback channels (e.g., proprioception or touch) are not accurate enough. Therefore, in order to create, improve or verify the mental model of the system the user has to check permanently, whether a certain input leads to the anticipated system reaction or not. The more confident the mental model is, the less verification of the system reaction is required.

For further investigations of these two processes, which concurrently influence natural gaze behavior during human-computer interaction, alignment of gaze data with the task and system state is required.

2.3   Methods for alignment of gaze data

To align gaze data with the model presented above we use both, absolute position and movement of gaze. Typically gaze movements are separated into two different components: *fixations* and *saccades*. While saccades are rapid eye movements used to locate the gaze at a certain position, gaze remains almost still during fixations to enable retrieval of visual information. Two different algorithms have been implemented for automated fixation detection. Both algorithms "I-DT" (Dispersion-Threshold Identification) and "I-VT" (Velocity-Threshold Identification) are taken from [SG00]. The first algorithm clusters gaze points according to their spatial distribution, the second one according to the velocity of gaze movements.

In the following we present methods for interpretation of gaze data in an interactive environment with visual representation of object and system states on a 2-dimensional planar display. The state of an object in such an environment can be described by $q_t = (p_t, \alpha_t)$, where $p_t \in \mathbb{N}^2$ is the position of the visual representation of the object on the display and α_t describes further attributes of the object. Fixation positions are further denoted with $f_t \in \mathbb{N}^2$. In order to analyze gaze positions in the context of a task, we calculate the difference vector $v_t = f_t - p_t$. Additionally, we define the vector $w_t^i = \hat{p}_{t+1}^{\pi_i} - p_t$ with

$$\hat{p}_{t+1}^{\pi_i} = \operatorname*{argmax}_{p_{t+1}} \quad P^T(Q_{t+1} = (p_{t+1}, \alpha_{t+1})|Q_t = q_t, I_t = \pi_i(q_t)).$$

as the most probable next object state given a certain policy π_i. w_t^i also could be calculated by not only considering one but cumulating multiple steps of the policy until a certain horizon of predicition.

Every fixation further is classified into one of the following categories:

$$P^{f,i} : (\|v_t\| > v_o) \wedge (\measuredangle(v_t, w_t^i) \leq \beta_{max})$$
$$O^{f,i} : (\|v_t\| \leq v_o) \wedge (w_t^i = 0)$$
$$N^f : (\|v_t\| > v_o) \wedge (\forall i : \measuredangle(v_t, w_t^i) > \beta_{max})$$
$$O^f : (\|v_t\| \leq v_o) \wedge (\forall i : w_t^i \neq 0)$$

Fixations of category $P^{f,i}$ are proactive with respect to policy π_i. Category $O^{f,i}$ contains fixations on objects along a certain policy with no changes in object position, while O^f describes all other fixations on an object. N^f contains all fixations belonging to none of the other categories.

The criteria for the different categories only depend on system states at one single point in time. The time delay for fixation classification induced by a previous approach presented in [BVK09] can therefore be avoided.

Taking only absolute fixation positions into account for gaze analysis may lead to problems if gaze position measurement is subject to drift, as it is often the case with current eye tracking hardware. Therefore, we also classify gaze movements according to their spatial relation to object and target positions as well as to possible policies. We define saccades as $\Delta f_t = f_t - f_{t-1}$ and assign them to one of the following classes:

$$P^{s,i} : (\|v_t\| > \|v_{t-1}\|) \wedge (\measuredangle(\Delta f_t, w_t^i) \leq \beta_{max})$$
$$P^s : (\|v_t\| > \|v_{t-1}\|) \wedge (\forall i : \measuredangle(\Delta f_t, w_t^i) > \beta_{max})$$
$$R^s : (\|v_t\| \leq \|v_{t-1}\|)$$

Categories $P^{s,i}$ and P^s contain proactive, R^s reactive saccades. Too small saccades or those ones too far away from an object are filtered out by the conditions $\|\Delta \boldsymbol{f}_t\| > \Delta f_{min}$ and $\|\boldsymbol{v}_t\| \leq v_s \vee \|\boldsymbol{v}_{t-1}\| \leq v_s$, where Δf_{min} is the minimal length of a saccade and v_s the maximal distance to an object.

Proactive gaze behavior which can be assigned to a certain policy (categories $P^{f,i}$, $O^{f,i}$ and $P^{s,i}$) can be used for estimating user's intention. Especially for tasks with multiple possible policies the policy which will be chosen by the user could be identified previous to any object movement, allowing for designing new proactive interaction techniques. Additionally, knowing which policy is chosen by the user according to his gaze movements, a model mismatch can be detected if a different policy is actually executed. In order to reduce training time and to resolve the model mismatch a hint could be displayed to the user in such a case. More generally speaking, the interface can automatically adapt to novice or expert users.

Reactive gaze movements are not of value for intention recognition, since they do not convey any additional information not already available through observation of system state changes. However, a high amount of reactive fixations might indicate uncertainty of the user.

3   Evaluation

3.1   Participants and Task

We evaluated the proposed model with a small user study. Four participants were asked to perform an indirect object manipulation task as fast as possible. The goal was to move a point from its initial position into a target area as shown in Figure 3.1(a). We distinguish between four types of tasks (A,B,C,D) depending on the location of the target area on the screen (see Figure 3.1(b)). Subgoals for the two policies with a minimal number of changes in movement direction of the object were indicated for each task as small dots.

3.2   Apperatus and system model

The size of the display is 12.1 inches with a resolution of 1024×768 pixels. As input devices we use one single key of a keyboard and a pen tablet, while only horizontal movements of the pen on the tablet were used. Hence, we obtain the set of possible inputs $\mathcal{I} = \{0,1\} \times \mathbb{N}$ with elements $\boldsymbol{i} = (i^k, i^d)$, where $i^k \in \{0,1\}$ indicates whether the key is pressed (1) or not (0) and $i^d \in \mathbb{N}$ is the relative

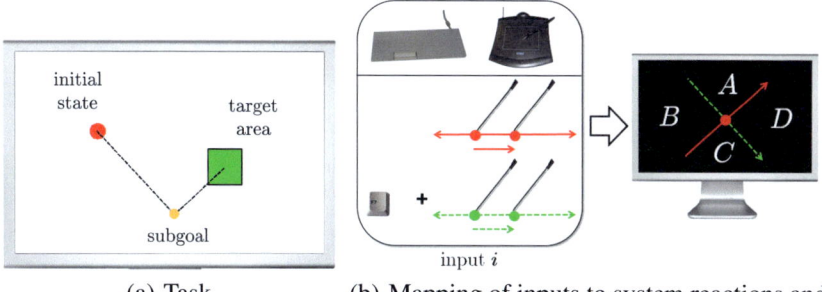

(a) Task

(b) Mapping of inputs to system reactions and target quadrants A,B,C and D

Figure 3.1: Experimental task (a) and mapping of input devices (b).

movement of the pen in horizontal direction to the left (< 0) or to the right (> 0). The position of the point after a state transition is defined by

$$\boldsymbol{p}_{t+1} = \begin{cases} \boldsymbol{p}_t + i_t^d \cdot \boldsymbol{a}_0 & \text{if } i_t^k = 0, \\ \boldsymbol{p}_t + i_t^d \cdot \boldsymbol{a}_1 & \text{if } i_t^k = 1, \end{cases}$$

where $\boldsymbol{a}_0$ and $\boldsymbol{a}_1$ are the two possible movement directions of the object. The mapping between inputs and system state transitions is graphically illustrated in Figure 3.1(b). The mapping was chosen to be distinct from any standard mapping potentially known by the participants in order to being able to study gaze behavior under uncertain mental models $P^M \neq P^T$ of the users.

Figure 3.2 shows the two policies π_1 and π_2 for a task of type D with minimal number of changes in movement direction of the object. Note that the arrows in Figure 3.2 are not the inputs delivered by the policy functions, but indicate the direction of movement of the visual representation of a manipulated object induced by a certain input of the policy.

Participants' eye movements were captured by a SMI iViewX™ HED [Sen03] head mounted eye tracking system. For transforming gaze positions into screen coordinates a video-based marker detection and tracking system was used (see [BVK09] for details).

3.3 Procedure

The participants had to execute 60 tasks of different types (A,B,C,D) in random order, while the order was equal for all participants. Previous to the first task,

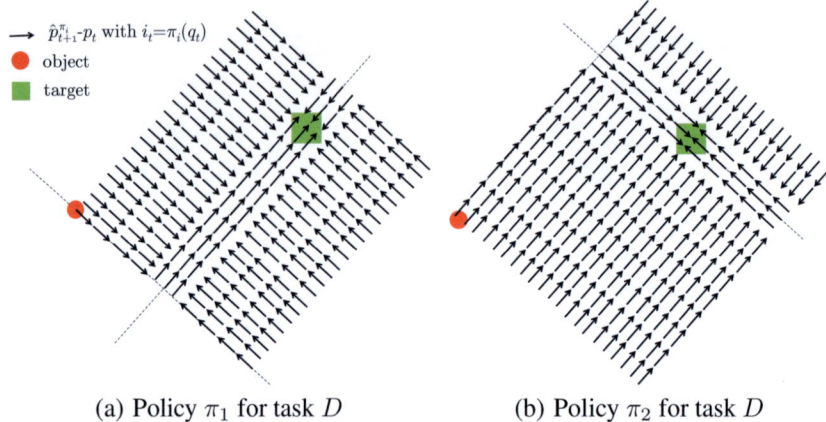

(a) Policy π_1 for task D (b) Policy π_2 for task D

Figure 3.2: Two policies for task of type D with minimal number of changes in movement direction of the manipulated object.

every user was told that only horizontal movements of the pen are interpreted by the system and the key of the keyboard has "some additional function". Additionally, users had time to practice interaction with the pen in a separate application, where horizontal movement of the pen changed the background color of the screen. Hence, no mental model could be build about the mapping between input and object movement during practice.

3.4   Data Analysis

In the study described here we focus on analyzing gaze movements, which occur previous to any object movement. Such *pre-object gaze movements* are particularly interesting for estimating user's intention and model mismatches.

Both, fixations and saccades are classified as described in 2.3. In order to obtain an estimate of user's intention, information about all pre-object gaze movements is cumulated by

$$\hat{\Pi}^{\mathcal{G}} = \{\pi_{j_1}^{\mathcal{G}}, ..., \pi_{j_M}^{\mathcal{G}}\}$$

with

$$j_k \in \{i \in \{1, ..., N_\pi\} | \#P^{f,i} + \#P^{s,i} = \text{maximum}\},$$

where $\#P^{f,i}$ and $\#P^{s,i}$ denote the number of pre-object proactive fixations/saccades assigned to the respective policy $\pi_i^{\mathcal{G}}$. In our experiments we only consider the two different policies shown in Figure 3.2 ($\Rightarrow N_\pi = 2$). If there are no proactive gaze movements, intention can not be estimated and $\hat{\Pi}^{\mathcal{G}} = \{\}$. If the number of fixations/saccades assigned to two or more distinct policies is equal ($|\hat{\Pi}^{\mathcal{G}}| > 1$), also no decision for one single policy is possible.

The policy actually taken by the user is determined by aligning the sequence of inputs $i_{t_1}, ..., i_{t_{N_I}}$ with the different policies. We calculate a score s_i for every policy π_i of a given task according to

$$s_i = \sum_{k=1}^{N_I} < p_{t_k+1} - p_{t_k}, \hat{p}^{\pi_i}_{t_k+1} - p_{t_k} >$$

The policy $\pi_m^{\mathcal{G}}$ ($m = \underset{i}{\mathrm{argmax}}\, s_i$) with the highest score is considered to be the policy, which was chosen by the user for executing the task.

We assume a mismatch between the mental model of the user and the real system if the estimated user intention differs from the policy actually taken:

$$\text{model mismatch} := (\hat{\Pi}^{\mathcal{G}} \neq \{\}) \wedge (\pi_m^{\mathcal{G}} \notin \hat{\Pi}^{\mathcal{G}})$$

3.5 Results

Figures 3.3 and 3.4 show target areas, object movements, and the last pre-object gaze positions in each task for two different participants. Data from earlier tasks of the experiments are drawn in light gray, later tasks in dark gray and black, respectively. In the left figures only data from tasks of type B and in the right figures only from tasks of type D are shown. For both of the two different tasks the policies used by the user converged towards a certain policy. However, gaze behavior differed significantly for the different users and for the tasks.

Figure 3.3 shows data captured from a user ("*User 1*") who used *proactive gaze behavior*. In the right Figure 3.3 (b) proactive gaze positions are distributed along policy π_2, which at the same time is the policy most frequently chosen by the user. In the left Figure 3.3 (a) gaze positions are also proactive, but most of them are distributed along π_1, while the most frequently used policy is π_2. Hence, the figure for task B indicates a model mismatch, since pre-object gaze movements indicate that a wrong system reaction was anticipated by the user.

The user who's data is shown in Figure 3.4 ("*User 2*") almost exclusively used *reactive gaze behavior* at the beginning of the task sequence. For both tasks last pre-object gaze positions are concentrated around the initial object position. Additionally, object paths in Figure 3.4 show much more deviation from one of the

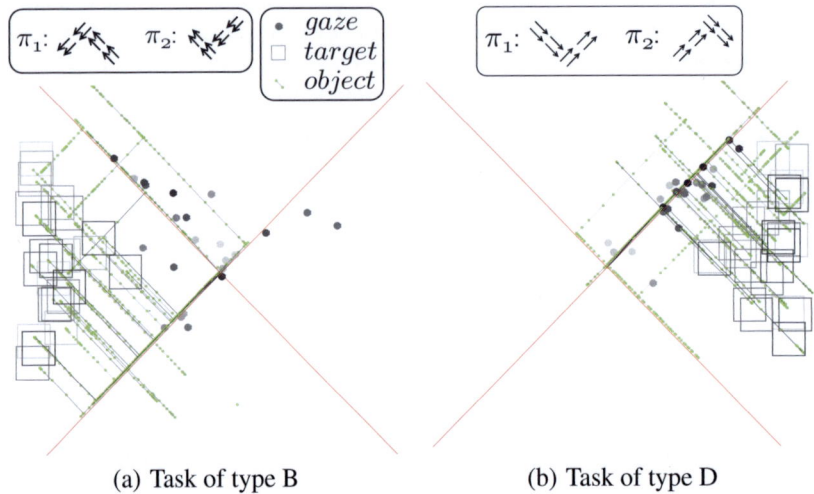

(a) Task of type B   (b) Task of type D

Figure 3.3: Object paths and last pre-object gaze positions for *"User 1"* showing predominantly *proactive gaze behavior* for tasks of type B (a) and D (b)

two "optimal paths" compared to those in Figure 3.3. This indicates that the user with proactive gaze behavior has built a better mental model than the user with reactive gaze behavior or, the other way round, the user with the better model uses proactive gaze behavior while the user with the worse model uses a reactive one.

At the end of the task sequence for task D *"User 2"* switched from reactive to proactive gaze behavior (see Figure 3.4(b)). This also supports the proposition that a better mental model build over time leads to more proactive gaze behavior.

In order to evaluate the proposed model more formally all pre-object fixations and saccades are classified as described in 2.3 and 3.4. Further, user's intention is estimated as the set of most probable policies $\hat{\Pi}^{\mathcal{G}}$ based on the gaze data and is compared with the true policy $\pi_m^{\mathcal{G}}$ chosen by the user. Note that for calculating $\hat{\Pi}^{\mathcal{G}}$ not only last pre-object fixation as shown in Figure 3.4 and 3.3 is considered, but all pre-object fixations and saccades are used as described in 3.4. The results of this evaluation for data collected from four participants are shown in Figure 3.5. The data in Figure 3.3 corresponds to *User 1* and the data in Figure 3.4 to *User 2*.

Pre-object gaze movements of *User 1* and *User 4* deliver good estimates of the policy actually chosen by the user for task D. The amount of tasks of type D with $\hat{\Pi}^{\mathcal{G}} \neq \{\}$ is 95.83% for *User 1* and 66.67% for *User 4*. For task B this percentage is lower for *User 1* (52.12%) and similar for *User 4* (69.57%). However, especially

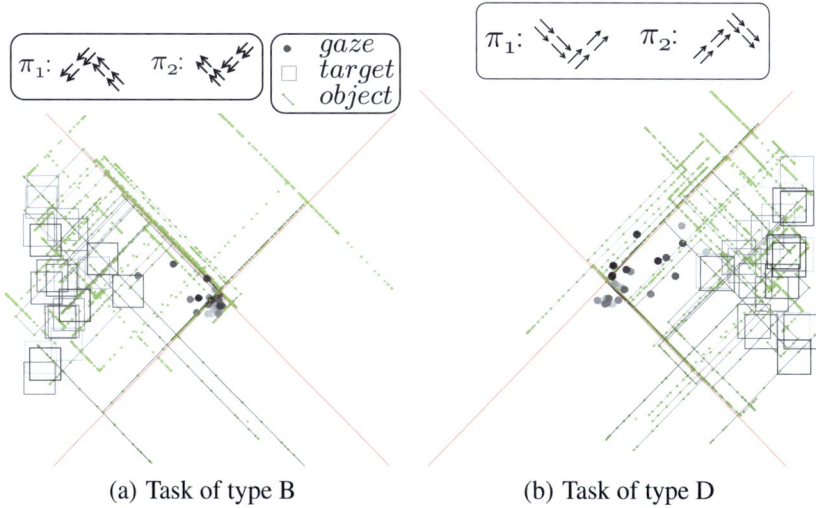

(a) Task of type B   (b) Task of type D

Figure 3.4: Object paths and last gaze position previous to first object movement for *User 2* showing predominantly *reactive gaze behavior* for tasks of type B (a) and a switch from *reactive to proactive behavior* for tasks of type D. (b)

User 4 shows many proactive fixations and saccades indicating a different policy than the one actually chosen (see Figure 3.5(a)). This indicates the existence of a model mismatch for task B.

For *User 2* the number of tasks with $\hat{\Pi}^{\mathcal{G}} \neq \{\}$ increased with the time from 50% for task D (34.78% task B) in the first half of the task sequence to 75% (60.87% task B) in the second half (complete task sequence: 62.5% task D, 47.83% task B). However, as we can see in Figure 3.5(b), *User 2* produced a lot of mismatches between gaze and actual object movement at the end of the task sequence.

User 3 shows a similar development of gaze behavior as *User 2* (at least for task B), however, with a lower amount of tasks with proactive gaze behavior allowing for estimating user's intention (task B: 1st half 17.39%, 2nd half 60.87% total 39.13%; task D: 1st half 33.33%, 2nd half 33.33%, total 33.33%).

3.6   Discussion

The above results show that the proposed model provides a good basis for analyzing gaze data in the context of a task and in a dynamic environment. The small

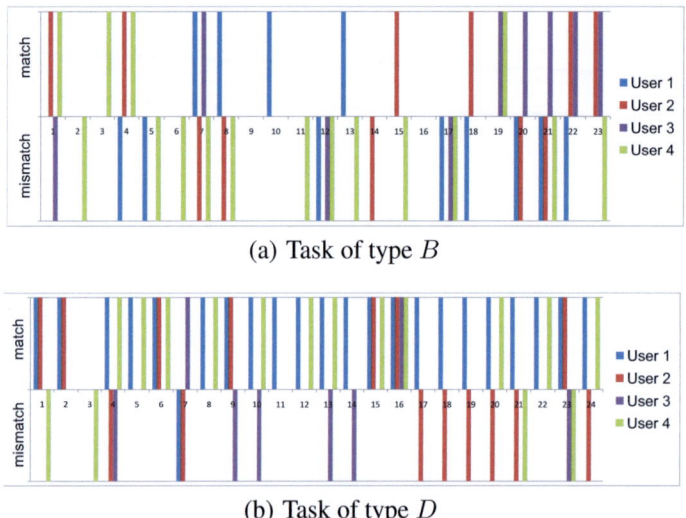

(a) Task of type B

(b) Task of type D

Figure 3.5: Comparison of estimated policy and true policy chosen by the users for all tasks of type D. Bars above the horizontal axis indicate a match of estimated intention and true policy, bars below indicate a mismatch. Missing bars indicate that no intention estimation was possible.

study for evaluating our model already revealed some interesting findings which need to be verified in further, more extensive studies.

Building the correct mental model for task B seems to be more difficult than for task D. All of the four participants showed more mismatches for task B. Also more proactive fixations and saccades could be observed for task D than for task B. The difficulties users had with task B could be explained by a wrong mental model about the functionality of the key, namely that the key determines whether the point moves upwards or downwards instead of along one of the two diagonal axes as shown in Figure 3.1. However, when asked after the experiments, all users explained the functionality of the key correctly.

Gaze behavior strongly varied among different users. However, also similarities between *User 1* and *User 4* as well as *User 2* and *User 3* could be observed. The differences between the two groups of users seem to be correlated with the quality and certainty of the user's mental model. This dependency, if verified in further studies, could be used for automatically adapting the human-computer interface according to the quality of the user's mental model. For users with a correct mental model proactive gaze behavior could be used for intention recognition and for realizing proactive interaction techniques. Users with an uncertain or wrong mental model could be supported by adequate hints, which help to improve or correct their mental representation of the system.

Based on the considerations from 2.2 we would expect the user to look at a certain location on the screen for one or both of the two reasons: "control of input" and/or "verification of system reactions or states". The results of our study can be interpreted in the following way: the more proactive gaze behavior of "experienced" users is caused by a switch from verification of system reactions for learning purposes to indirect control of absolute positioning of the object at key points of the task.

4 Conclusion

The proposed model allows for analysis of gaze data in the context of a task currently executed by the user. Uncertainty of the mental model of the user can be modeled and therefore it also provides a basis for studying the influence of learning processes on natural gaze behavior. We have demonstrated how it can be used to provide an explanation for "why we look where we look" and as a general framework for analyzing gaze data in context.

The evaluation of the model in a small user study has been shown that the various kinds of visual control strategies of the user can be captured by the model and thus can be made available for further analysis. We have observed that gaze behavior is both, task- and user-specific. The results indicate, that a better mental model leads to more proactive gaze behavior, allowing for intention recognition when aligned with the task. This allows for designing new *proactive user interfaces* and improvement of uncertain input devices (see also [BVK09]). However, the study also revealed that not only a correct but also a wrong mental model leads to proactive gaze behavior. We have demonstrated that such a model mismatch can be detected with the proposed framework at an early stage, which allows for designing *adaptive systems* providing help to the user automatically.

In future work the proposed model needs to be evaluated on larger data sets and with more complex tasks. In this paper we have only focused on pre-object gaze data. However, the model also can be used for analyzing gaze data during object movement phases which contain further valuable information about user's cognitive processes. Finally, new user interfaces based on the proposed model need to be implemented and evaluated. In this context the proposed model also provides a good basis for real-time recognition of user's intention and cognitive states.

Bibliography

[BRS03]   Liana E. Brown, David A. Rosenbaum, and Robert L. Sainburg. Limb position drift:
           Implications for control of posture and movement. *Journal of Neurophysiology*, 90:3105–
           3118, 2003.

[BVK09]   Thomas Bader, Matthias Vogelgesang, and Edmund Klaus. Multimodal integration of
           natural gaze behavior for intention recognition during object manipulation. In *Proceedings
           of ICMI-MLMI*, pages 199–206. ACM, November 2009.

[FJ03]   Randall Flanagan and Roland S. Johansson. Action plans used in action observation.
           Nature, 424:769–771, 2003.

[GBOF08]   Benno Gesierich, Angela Bruzzo, Giovanni Ottoboni, and Livio Finos. Human gaze be-
           haviour during action execution and observation. *Acta Psychologica*, 128:324–330, 2008.

[HMR03]   A. Hyrskykari, P. Majaranta, and K. Räihä. Proactive response to eye movements. In
           M. Rauterberg, editor, *Human Computer Interaction INTERACT 2003*, pages 129–136.
           IOS Press, September 2003.

[Joh90]   Bonnie E. John. Extensions of goms analyses to expert performance requiring perception
           of dynamic visual and auditory information. In *CHI '90: Proceedings of the SIGCHI
           conference on Human factors in computing systems*, pages 107–116, New York, NY, USA,
           1990. ACM.

[JWBF01]   Roland S. Johansson, Göran Westling, Anders Bäckström, and J. Randall Flanagan. Eye-
           hand coordination in object manipulation. *The Journal of Neuroscience*, 21(17):6917–
           6932, 2001.

[Lan00]   Chris Lankford. Effective eye-gaze input into windows. In *ETRA '00: Proceedings of the
           symposium on Eye tracking research & applications*, pages 23–27, New York, NY, USA,
           2000. ACM.

[LL94]   Michael F. Land and D. N. Lee. Where we look when we steer. *Nature*, 369:742–744,
           1994.

[LM00]   Michael F. Land and Peter McLeod. From eye movements to actions: how batsmen hit the
           ball. *Nature Neuroscience*, 3:1340–1345, 2000.

[PHL01]   Jeff Pelz, Mary M. Hayhoe, and Russ Loeber. The coordination of eye, head, and hand
           movements in a natural task. *Exp Brain Res*, pages 266–277, 2001.

[SA00]   Dario D. Salvucci and John R. Anderson. Intelligent gaze-added interfaces. In *CHI '00:
           Proceedings of the conference on Human factors in computing systems*, pages 273–280.
           ACM Press, 2000.

[SA01]   Dario D. Salvucci and John R. Anderson. Automated eye-movement protocol analysis.
           Hum.-Comput. Interact., 16(1):39–86, 2001.

[Sen03]   SensoMotoric Instruments GmbH (SMI), Warthestrassee 21 D-14513 Teltow/Berlin. *iView
           X Manual Version 1.03.09*, September 2003.

[SG00]   Dario D. Salvucci and Joseph H. Goldberg. Identifying fixations and saccades in eye-
           tracking protocols. In *ETRA '00: Proceedings of the symposium on Eye tracking research
           & applications*, pages 71–78. ACM, 2000.

[SHAZ00]   Barton A. Smith, Janet Ho, Wendy Ark, and Shumin Zhai. Hand eye coordination patterns
           in target selection. In *ETRA '00: Proceedings of the symposium on Eye tracking research
           & applications*, pages 117–122. ACM, 2000.

[ZMI99]   Shumin Zhai, Carlos Morimoto, and Steven Ihde. Manual and gaze input cascaded (magic)
           pointing. In *In CHI99*, pages 246–253. ACM Press, 1999.

Probabilistic Localization and Mapping for Mobile Robots

Thomas Emter

Vision and Fusion Laboratory
Institute for Anthropomatics
Karlsruhe Institute of Technology (KIT), Germany
thomas.emter@iitb.fraunhofer.de

Technical Report IES-2009-07

Abstract: The essential key capabilities for a mobile robot are to determine where it is located and gather an idea of its surroundings. For precise self localization several sensors are needed as due to noisy measurements no single sensor is sufficient. The data from the sensors is fused to a combined estimate resulting in a more accurate localization. As in most situations positioning sensors like odometry and GPS alone are still insufficient, for example in case of collision avoidance, it is preferable to incorporate exterozeptive sensors as well. Furthermore it is possible to use these sensors to localize the robot in a map. If a map of an area is unavailable, the robot has to build it while exploring the environment. This exploration and mapping is a very challenging problem because of noise in the sensor measurements and approaches to solve this so called simultaneous localization and mapping (SLAM) problem exist.

1 Introduction

The AMROS (**A**utonomous **M**ultisensoric **Ro**bots for **S**ecurity Applications) system, currently developed at Fraunhofer Institute for Information and Data Processing (IITB), is an autonomous mobile robotic system for multi sensor outdoor surveillance of real estates and building complexes [EMF+07]. To perform autonomous surveillance and security inspection the robot must be able to patrol around a building or navigate to certain points of interest.

The essential key capabilities for the mobile robot to be able to patrol autonomously is to determine where it is located and perform path planning and following. For precise self localization several sensors are combined by means of multi-sensor fusion resulting in a more accurate localization. In addition to positioning sensors exterozeptive sensors are incorporated as well, for example for collision avoidance. Furthermore, the exterozeptive sensors can be used to localize the robot in a map. These maps can be built from raw sensor data yielding a dense map or with an additional feature extraction step resulting in a map consisting of distinct landmarks. In the former case the dense map can be interpreted as a single landmark.

1.1   Sensors for Localization

To localize itself in the environment the mobile robot platform is equipped with several sensors. The easiest way to perform localization is dead-reckoning, i.e., to use the odometry sensors (wheel encoders) of the robot by incrementally incorporating the measured revolutions of the robot's wheels from a known starting position. As these encoders only deliver relative measurements and all sensors are subjected to errors, the uncertainty of the pose grows boundlessly over the covered distance. In outdoor environments navigation sensors like GPS and compass can be used. They are measuring absolute quantities and therefore are not suffering from error accumulation but are prone to be disturbed locally by surrounding objects. The measurements of the compass are degraded by disturbances of the terrestrial magnetic field, e.g., by metal fences or ventilation fans of air condition systems. Using a Differential GPS receiver the significant remaining source of error is the multipath propagation due to reflections and shadowing effects of large objects like buildings. As the multipaths are dependent on the constellation of the receiver and the satellites relative to nearby reflecting surfaces the errors are time variant and locally varying [EFK08].

In addition, sensors which observe the environment like a laser scanner or camera can be used for localization in a map. For navigation, a map is also advantageous as it provides the possibility of path planning beyond the actual sensor coverage. The required map can be provided by an official site plan of the real estate. However the main disadvantage with this approach is that it is not granted that the sensors detect the same objects as specified by the given map. Hence, in most cases, it is better to create a map from the sensor data the robot gathers while exploring the environment for the first time. This is a very challenging problem because of uncertainties in the sensor measurements as can be seen in Figure 1.1. Because all sensor measurements contain errors and the estimate of the robot's pose depends on the map and vice versa, the resulting map may become inconsistent [DWB06a].

The map was built as occupancy grid map by naïve recording of the sensor data, i.e., the robot's odometry and a 180° 2D laser scanner (SICK LMS 200). It represents the world discretely as a 2D matrix. Its cells are considered independent and

Figure 1.1: Naïve recording of the sensor data and the robot's path, estimated by odometry only.

contain the probability of being occupied. A simple algorithm based on a frequentist approach is used for updating the cells: Each cell $c^{x,y}$ of the map contains two values, one to count how often the cell has been inspected ($i^{x,y}$) and the other one counts how often the cell has been found occupied ($o^{x,y}$). Each laser beam can be described by a line from the sensor's origin to the endpoint. The cell containing the endpoint is deemed occupied, thus $i^{x,y}$ and $o^{x,y}$ are both incremented. For all other cells being crossed by the line, only $i^{x,y}$ is incremented. The probability of the cell being occupied is

$$p^{x,y} = p(c_k^{x,y}) = \frac{i_k^{x,y}}{o_k^{x,y}} \tag{1.1}$$

with k indicating the time. In Figure 1.1, dark areas show a low probability of occupation, while the bright ones are occupied with high probability and gray indicates no information. It can clearly be seen that the noise of the sensor data results in an inconsistent map as the robot's return path shows a second corridor where there is only one.

2 Probabilistic Simultaneous Localization and Mapping

To build a precise and correct map, the robot has to simultaneously localize itself in the so far registered map which contains errors and has to update it continuously.

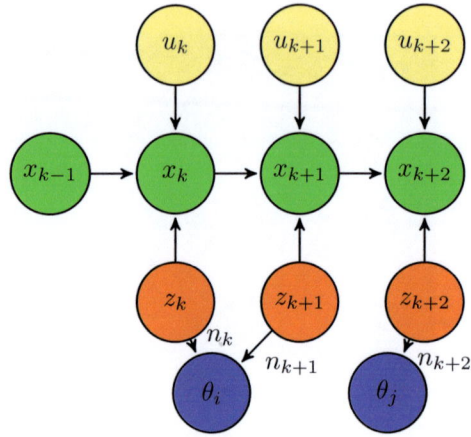

Figure 2.1: The SLAM problem as a Dynamic Bayes Network.

Consequently, the map built becomes inconsistent unless the dependencies between the uncertainty in the pose and the errors in the map are taken into account. By observing areas or features of the map several times, the uncertainties in the map are decreased and the map converges to a better solution. Several approaches of probabilistic mapping exist to solve this so called simultaneous localization and mapping (SLAM) problem [DWB06a]. The SLAM problem and its dependencies between the state variables can be modeled as random variables in a Dynamic Bayes Network (DBN), see Figure 2.1 [TBF05]. The path x of the robot is depicted in green, while k denotes the time steps. The position sensor measurements are denoted as control inputs u and are shown in yellow. The measurements z of the sensors observing the environment, so called exterozeptive sensors, are shown in orange. They measure features θ of the environment. These features are also called landmarks. The data association n is a very important auxiliary requirement as it represents the correct associations between observations and landmarks in the map. A SLAM algorithm has to estimate the full SLAM posterior

$$p(x^k, \Theta | z^k, u^k, n^k)$$

where $\Theta = \theta^N = [\theta_1, \theta_2, ..., \theta_N]$ is the map consisting of all N landmarks θ. A variable with superscripted time like x^k denotes the set of all its instances up to time k.

There are several criteria for an algorithm solving the SLAM problem to converge to a better solution when re-observing known parts of the map: The first criterion is the incorporation of the dependencies between the pose of the mobile robot and the map or landmarks respectively and between landmarks themselves. Secondly, a robust data association is important as wrong associations can lead to catastrophic failures. Thirdly, in dynamic environments the detection of moving objects has to be considered as they have to be eliminated from sensor data prior to mapping. If data from dynamic objects is used for landmarks the map will most likely contain spurious information or will even be completely incorrect.

Solving the DBN problem directly is computationally demanding as the effort grows exponentially with time k. But the problem can be also seen as Markov chain, cf. Figure 2.1. Given the Markov assumption that the present state is fully described by the previous state and the current measurements, the problem can be computed recursively and the map is built incrementally. This recursive update scheme is also known as Bayes filter. In most cases the recursive update is not solvable in closed form, meaning approximations are inevitable. By restricting the SLAM posterior, the motion model, and the measurement model to multivariate Gaussian distributions the well known Extended Kalman Filter (EKF) can be used to estimate the full SLAM posterior [DNC$^+$01]. Neglecting the state of the robot, its memory requirement is quadratic in the number of landmarks while the computational complexity is even greater than $\mathcal{O}(N^2)$ as the covariance matrix has to be inverted. Due to the high dimensionality of the problem when dealing with maps containing a lot of landmarks the EKF can become computationally infeasible. Furthermore only unimodal distributions can be modeled and only a single hypothesis in data association can be maintained. This renders the algorithm susceptible to ambiguous situations and incorrectly incorporated observations cannot be removed. If many wrong associations occur, the algorithm will diverge. To reduce the impact of wrong data associations in target tracking applications the Multi Hypothesis Tracking (MHT) approach has been introduced [Rei79]. In situations where several association hypothesis are probable, new EKFs are instantiated according to each hypothesis, multiplying the computational effort. To keep the number of filters from increasing steadily, heuristics are needed to remove improbable hypotheses over time.

In contrast to the Kalman filter approaches being parametric approximations an alternative method is discretization of the probability distribution. The complete discretization of the state space would lead to either a very coarse representation or incredibly high demand for computational power and memory. A more efficient discretization strategy can be achieved with particle filters. Particle filters represent distributions with a finite set of samples, whereas the density of the samples is proportional to the probability of the state. They have the capability to model multi-modal distributions and implicitly incorporate multiple hypotheses over data associations. On the other hand standard particle filters are only suitable for low dimensional problems as in the worst case the required number of particles grows exponentially with the dimension of the state space. The dimensionality of the SLAM problem also grows with the number of landmarks and the particle filter may become inapplicable. However, it is possible to condition the landmark estimates on the robot's path allowing the SLAM problem to be factored into independent landmark estimation problems, which is an instance of the Rao-Blackwellized particle filter [DdFMR00].

3   Rao-Blackwellized Particle Filter SLAM

3.1   Factorization of the SLAM Posterior

An implementation of a Rao-Blackwellized particle filter algorithm in the context of SLAM known as FastSLAM, was presented by Thrun *et al.* [MTDW02]. Regarding the Dynamic Bayes Network in Figure 2.1 it becomes evident that if the robot's path is known, the landmarks become conditionally independent from each other. Applying this condition to the particle filter, each particle represents a hypothesis of the true path of the robot, meaning the landmarks can be estimated independently, i.e., the SLAM posterior can be factored in the following way [TBF05]:

$$p(x^k, \Theta | z^k, u^k, n^k) = p(x^k | z^k, u^k, n^k) \prod_{n=1}^{N} p(\theta_n | x^k, z^k, u^k, n^k) \, .$$

The particles sample the distribution of the path posterior

$$p(x^k | z^k, u^k, n^k) \, . \tag{3.1}$$

Each particle has N independent landmark estimators attached to it, meaning every particle is carrying its own map. If the errors of the observations of the landmarks are modeled as Gaussians these estimators are EKFs. The cross-correlations between landmarks do not have to be maintained explicitly like in the full EKF-SLAM, but are merely implicitly incorporated by the condition of known paths.

It is not possible to directly sample from the target distribution, i.e., the path posterior (3.1). Therefore the M samples are drawn from the probabilistic motion model $p(x_k | u_k, x_{k-1}^{[m]})$ for each particle $[m]$ separately. The propagation of the particle with the motion model in combination with the assumption that the particles from the previous time step are distributed according to $p(x^{k-1,[m]} | z^{k-1}, u^{k-1}, n^{k-1})$ yields the proposal distribution

$$p(x^{k,[m]} | z^{k-1}, u^k, n^{k-1,[m]}) = p(x_k^{[m]} | u_k, x_{k-1}^{[m]}) p(x^{k-1,[m]} | z^{k-1}, u^{k-1}, n^{k-1}) \, .$$

In addition, each sample is given an importance weight which is the ratio of the target distribution and the proposal distribution. This ratio is proportional to the observation likelihood. Thus the set of weighted particles represents the probability distribution of the full SLAM posterior. As the landmark estimators are EKFs, the importance weights can be calculated by means of innovation, which is the difference between the current observation z_k and the predicted observation $\hat{z}_{n_k^{[m]}}$ based on the map

$$
\begin{aligned}
w_k^{[m]} &= \frac{\text{target distribution}}{\text{proposal distribution}} = \frac{p(x^{k,[m]}|z^k, u^k, n^{k,[m]})}{p(x^{k,[m]}|z^{k-1}, u^k, n^{k-1,[m]})} \\
&\propto p(z_k|x^{k,[m]}, z^{k-1}, u^k, n^{k,[m]}) \\
&= \frac{1}{\sqrt{|2\pi Z_{n_k^{[m]},k}|}} \exp\left(-\frac{1}{2}(z_k - \hat{z}_{n_k^{[m]},k})^T Z_{n_k^{[m]},k}^{-1}(z_k - \hat{z}_{n_k^{[m]},k})\right),
\end{aligned}
$$

(3.2)

$Z_{n_k^{[m]},k}$ being the innovation covariance matrix

$$
Z_{n_k^{[m]},k} = H P_{n_k^{[m]},k-1}^{[m]} H^T + R
$$

(3.3)

with the linearized measurement model H, the covariance of the observed landmark $P_{n_k^{[m]}}$ and the measurement noise R [MT07]. The observed landmarks are updated separately with an EKF. If several landmarks are observed at once, they can be computed sequentially as the are conditionally independent.

If this recursive algorithm is processed for a long time it may suffer from degeneration of the particle weights, i.e., most of the w_k become very small. To avoid the degeneration an algorithm called Sequential Importance Resampling (SIR) was introduced by Rubin [Rub88]. Therein, a new set of unweighted particles is drawn from the present set by sampling with replacement with probability proportional to w_k. Afterwards the importance weights are reset to $w_k = 1/M$, which means the set now consists of unweighted samples.

3.2 Consequences of Resampling

The necessary resampling has some drawbacks on the performance and convergence speed of the algorithm. In the resampling step particles are thrown away while others are duplicated possibly several times. This so called *sample impoverishment* or *particle depletion* reduces the sample diversity and thus the performance of the algorithm degrades. As the dependencies between the landmarks are not used explicitly but merely bound to the condition of a known path, this leads to an underestimation of the landmarks covariances and a slower convergence speed of the algorithm or even a complete failure.

There are several reasons for sample impoverishment. If the robot is equipped with noisy position sensors and accurate measurements of landmarks, the proposal and target distribution do not match very well in the sense that many particles will get very low importance weights and will be thrown away in the next resampling step with high probability. A sensor configuration like this is found very often in mobile robotics as most odometry sensors are not very accurate. An extension to the presented algorithm, the FastSLAM 2.0 algorithm, dealing with this problem has been introduced by Montemerlo et al. [MT07]. It addresses the dissimilarity of proposal and target distribution by introducing a new proposal distribution incorporating the present sensor measurement. This will be discussed in Section 3.3.

A situation where a lot of samples are thrown away is the closure of large loops. Due to error accumulation of relative position sensors like odometry the uncertainty in the robot's path grows while traveling through unknown areas. While closing a loop the robot enters known territory and the uncertainty in pose becomes very low. Thus a lot of particles are deleted from the set. Another aspect regarding the growth of uncertainty in the context of closing large loops is the required amount of particles to ensure their diversity. The larger the loop the more samples are required. To address this issue, the fusion of relative measuring sensors with absolute measuring sensors like GPS and compass to confine the global error has been investigated in [EFK08].

Another reason are ambiguities in data association when dealing with densely spaced point landmarks or in situations where the uncertainty in pose is very high. The latter is especially prominent when closing loops while only using relative sensors as the uncertainty in the pose steadily increases while driving in previously unknown territory. The problem originates from modeling the landmarks as points. It can be very difficult to distinguish landmarks in the aforementioned situations as the only discrimination possible is by the positions of the landmarks. It is apparent, that an additional appearance-based attribute could improve the robustness of the data association. The idea of an extended data association will be presented in Section 4.

3.3   Gridmapping with FastSLAM 2.0

Particle filters yield good results when the proposal and posterior distributions are similar. Thus sampling from the motion model can be disadvantageous when the robot's motion is very noisy compared to the ambient sensors. In this case many particles are discarded in the resampling step, degrading the performance of the filter.

To obtain a proposal distribution that better matches the target distribution the most recent sensor observations are incorporated into the proposal distribution. The particles $x_k^{[m]}$ are thus drawn proportional to $p(x_k|x^{k-1,[m]}, z^k, u^k, n^{k,[m]})$. The new sampling distribution is obtained in an EKF estimation step per particle. The prior distribution for the EKF is provided by the linear Gaussian propagation of the particle of the previous time step. The likelihood of the measurement z_k is fused in the standard EKF update step and a new particle is drawn from the resulting Gaussian.

The path posterior of the previous time step is assumed to be distributed according to $p(x^{k-1,[m]}|z^{k-1}, u^{k-1}, n^{k-1})$ as before. Together with the new sampling distribution the proposal distribution is now given by the product

$$p(x_k^{[m]}|x^{k-1,[m]}, z^k, u^k, n^{k,[m]})p(x^{k-1,[m]}|z^{k-1}, u^{k-1}, n^{k-1,[m]}) \,.$$

The importance weights have to be adapted accordingly, since the proposal distribution has been changed:

$$
\begin{aligned}
w_k^{[m]} &= \frac{\text{target distribution}}{\text{proposal distribution}} \\
&= \frac{p(x^{k,[m]}|z^k, u^k, n^{k,[m]})}{p(x_k^{[m]}|x^{k-1,[m]}, z^k, u^k, n^{k,[m]})p(x^{k-1,[m]}|z^{k-1}, u^{k-1}, n^{k-1,[m]})} \\
&\propto p(z_k|x^{k-1,[m]}, z^{k-1}, u^k, n^{k,[m]}) \,.
\end{aligned}
$$

As several concurrently observed landmarks are incorporated one after another, the data association is done sequentially also. Thus the association of the first landmark will still be difficult as at this point only knowledge from the motion model is available which is very noisy, i.e., in FastSLAM 2.0 the order of incorporating several landmarks has to be considered [MT07].

An instance of FastSLAM 2.0 was implemented with a laser scanner and occupancy gridmaps similar to the algorithm found in [GSB07]. To compute the observation likelihood a scan matching step is performed per particle to find the best match between the present sensor measurement and the map. The match is evaluated by computing the correlation between a local map built from the present laser scan and the global map according to

$$\rho = \frac{\sum_{x,y}(p^{x,y,\text{global}} - \bar{p}) \cdot (p^{x,y,\text{local}}(x_k) - \bar{p})}{\sqrt{\sum_{x,y}(p^{x,y,\text{global}} - \bar{p})^2 \sum_{x,y}(p^{x,y,\text{local}}(x_k) - \bar{p})^2}} \,, \tag{3.4}$$

Figure 3.1: Map of the best particle and the robot's path in red.

with

$$\bar{p} = \frac{1}{2L} \sum_{x,y} p^{x,y,\text{global}} + p^{x,y,\text{local}}$$

being the average map value [TBF05]. $p^{x,y}$ is the probability of the cell being occupied, cf. Equation (1.1). Whereas global indicates the map and local indicates a local section based on the actual laser scan. L is the number of cells being covered by both the local and global map.

To find the best match, a gradient descent search is performed. Afterwards, a local Gaussian approximation is computed around the found maximum for the integration in the proposal for the EKF. The gridmaps are updated with the scheme explained in Section 1 assuming the cells being independent and the importance weights are computed according to equation (3.4).

Resampling is necessary to counteract degeneration of the importance weights, but it can intensify the particle depletion mentioned earlier. Thus resampling should only be carried out when the particles do not approximate the target distribution well. This is the case when the variance in the importance weights grows, as directly sampling from the target distribution leads to equal weights for all particles. A measure for the quality of the approximation can be estimated by the *effective sample size*

$$\hat{M}_{\text{eff}} = \frac{1}{\sum_{m=1}^{M} \left(w_k^{[m]} \right)^2}$$

as formulated by Doucet *et al.* [DGA00]. Resampling is performed only if $\hat{M}_{\text{eff}}$ is below a predefined threshold.

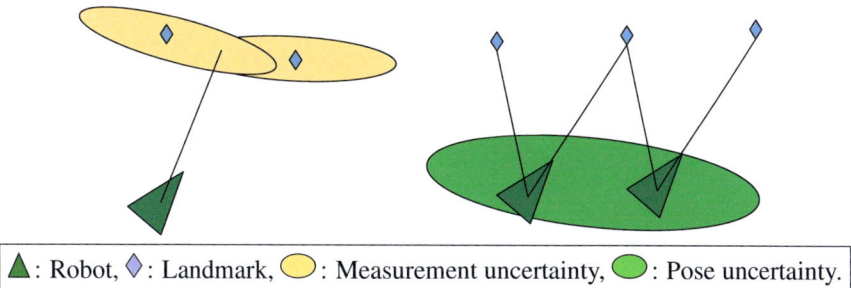

: Robot, ◈ : Landmark, ◯ : Measurement uncertainty, ⬤ : Pose uncertainty.

Figure 4.1: Measurement ambiguity on the left and motion ambiguity on the right.

Figure 3.1 shows that the algorithm works very well. The sensor data is the same used to build the map in Figure 1.1. The SLAM algorithm is capable of re-localizing the robot in the map and thus generating a consistent map. An advantage of this algorithm is that it also considers the free-space. Dense maps also have a great advantage for path planning as they also contain information of free-space while feature-based maps are normally sparse. Feature-based maps contain only landmarks matching a given model extracted from raw sensor data discarding information about the space in-between the landmarks. On the other hand, calculating the correlation (3.4) is computationally highly demanding. Furthermore, for calculating the correlation the normalized quadratic distance between maps is compared, which has no physical justification as it does not model the noise characteristic of laser scanners.

4 Data Association

A reliable data association between observations and the contents of the map is the second convergence criterion for SLAM algorithms, cf. Section 2. There are two factors affecting the reliability, namely motion noise and measurement noise both leading to ambiguities as depicted in Figure 4.1. While measurement noise may lead to single wrong data associations, motion noise may lead to several erroneous associations at once. In addition, motion noise is often stronger as pointed out above.

4.1 Robust Data Association

In case of feature-based maps and a Gaussian error model of landmark attributes the probability of an observation can be computed by a function of the innovation:

$$\hat{n}_k^{[m]} = \arg\max_{n_k^{[m]}} p(z_k | n_k^{[m]}, \hat{n}^{k-1,[m]}, x^{k,[m]}, z^{k-1}, u^k) \tag{4.1}$$

$$= \arg\max_{n_k^{[m]}} \frac{1}{\sqrt{|2\pi Z_{n_k^{[m]},k}|}} \exp\left(-\frac{1}{2}(z_k - \hat{z}_{n_k^{[m]},k})^T Z_{n_k^{[m]},k}^{-1}(z_k - \hat{z}_{n_k^{[m]},k}) \right).$$

with $Z_{n_k^{[m]},k}$ according to equation (3.3). This is an instance of a Maximum Likelihood (ML) estimator for multivariate Gaussians. If the likelihood of matching the observed landmarks to any landmark in the map is below a certain threshold a new one is placed in the map. If this threshold is too high, many landmarks will be erroneously instantiated several times despite already existing in the map. Being too low, newly observed landmarks will be associated wrongly to existing landmarks in the map.

A particle filter implicitly represents multiple hypotheses over data associations as the association is done per particle. Particles with wrong data associations will obtain low importance weights and thus are more likely to be thrown away in a resampling step at a later time. This can be considered as a delayed decision making in statistically justified manner with no need for heuristics, as it is the case with MHT. Although this is a great advantage, it might have an impact on the sample impoverishment when too many wrong data associations occur and thus indirectly affects the first convergence criterion.

Especially in ambiguous situations an improvement can be achieved with joint consideration of multiple data associations per time step, as it is done for example in the Combined Constraint Data Association (CCDA) algorithm of Bailey [Bai02]. Another possibility is to exploit the multi hypotheses property of the particle filter further with Monte Carlo data association. The key idea of Monte Carlo data association is to perform the associations probabilistically with probabilities proportional to their likelihood. In this way it accounts for ambiguous situations where several association hypotheses are probable but needs more particles to achieve the same accuracy [MT07].

A further addition is the usage of negative information to remove erroneously instantiated or outdated landmarks from the map, which is beneficial in case of dynamic objects, erroneous measurements or changes in the environments. For this purpose an additional value for the probability of its existence is attached to every landmark. Positive evidence is found when reobserving a landmark and negative evidence when a landmark of the map is in sensor coverage but is not observed. If this probability drops below a certain threshold the according landmark will be deleted from the map. The existence probability can also be used for delayed instantiation of landmarks by introducing another threshold which has to be exceeded. This is especially useful for FastSLAM 2.0 as the sequential data association is more robust when using landmarks with low uncertainties, i.e., landmarks which have been observed repeatedly [MT07].

4.2   Extended Data Association

In the original FastSLAM algorithms 2D point features possessing two coordinates as attributes are used as landmarks, which renders the data association susceptible to ambiguities in areas where landmarks are dense and especially in situations when closing a loop. The reason for the latter is the growth of uncertainty in the robot's path and map while the robot travels in unknown environments. It seems apparent that an additional visual signature-based or appearance-based attribute could enhance the distinction between landmarks [DWB06b]. Especially in situations where landmarks are densely spaced or the pose uncertainty of the robot is very high, the appearance of the landmarks could greatly improve the data association.

Landmarks are features of the environment and can be modeled as objects with several attributes, i.e., an object-oriented representation of the the landmarks. Attributes with Gaussian error distributions can be incorporated directly in the ML estimator (equation (4.1)) and the importance weights (3.2). If the attributes are non-Gaussian but independent of the position, the ML estimator is able to incorporate the measurements of position z_{pos} and appearance z_{app} of the landmark independently:

$$
\hat{n}_k^{[m]} = \arg\max_{n_k^{[m]}} \left(p\big(z_{\text{pos},k} \big| n_k^{[m]}, \hat{n}^{k-1,[m]}, x^{k,[m]}, z_{\text{pos}}^{k-1}, u^k\big) \right.
$$

$$
\left. p\big(z_{\text{app},k} \big| n_k^{[m]}, \hat{n}^{k-1,[m]}, x^{k,[m]}, z_{\text{app}}^{k-1}, u^k\big) \right).
$$

The likelihood is computable if a measure for the difference between the observation z_{app} and the expected observation $\hat{z}_{\text{app}}$ can be computed.

Simulations have been performed to compare data association robustness and their impact on overall performance of the SLAM algorithm between point landmarks and landmarks with an additional appearance-based attribute. The implementation is based on MATLAB code by Tim Bailey, which was extended by a ML data association estimator according to (4.1). All motions of the robot and sensor measurements are affected by additive Gaussian noise. For comparison simulations

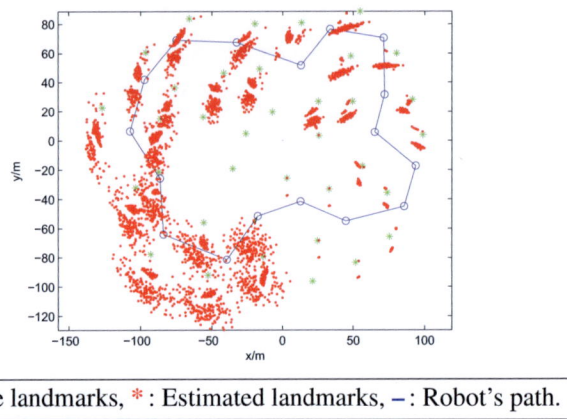

* : True landmarks, * : Estimated landmarks, – : Robot's path.

Figure 4.2: Simulation with position attributes only.

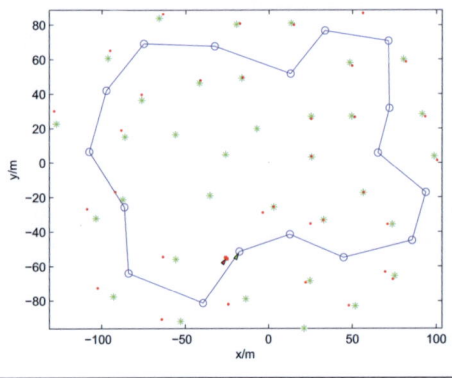

* : True landmarks, * : Estimated landmarks, – : Robot's path.

Figure 4.3: Simulation with additional appearance-based attribute.

with position attributes only and with an additional appearance attribute respectively were performed. The corresponding results are shown in Figure 4.2 and 4.3 showing the estimated maps of all particles as red dots.

The simulations were conducted with 200 particles and the same parameters. The robot travels twice along the dark blue path. While the real landmarks are depicted in green their estimates are shown in red. As every particle posses its own map 200 maps exist in the particle filter. The following results are summarized for all maps.

In case of the position-only attributes 11303 wrong data associations occurred and 4200 times an already mapped landmark was erroneously instantiated. The robot could not successfully close the loop in the second round leading to divergence and failure of the mapping process.

With the additional appearance attribute all data associations were correct but it still happened 430 times that an already mapped landmark was erroneously instantiated, leading to three landmarks being mapped twice. Nonetheless the robot could successfully close the loop and build a consistent map except for the three duplicated landmarks. Further improvement could be achieved by including joint considerations of data association hypotheses, Monte Carlo data association and inclusion of negative information as mentioned in Section 4.1.

5 Conclusion & Outlook

An introduction to the SLAM problem has been given and methods of probabilistic SLAM based on Bayesian filters have been discussed. The FastSLAM algorithm with its properties making it very flexible and powerful was explained in detail regarding its advantages and shortcomings. Three approaches to improve the limitations of the algorithms have been illustrated. The advantage of an improved proposal distribution has been explained. Besides the incorporation of absolute sensors to confine the global error, the idea of an extended data association has been presented. The addition of an appearance-based attribute allows for a more robust data association. In consequence the particle depletion caused by wrong associations can be alleviated, wrongly instantiated landmarks occur less frequently and the loop closure becomes more robust.

In future investigations the simulation results will be experimentally verified. As additional sensor for the appearance-based attribute, a stereo camera in combination with the laser scanner is considered. From the sensor data, landmarks are to be extracted with attributes for position and an additional appearance-based attribute which is independent from position. The appearance attribute should be independent from viewing angle and statistically assessable for the data association and computation of the importance weights. To avert the restriction of independence from the angle of view and position an auxiliary algorithm to cope with partial observability including the extension, splitting and merging of landmarks has to be considered later on.

The object-oriented modeling of the landmarks allows for straight forward integration of different heterogeneous sensors. As a minimum requirement the position must be extractable from sensor data in order to place the landmarks in a map.

Thus the SLAM algorithm has the capability of fusing information from different sensors into a single representation, for example the combination of sparse feature-based (landmark-based) maps with dense gridmaps.

Bibliography

[Bai02]   Tim Bailey. *Mobile Robot Localisation and Mapping in Extensive Outdoor Environments*. PhD thesis, University of Sydney, 2002.

[DdFMR00]   Arnaud Doucet, Nando de Freitas, Kevin Murphy, and Stuart Russel. Rao-Blackwellised Particle Filtering for Dynamic Bayesian Networks. *Proceedings of the Sixteenth Conference on Uncertainty in Artificial Intelligence*, 2000.

[DGA00]   Arnaud Doucet, Simon Godsill, and Christophe Andrieu. On sequential Monte Carlo sampling methods for Bayesian filtering. *Statistics and Computing*, 10, July 2000.

[DNC+01]   M.W.M. Gamini Dissanayake, Paul Newman, Stuart Clark, Hugh F. Durrant-Whyte, and Michael Csorba. A solution to the simultaneous localization and map building (SLAM) problem. *IEEE Transactions on Robotics and Automation*, 17, June 2001.

[DWB06a]   Hugh Durrant-Whyte and Tim Bailey. Simultaneous localization and mapping: Part I. *IEEE Robotics & Automation Magazine*, 13, June 2006.

[DWB06b]   Hugh Durrant-Whyte and Tim Bailey. Simultaneous localization and mapping: Part II. *IEEE Robotics & Automation Magazine*, 13, September 2006.

[EFK08]   Thomas Emter, Christian Frey, and Helge-Björn Kuntze. Multisensorielle Überwachung von Liegenschaften durch mobile Roboter - Multi-Sensor Surveillance of Real Estates Based on Mobile Robots. *Robotik 2008: Leistungsstand - Anwendungen - Visionen - Trends*, June 2008.

[EMF+07]   Thomas Emter, Eduardo Monari, Christian Frey, Thomas Müller, Helge-Björn Kuntze, Astrid Laubenheimer, and Markus Müller. AMROS - an Autonomous Mobile Robotic system for Multisensor Surveillance of Real Estates. *Proc. Future Security, 2nd Security Conference*, Septempber 2007.

[GSB07]   Giorgio Grisetti, Cyrill Stachniss, and Wolfram Burgard. Improved Techniques for Grid Mapping with Rao-Blackwellized Particle Filters. *IEEE Transactions on Robotics*, 23, February 2007.

[MT07]   Montemerlo Michael and Sebastian Thrun. *FastSLAM - A Scalable Method for the Simultaneous Localization and Mapping Problem in Robotics*, volume 27 of *STAR - Springer Tracts in Advanced Robotics*. Springer Verlag, Berlin Heidelberg New York, 2007.

[MTDW02]   Montemerlo Michael, Sebastian Thrun, Koller Daphne, and Ben Wegbreit. FastSLAM: A Factored Solution to the Simultaneous Localization and Mapping Problem. *AAAI-02 Proceedings*, 2002.

[Rei79]   Donald B. Reid. An algorithm for tracking multiple targets. *IEEE Transactions on Automatic Control*, 24, December 1979.

[Rub88]   Donald B. Rubin. Using the SIR algorithm to simulate posterior distributions. *Bayesian Statistics 3*, 1988.

[TBF05]   Sebastian Thrun, Wolfram Burgard, and Dieter Fox. *Probabilistic Robotics*. The MIT Press, Cambridge, Massachusetts, 2005.

Smart Surveillance: A Holistic Approach for Future-Proof Solutions

Hauke Vagts

Vision and Fusion Laboratory
Institute for Anthropomatics
Karlsruhe Institute of Technology (KIT), Germany
vagts@kit.edu

Technical Report IES-2009-08

Abstract: Surveillance systems have become increasingly powerful. Conventional camera-based systems are extended with all kind of sensors, the number of data sources increases, hardware and algorithms improve, and data can potentially be shared between interlinked networks. Smart surveillance systems take advantage of these developments and do not threaten solely the protection of privacy; they also provide an opportunity to achieve data and privacy protection on a new level. The current legal situation for 'obsolete' surveillance deployments has not been explored and is quite heterogeneous. Hence the *Fair Information Principles (FIP)* are still the minimum privacy requirements for surveillance systems.

This contribution identifies the key challenges for security and privacy in smart surveillance that must be mastered in any future-proof system. Subsequently two potential solutions are presented that solve two of them. Privacy issues are addressed by the *Privacy Manager (PM)*, a framework for privacy enforcement in smart surveillance architectures that achieves compliance with the FIP. Authenticity of surveillance sensors is a security challenge, and a *Web of Trust for smart Surveillance Sensors* is proposed that can be established between surveillance operators.

1 Introduction

Many factors, such as decreasing prices, increasing capabilities, and the 'war on terror' lead to a growing number of surveillance installations. The major cause for deployment is crime prevention and most systems are still video based. Legacy systems are typically closed-circuit, have few (analog) cameras and do not assist the user. Modern installations are IP-based, can integrate a high number of cameras and assist the operator. Systems become not only more powerful and frightening at the same time, but also more vulnerable. To assure success of surveillance solutions security and privacy objectives must be achieved.

Surveillance is popular in the United Kingdom, and the current number of cameras can only be 'guesstimated', they differ between one million and 4.2 millions. By comparison, Germany has about 30,000 cameras in public places and 400,000 in industrial environments. In some places, e. g., the central station in Frankfurt (150 cameras) or Leipzig (120 cameras), the concentration of surveillance sensors is comparable to the UK. Even if these impressive numbers[1] are estimated, an extreme tendency towards surveillance is undeniable and it must be accepted that the cameras will not disappear. Conventional surveillance systems cannot handle the mass of information gained by the increasing number of sensors and smart surveillance and become a popular area of research. Several approaches have been presented , e. g., [HBC$^+$05] [BEE$^+$08]).

The paper is organized as follows. After a short motivation for addressing privacy and security issues, the author shows, why a holistic approach is required to achieve security and privacy in modern surveillance systems. Afterwards the identified key challenges for privacy and security are highlighted and two potential solutions are presented. Concluding the solutions are discussed and future work is proposed.

2   Motivation

Conventional surveillance systems consist of n cameras, a video recording server and an user interface that can either display one ore more of the n cameras or can be used to search the stored video information. Most of these systems still contain many analog cameras and do not contain other sensors. Such installations can be secured by physical isolation and access controls. Furthermore manipulation of the collected data is difficult, costintensive and hence not worthwhile in most cases. To reduce deployment costs modern installations are integrated into existing IT-infrastructures, which allows easy usage and data exchange. By contrast, a surveillance system is opened for attacks on security and malicious operators can relate personal data to other data sources. Due to the open nature of modern surveillance deployments, they can can easily be extended with new sensors and can be interconnected to huge surveillance networks that are used by different parties. In the UK surveillance systems are run together by the municipality, private security providers and the police. The state has lost track of existing deployments.

---

[1]References and more details can be found in [VB09]

These modern systems that get smarter inch by inch threaten privacy and data protection. To prevent 'total surveillance' and misuse of personal data new solutions for privacy and security are required. These solutions must be compliant with law and must be accepted by Society, hence an interdisciplinary (holistic) approach for surveillance is required. Identified key challenges in security and privacy are highlighted in Section 5. All of challenges must be mastered to develop future-proof surveillance solutions that can be used in practice. Technological developments, as the approaches presented in this work, must be discussed with lawyers, sociologists, and system operators.

3 Related Work

Privacy in surveillance is a recent area of research and new solutions are required. In the branch of video surveillance some approaches exist to ensure privacy and security, most of the approaches blur regions of interest (RoI) that might imperil privacy. In [SPH+05] Senior et. al. purpose a "privacy-preserving console" for video surveillance. The console rerenders the video stream and hides sensitive details, detected by video analysis. Depending on the authorization level, access is granted to rerendered videos (e. g. with blurred faces or even enriched with additional information) or the raw video stream. They also purpose a "privacy cam", which processes the video sources and transmits encrypted information streams. In [CB07] Chattopadhyay and Bould also present a privacy cam, which is implemented on a Blackfin DSP and blurs RoI based on PICO [Bou05]. Another scrambling approach is presented in [DE06]. Fleck's approach to privacy [FS08] is based on smart cameras, which transmit events instead of video data. Fidaleo et. al. present in [FNT04] a privacy enhanced software architecture with a centralized server that hosts a privacy buffer, which can remove private or identifiable information from the stream.

Approaches for security also exist, and just as in the field of privacy research the approaches focus on video surveillance systems. One way to provide confidentiality, integrity and authenticity (CIA, e. g. [DNVHC05]) is to use video independent solutions that have been proved to be successful, as symmetric and asymmetric encryption, signatures, certificates and public key infrastructures (PKI), and existing security protocols (SSL, IPSec, Kerberos, etc.). However, in case of video data more specific approaches have been proposed that take advantage of video characteristics. To ensure authenticity of images and video, a lot of research has been done in the area of (robust) watermarking, e. g., [DF02] [TT01]. To achieve confidentiality of transmitted video data several approaches exist that achieve better performance by utilizing video characteristics, e. g., [CP09].

4 Holistic Approach

To develop efficient (adequate for several specific surveillance tasks) and accepted surveillance technologies, a holistic approach for privacy and security is required that considers legal and social aspects. Generally, technology improves at first and subsequently the real potential emerges, alarms society and is then limited by law. On the one side, relevant technologies improve with great speed and the gap to areas as social networks or ubiquitous applications is closing. On the other side perception and assessment of privacy change (extensive use of Twitter, Facebook, etc.), and the question is, whether data protection will exist in future and if so, a change towards enhanced data preservation is probable. Beside law and technology, social acceptance is essential for surveillance technology. Surveillance must be more transparent to archive more confidence and must redress the balance of the asymmetric relationship of vision between data controllers and data subjects [HT04]. Observed subjects need easy ways to interact with the system (or control it). However, a holistic approach is required that considers law and social acceptance from the beginning. To achieve a future-proof solution a control loop must be established between the three disciplines. It must be assumed that the potential of surveillance technology is exploited, even if it is prohibited by law. Hence prohibition is insufficient, security and privacy compliant solutions must be available, affordable and easy to use, so that no appeal exists for purchasing and abusing an overpowered surveillance system. It is important to consider social and legal changes that might happen or would do well in future and surveillance systems must follow realistic requirements. Technological enhancement also provides new possibilities to achieve social acceptance and even better privacy [VB09].

5 Key Challenges in Privacy and Security

This work highlights the *security and privacy challenges* that must be mastered in modern surveillance systems; seven key challenges exist, four for security and three for privacy. Exact requirements for future surveillance systems are uncertain. Hence a holistic approach must be followed that covers tendencies and surveillance systems. The approach must be adaptable to specific surveillance scenarios, i. e., privacy and security guidelines and must be adaptable to the circumstances and the surveillance task. Following the identified seven key challenges are described.

5.1   Security

As modern surveillance systems are distributed and IP-based, they face the same security issues as distributed systems (*Secure architecture*). Additionally other issues arise that result from the flexibility and size of modern surveillance systems (*Flexible Architecture and Trust*), the interconnection of surveillance systems and sharing of information (*Access Controls and Information flow*), and the trust of the users and validity in court, respectively (*Certification*).

Secure Architecture: It must be guaranteed that surveillance data cannot be stolen or changed and it must be infeasible to prevent storing (authenticity, integrity, availability). Any access to the storage must be logged, and access to data must be granted according to the proper authorization level. To provide security for a single component is manageable, but to provide security for an entire surveillance deployment is a difficult task, which becomes even more complex in huge or flexible systems (changing users, tasks or sensors). To validate security properties and to build trust, deployments can be built by using an open architecture or by certification of the entire system.

Certification: Up to now, no appropriate certification for modern surveillance systems exist. There is no international standardization for certification of such systems. It is estimated that manipulation is very challenging and can also be identified by experts. Even if it is hard to gain access to the system, manipulation becomes easier and the first law case about the authenticity of video data is only a matter of time. An affordable international certification for entire systems is required. Components from different distributors must be interoperable and system operators must be assisted during deployment (selection of protocols, sensors, etc.).

Access Controls and Information Flow: Access controls must prevent unauthorized access to any information provided by a surveillance system that includes access to raw data and meta data. Any access by a user or task must be granted according to least privilege, i. e. only data concerning a specific surveillance task or even subtask is accessible and access should only be provided as long as necessary. Dynamic allocation of authorizations is challenging in huge, flexible networks or if data is exchanged between surveillance systems. It must be ensured that data from different tasks cannot be combined and any forbidden information flow must be prevented. Beside access controls for data access, access controls for injection of sensor data must also be established.

Flexible Architecture and Trust: Trust in a flexible infrastructure, sensors, tasks and other components can not easily be achieved. Definition and evaluation of trust models is difficult and no sufficient model for a (multi-party) surveillance scenario exists. It is also an open question how existing systems must be extended to provide trust. Prior unknown partners, spontaneous interconnection and a changing number of sensors make it difficult to validate integrity and authenticity of the system state or specific sensors (insertion, removal). Using wireless sensors makes integration of sensors easier, but it must still be ensured that detected events and control data is reliably transmitted.

5.2 Privacy

Privacy is a philosophical term and everybody has its own definition of it. In terms of surveillance, the FIP provide minimum requirements and national law must be considered as well. However, the sense of privacy changes with the surveillance context (task) and over time. Hence systems must be adaptable to changing privacy requirements. The Privacy challenges in surveillance are: *data protection*, *trust in surveillance* and privacy-aware *data exchange and communication*.

Data Protection: Any surveillance task must be specified exactly, and only data concerning this task must be generated and collected by the surveillance system. Hence any data must refer to its surveillance task(s). For applicable solutions access controls must be quickly adaptable (granting and prohibition) to new surveillance tasks. The FIP require data minimization. In modern surveillance systems this can be divided in *minimization of data collection*, *data processing* and *data storing*. To minimize data collection, only required (as few as possible) sensors must be used and irrelevant data must be deleted instantly (at sensor level). This prevents area-wide surveillance and the creation of movement profiles. To ensure privacy as few as possible of the collected data and prior knowledge must be processed (semantic level). If, for instance, an identified object is processed, only relevant attributes must be accessible. Again, non-useful data must be deleted instantly. In the end surveillance data is stored, which is also done in a data minimizing way. Only relevant events and only sensor data must be stored. The sensor data must be stored privacy-compliant, i. e., according to authorization levels, only a subset of the stored data is accessible. Access to stored data must be as granular as possible. Additionally, to be compliant with law, any observed subject can request information about the personal data related to him and can dispose correction or erasing. Deployments that are not aware of privacy will not be compliant with law and will not be accepted by the users (society). Modern systems have the potential to ensure privacy on an unrivaled level. Hence one component of the NEST (Network Enabled Surveillance and Tracking, [BEE+08]) architecture is the *Privacy Manager*, which is described below. A more detailed description about privacy in surveillance and the Privacy Manager can be found in [VBEB09].

Data Exchange and Communication: As mentioned above, data can potentially be used in another surveillance task, or for the same task in another surveillance system. To guarantee privacy, person related data must be secured against unauthorized usage. Lifetime and usage in surveillance tasks must be restricted. Hence a form of *digital rights* must be embedded in the surveillance data. In modern surveillance any kind of personal information can be exchanged (video, location, relations, etc.) and can be fused in a new data type for surveillance. Hence digital rights for surveillance meta data are required.

Trust of the Surveillance Subjects: For observed objects it must be comprehensible that their privacy is respected and person related data is protected. Trust in a system might follow irrational reasons and it cannot be said which mechanisms enhance trust in privacy. Openness of the system architecture and certification of privacy-compliance seem to be adequate solutions. Functionality of surveillance system must be specified exactly and must be restricted to its purpose and technical mechanisms for privacy enforcement must be certified by a trusted instance. 'Control of controllers' and control of one's personal data collected by the systems will also enhance trust in the surveillance system.

A modern surveillance system must consider all of the challenges that have been named above and the issues must be addressed right from the beginning—*security by design* and *privacy by design*. In case of surveillance both is recent research and innovative surveillance technology requires innovative security and privacy solutions.

6   A Framework for Privacy Enforcement

The Fair Information Principles are the minimum privacy requirements for the processing of person related data. Following a framework for privacy enforcement is presented that is compliant with the FIP.

6.1   Fair Information Principles

The Guidelines on the Protection of Privacy and Transborder Flows of Personal Data serve as a rule for the EU directives on data protection (95/46/EC, 2002/58/EC), which must be enforced by the member states. The guidelines have been published by the OECD in 1980. Even if the legal situation concerning privacy and data protection should be the same throughout the EU, surveillance and data protection is handled differently in any state. The legal status in the US is also different. The Guidelines contain eight principles for privacy (see below), which should be considered by any legislation. Due to the inhomogeneous law, these principles can be considered as minimum requirements for surveillance systems. Solutions that enforce privacy must deal with all principles, but must be flexible enough to adapt privacy according to future (legal and sociological) requirements.

(P1) Data Collection Limitation Principle: There should be limits to the collection of personal data and any such data should be obtained by lawful and fair means and, where appropriate, with the knowledge or consent of the data subject.

(P2) Data Quality Principle: Personal data should be relevant to the purposes for which they are to be used, should be accurate, complete and kept up-to-date.

(P3) Purpose Specification Principle: The purposes for which personal data are collected should be specified not later than at the time of data collection.

(P4) Use Limitation Principle: Personal data should not be disclosed made available or otherwise used for purposes other than those specified in accordance with P3. Excep with consent of the data subject, or by the authority of law.

(P5) Security Safeguard Principle: Personal data should be protected by reasonable security safeguards against such risks as loss or unauthorized access, destruction, use, modification or disclosure of data.

(P6) Openness Principle: There should be a general policy of openness about developments, practices and policies with respect to personal data.

(P7) Individual Participation Principle: An individual should have the right to obtain confirmation of whether or not data relating to him has been collected.To challenge data relating to him and, if the challenge is successful to have the data erased, rectified, completed or amended.

(P8) Accountability Principle: A data controller should be accountable for complying with measures which give effect to the principles stated above.

In the following sections the author explains, how the eight principals (P1-P8) are achieved by a framework for privacy management and a task-oriented approach. Security and privacy are closely related (see P5) and besides these privacy requirements, security challenges exist that must be addressed by smart surveillance systems.

6.2   The NEST Architecture

In the smart surveillance architecture NEST an operator specifies surveillance tasks. He must not observe a great number of monitors and other sensors, the system notifies him about events concerning his tasks (*management by exception*). NEST is a Service Oriented Architecture (SOA) and the operator can create any surveillance task by composing services, e. g. path finding or person tracking services. Due to the flexible SOA design different sensor types can be integrated and a huge amount of data sources can be linked into the system. Any information is stored in the central *Object Oriented World Model* (OOWM) [BEVB09], it is extracted from the sensors and fused on a higher level of abstraction. Hence the OOWM is a good starting point to establish privacy and security.

Another unique characteristic of the NEST architecture is plug and protect. If a sensor is plugged into the network, it automatically registers in the surveillance deployment and transmits its configuration details. In an open-world scenario many sensors are not known beforehand, authenticity of sensors and trust in the corresponding data is challenge. In NEST a web of trust for surveillance sensors is established to build trust in the deployed sensors. In the NEST framework focus is on the key challenges that match the unique characteristics of the NEST architecture—privacy and data protection via the Object Oriented World Model, SOA security for surveillance deployments and plug and protect. In the following the approaches for privacy enhancement and trust in surveillance sensors are presented.

6.3   Task-Oriented Approach for Privacy Enforcement

In a task-oriented surveillance system the usage of a resource and each processing step are assigned to a concrete surveillance task. The approach has two great advantages. On the one hand resources can be used more efficiently and on the other hand data can be processed in according to the FIP. For instance, if one specific person should be tracked in a central station. A sensor-oriented approach examines the entire scene including the requested person. A task-oriented approach monitors only the relevant person and ignores the others. It is required by law and the FIP (P3) that the purpose of a surveillance task is specified before the task is executed. If a task is specified strictly according to the purpose, a task-oriented System as NEST can ensure best possible privacy and data protection for the user subjects. As processing is task-related, person related data can be isolated in case of multiple surveillance tasks and privacy protection mechanism can be established very granularly according to the requirements of the task. Hence a task-oriented system is efficient and privacy-aware. Essential for privacy enforcement is the OOWM that is encapsulated by a privacy framework—the *Privacy Manager* (PM), which is shown in Figure 6.1.

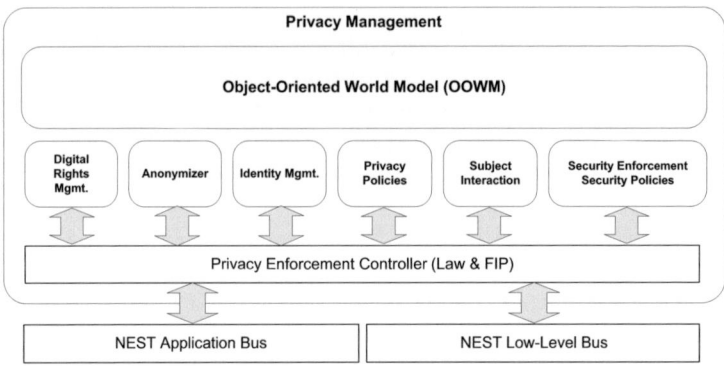

Figure 6.1: The Privacy Manager

6.4   Framework for Task-Oriented Privacy Enforcement

The PM enforces compliance with privacy guidelines by restricting the access to the OOWM according to the deployed privacy policies for guidelines and law. It is directly linked the World Model and hosts a *Security Enforcement Sub-Module* (*SESM*). The latter enforces the actual access controls that are derived from the privacy policies, performs authenticity checks and manages cryptographic keys. Beside the *Task Management* (*TM*), the *Low-Level Sensor Planer* (*LLSP*) is also essential for privacy enforcement; they are connected via the application and low-level bus, respectively. The framework contains modules for anonymization, identity management and user interaction (erasure or correction of personal data) and a policy repository. If data is exchanged with other surveillance systems the PM attaches digitals rights to ensure that information can only be used for a specific task. All components in the PM are geared to task-orientation and enforce privacy according to the FIP.

Privacy Enforcement Controller (PEC): The *Privacy Enforcement Controller* is the central interface; it receives and processes data requests from high-level services and controls all privacy-related modules (achievement of the FIP is shown below). Request are handled according to predefined privacy policies that specify legal guidelines. To control and minimize data collection at sensor level the PEC also interacts with the LLSP and the TM. The SESM is also controlled by the PEC.

Identity Management (IdM): To guarantee privacy, the *Identity Management* performs *multi-layer identity management*, i. e., the IdM handles Object IDs at three levels: *sensor level*, *operational level* (in the OOWM) and *access level* (semantic level). For the latter, the IdM keeps track of surveillance tasks, and creates virtual IDs to anonymize user data to apply least privilege on privacy sensitive data. Additionally it must be infeasible to combine information of different surveillance tasks, separation is also addressed by virtual IDs. Problems occur at the operational level, if access controls change dynamically. At sensor level, it must be ensured that gained information is assigned to the proper objects in the OOWM. Problems occur, if objects are split up or fused due to misinformation.

Anonymizer (AM): The *Anonymizer* is closely linked to the IdM and ensures privacy conform access on information about objects. The AM enforces maximum privacy for different accesses by anonymization. If possible (depending on the surveillance task) location requests and attribute requests are anonymized. In most cases access to sensitive attributes is restricted to a subset of services of a surveillance task. In general, as less as possible information of an object should be provided to a service. Depending on the surveillance task, imprecision or intentional errors can be added intentionally.

Digital Rights Management (DRM): Task of this module is to attach digital rights to any information that is sent to a service or to another surveillance deployment (OOWM). This guarantees that data is only accessible during execution of a surveillance task or even just a subtask. Lifetime of data is restricted and data is only available for authorized services. However, even if the information flow can be controlled, services must be trusted. Once information has been observed, it might be reproduced and misused.

Subject Interaction (SI): The Subject Interaction module handles the interaction between an observed subject and the surveillance system. The subject can request personal data related to him and can induce correction or erasure. In some surveillance scenarios a subject can import his own policies. Different options for interaction with a surveillance system can be imagined, for instance: a personal device, a kiosk or simply pen and paper.

Privacy Policies (PP): Privacy policies ensure a certain level of privacy for the surveillance deployment. Policies concern one or more surveillance tasks (global policies) or can be user specific (personal policies). Global policies are enforced to achieve compliance with data protection law and the FIP. By using personal policies the observed subject can specify a personal trade-off between functionality and privacy.

Security Enforcement and Security Policies: As mentioned, security is closely related to privacy. However, the SESM manages cryptographic keys and certificates, ensures authenticity of service end points and confidentially of transmitted data. The SESM also logs any (attempted) access to the world model. The SESM deploys and enforces the access controls derived from the privacy and security policies. The latter specify authorizations for services and resources that are not privacy related.

6.5 Achievement of the Fair Information Principles

Principle P3 and P6, can by definition not be achieved by the PM. The purpose for which personal data is collected must be specified before the surveillance task is started. Most legislations require that the entire surveillance task (purpose) is specified before it is started. P6 cannot be achieved by the PM and SM as well. Information about the architecture, policies and operators must be easily accessible for surveillance subjects.

Data Collection Limitation Principle (P1): The collection of data is firstly minimized at sensor level, i. e., the sensor services only select the potentially required sensors for a surveillance task. As a result only potential relevant information is fused in the OOWM and the relation to a specific task exists right from the start. However, sensors can still deliver too much information for a specific surveillance task that is not required. Hence the AM removes irrelevant information before the response or event is sent back.

Data Quality Principle (P2): Relevance of data is already achieved by the task-oriented approach used in P1. Data Quality is achieved by a Data Quality Module in the SESM, i. e., it performs integrity checks of the existing data, especially if data has been altered by external services. The OOWM core, more exactly, the internal Instance Manager and the IdM are responsible for freshness and correctness of the instantiated objects (for details see [BEVB09]).

Use Limitation Principle (P4): Use of data is restricted according to the surveillance task. Therefore accesses controls are enforced by the SM, access is granted to all involved services during the duration of the task, and such general Security Policies are stored in the SESM. To enhance privacy, more specific Privacy Policies can be specified that describe which attributes are accessible by particular services. Data should only be used in a specific context and only during execution of the corresponding task. Hence any information that leaves the World Model is coupled with digital rights. This is done by the DRM. This is especially important, if data is exchanged between OOWMs. A service or OOWM must have the valid credential to process the requested data, e. g., if a credential has expired, the service or OOWM cannot process information of a subject and the credential must be requested again.

Security Safeguard Principle (P5): Established security mechanisms and protocols are used to achieve CIA in the NEST architecture. For instance, certificates

(Public Key Infrastructures) or IPSec. Although, these methods are sufficient, more specific security mechanisms would enhance efficiency. In Section 7 a web of trust for surveillance sensors is proposed to enhance trust in the authenticity of surveillance sensors. Hence only sensor services that are assumed to be trusted are allowed to deliver information into the OOWM.

Individual Participation Principle (P7): Besides the general privacy policies mentioned above (P4), data subjects can also specify personal privacy policies, i. e., a data subject can find his personal trade-off between efficiency and privacy. Naturally not all surveillance tasks (e. g., thievery protection) allow personalization. The SI handles interaction between the surveillance subjects and the surveillance system and empowers user subjects to request the personal data related to them. They can induce erasure (if it is compliant with the surveillance task) or correction of their personal data.

Accounting principle (P8): Any services performed by a module inside the OOWM, any external access by an actor and any data integration by a sensor is logged. If, for some reason, a violation of access rules occurs, the operator is notified about it. These logs cannot be altered by the operator. Hence they can be used to proof proper processing of personal data.

7 Web of Trust for Smart Surveillance Sensors

One challenge for modern surveillance systems is the establishment of trust in unknown partners and sensors, even the authenticity of self-introduced sensors cannot ensured. Potential surveillance partners might not trust each other and establishment of a common root CA can be difficult. Hence, we propose a *web of trust* for building trust into surveillance sensors. The idea of a web of trust has been used in PGP[2] to establish trust in digital signatures. In the case of surveillance, a web of trust can be used to assign trust to known surveillance operators, which is used to calculate authenticity of sensors. A surveillance system operator A collects public keys of other operators (parties) in his public key ring (K_{pub}^A) and sets the *owner trust* for other surveillance system operators. He can set the trust to *complete*, if he has full confidence in an operator B or to *marginal* in case of marginal trust. If A has given complete trust to B, he considers any sensor digitally signed by B to be authentic. In case of marginal trust, any sensor s_B signed by B is partly trusted, i. e. information gained by s_B is weighted less authentic. Another party C that is marginally trusted must sign s_B to achieve full authenticity of s_B. A sensor s is authentic, if $A(s) = \frac{x(s)}{X} + \frac{y(s)}{Y} \geq 1$, $x(s)$ denotes the

---

[2]http://www.ietf.org/rfc/rfc4880.txt

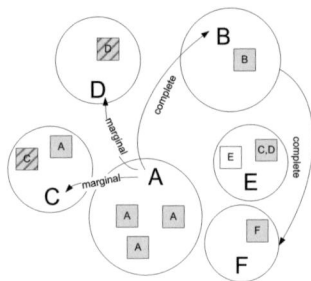

Figure 7.1: Web of Trust for Surveillance Sensors

marginal trusts and $y(s)$ denotes the complete trusts for s. X and Y denote the number of required trusts to achieve authenticity. If $A(s) \leq 1$, data received from s is not considered for surveillance tasks. As in PGP $X = 2$ and $Y = 1$ seem to be reasonable, but a surveillance operator can choose more restricted values. Optionally the information gained from s, can be weighted according to $A(s)$. A can also establish direct trust in s by signing the sensor directly. To extend his web of trust A can specify *trusted introducers*. If B is a trusted introducer of A, A trusts all operators b_i, $i \in \{1, \ldots, n\}$, trusted by B (marginal or complete). Figure 7.1 shows a web of trust with six surveillance parties (*A-F*). A has self-signed his own three sensors and one sensor run by C, hence they are all completely authentic. A has complete trust in B, resulting the sensor signed by B is also completely of authenticity. A marginally trusts C and D, hence in each domain one sensor is marginally authentic. The cumulative trust in C and D results in complete authenticity of one of the sensors operated by E. The other sensor is only signed by E, A does not know E, hence this sensor is not authentic. B is a trusted introducer of A, thus the sensor operated by F is completely authentic.

However, the major issue of a web of trust is that operators could carelessly trust in other operators to get a huge network of authentic sensors, instead of having a smaller but trustable sensor network. The authenticity that is achieved by a web of trust reflects the trust in a sensor by the view of a system operator, it is not a qualified signature, i.e. data gained by trusted sensors must be authenticated additionally to guarantee that it can be used in court.

8   Conclusion and Future Work

The proposed Privacy Manager can be used in task-oriented surveillance systems. Due to its flexibility it can be adapted to any privacy requirements. Future legal and social requirements must be specified and the approach must be discussed between the involved parties. Similar, the web of trust for surveillance sensors can (technologically) solve a security challenge, but it must be discussed with lawyers and system operators have to discuss its practicability.

Nevertheless a lot of research must be done in the area of privacy and security for surveillance systems. New anonymization techniques must be developed and explored in practice. New approaches for privacy polices are also necessary. Existing languages do not fit surveillance circumstances and do not provide sufficient mechanisms for automated derivation and flexible deployment. To enhance the web of trust, degrees of believe will be combined with authenticity mechanisms to couple trust, sensor signal quality and probabilities.

Bibliography

[BEE+08]   Alexander Bauer, Susanne Eckel, Thomas Emter, Astrid Laubenheimer, Eduardo Monari, Jürgen Mossgraber, and Frank Reinert. N.E.S.T. - Network Enabled Surveillance and Tracking. In Klaus Thoma, editor, *Future security: 3rd Security Research Conference*, pages 349–353. Fraunhofer IRB Verlag, September 2008.

[BEVB09]   A Bauer, T Emter, H Vagts, and J Beyerer. Object oriented world model for surveillance systems. In *Future security: 4th Security Research Conference*. Fraunhofer IRB Verlag, 2009.

[Bou05]   Terrance E. Boult. Pico: Privacy through invertible cryptographic obscuration. pages 27–38, November 2005.

[CB07]   Ankur Chattopadhyay and Terrance E. Boult. Privacycam: a privacy preserving camera using uclinux on the blackfin dsp. In *CVPR* [DBL07].

[CP09]   T. Chattopadhyay and Arpan Pal. Two fold video encryption technique applicable to h.264 avc. In *Advance Computing Conference, 2009. IACC 2009. IEEE International*, pages 785–789, March 2009.

[DBL07]   *2007 IEEE Computer Society Conference on Computer Vision and Pattern Recognition (CVPR 2007), 18-23 June 2007, Minneapolis, Minnesota, USA.* IEEE Computer Society, 2007.

[DE06]   Frédéric Dufaux and Touradj Ebrahimi. Scrambling for video surveillance with privacy. *Computer Vision and Pattern Recognition Workshop, 2006. CVPRW '06. Conference on*, pages 160–160, June 2006.

[DF02]   Rui Du and Jessica Fridrich. Lossless authentication of mpeg-2 video. In *Image Processing. 2002. Proceedings. 2002 International Conference on*, volume 2, pages II–893–II–896 vol.2, 2002.

[DNVHC05]   Dacfey Dzung, Martin Naedele, Thomas P. Von Hoff, and Mario Crevatin. Security for industrial communication systems. *Proceedings of the IEEE*, 93(6):1152–1177, June 2005.

[FNT04]   Douglas A. Fidaleo, Hoang-Anh Nguyen, and Mohan Trivedi. The networked sensor tapestry (nest): a privacy enhanced software architecture for interactive analysis of data in video-sensor networks. In *VSSN '04: Proceedings of the ACM 2nd international workshop on Video surveillance & sensor networks*, pages 46–53, New York, NY, USA, 2004. ACM.

[FS08]   Sven Fleck and Wolfgang Strasser. Smart camera based monitoring system and its application to assisted living. *Proceedings of the IEEE*, 96(10):1698–1714, October 2008.

[HBC⁺05] Arun. Hampapur, Lisa Brown, Johnathan Connell, A. Ekin, Norman Haas, Max Lu, Hans Merkl, and Sharath Pankanti. Smart video surveillance: exploring the concept of multiscale spatiotemporal tracking. *Signal Processing Magazine, IEEE*, 22(2):38–51, March 2005.

[HT04]   Leon Hempel and Erik Töpfer. CCTV in Europe. Final Report, Urbaneye Working Paper No. 15, August 2004.

          B Lo, J. Sun, and S.A. Velastin. Fusing visual and audio information in a distributed intelligent surveillance system for public transport systems.

[SPH⁺05] A. Senior, S. Pankanti, A. Hampapur, L. Brown, Ying-Li Tian, A. Ekin, J. Connell, Chiao Fe Shu, and M. Lu. Enabling video privacy through computer vision. *Security & Privacy, IEEE*, 3(3):50–57, May-June 2005.

[TT01]   Chih-Hsuan Tzeng and Wen-Hsiang Tsai. A new technique for authentication of image/video for multimedia applications. In *MM&Sec '01: Proceedings of the 2001 workshop on Multimedia and security*, pages 23–26, New York, NY, USA, 2001. ACM.

[VB09]   Hauke Vagts and Jürgen Beyerer. Security and privacy challenges in modern surveillance systems. In *Future security: 4th Security Research Conference*, 2009.

[VBEB09] Hauke Vagts, Alexander Bauer, Thomas Emter, and Jürgen Beyerer. Privacy enforcement in surveillance systems. In *Future security: 4th Security Research Conference*, 2009.

Multi-Modal Auto-Regressive Models for Inspection Tasks

Michael Mai

Vision and Fusion Laboratory
Institute for Anthropomatics
Karlsruhe Institute of Technology (KIT), Germany
mai@kit.edu

Technical Report IES-2009-09

Abstract: Analysis of data that are derived from advanced image acquisition techniques, gains more influence in the image processing industry. One major issue in the visual inspection in the industry is the detection of anomalies. Rather than detecting anomalies by describing them by features or detecting them by explicitly describing the non-anomaly case, the auto-regressive models provide a way to eliminate expected pattern and emphasize the not expected—the anomalies.

This paper introduces a new class of auto-regressive (AR) models that can handle data which contain different kinds of modalities, where the modalities represent different aspects of the inspected surface. The theoretical background of the AR models are presented, explained and analyzed.

1 Introduction

Recent developments in data acquisition, processing and not at least increased computational power, make it feasible and applicable to acquire and process more information of a specimen under examination. These additional information may provide additional clues for detection, recognition and identification of anomalies and structures in general. The original and additional information are refered here as multi-modal data.

The necessity for archiving data about the quality assess, reproducable objective decisions concerning the quality assess and the mere amount of products to assess are coercive reasons to assist man in this task. In the task of automated visual inspection, the detection could be simply accomplished in regions free of any structures. If the region is cluttered be structure, advanced methods are required instead.

One methology is to build a vector containing features that are derived from an image. These feature-vectors are classified for distinguishing regions that contains only expected structures and regions containing anomalies. Another methology is to model the expected structures, apply this knowledge and reduce the complexity of the remaining task. The *auto-regressive* (AR) models considered in this report allow modeling the expected structures by using statistical methods. With these models it is possible to capture the expectations (spatial as well as other information) in a statistically optimal way and render this knowledge useful in the inspection.

1.1   Contributions

The novelty of this paper are two flexible auto-regressive models that are adapted to multi-modal data. The combination of the ability of AR models to be adaptable to any pattern and multi-modal data, which can be obtained by emerging new technologies in image acquisition and processing, allow a robust and reliable emphazing of non-expected artifacts.

With the multi-modal AR models introduced in this report, the detection of structures is even possible, when the information required for detection is spread over different modalities and is only substantial in combination. The usage of the maximum accessible amount of information, enable the potentiality of a very reliable anomaly detection even in regions coated with other structures.

1.2   Related Work

Many procedures that are studied today and are deployed in the industry generates feature vectors that are adapted to the surface and structures currently examined. These vectors may be build from different feature generating processes. Each vector is subsequently classified for indicating a region that contain an anomaly or not.

[KP02] use Gabor wavelet features for the description of regions. Suitable Gabor filters are selected by comparing defect-free and defect regions, a simple thresholding is used for distinguishing these regions. [ZPY01] use specially designed wavelets for detection of defects on fabric. In [PP01], the outlier detection is conducted by using robust covariance matrices.

In the domain of auto-regressive models, the *VAR* (vector auto-regressive) model and *VARMA* (VAR moving average) model are the concepts closest to the multi-modal AR models proposed here. However, they are restricted to the one-dimensional case and are therefore useless in the process of detecting anomalies in multi-modal image data. Furthermore, they are not easily extensible to a high dimensional configuration.

2 Definition of Multi-Modal Data

Multi-modal contain on a baseline of understanding different kinds of information for a single location. In theory, there are no further requirements such as continuousity or equally spacing on the information if the data is discretized.

To derive a more manageable and appropriate data-structure for our case, we impose one additional constraint. We refer to data as multi-modal if for each spatial location (two-dimensional in image based data and three-dimensional in volume based data) serveral addition scalar information (identical in number) exist. Furthermore, we require that this information is equally spaced.

The structure of each location in a multi-modal dataset may be expressed as shown in Table 2.1.

Spatial system	Element at each location in the multi-modal data x
2-dimensional (images, ...)	$\underline{x}_{m,n} = \begin{pmatrix} x_{m,n,c=1} \\ x_{m,n,c=2} \\ \dots \end{pmatrix} \overset{\text{e.g.}}{=} \begin{pmatrix} \text{Grayvalue at } x, y \\ \text{Surface inclination at } x, y \\ \dots \end{pmatrix}$
s-dimensional	$\underline{x}_i = \begin{pmatrix} x_{i,c=1} \\ x_{i,c=2} \\ \dots \end{pmatrix}$ $i \in \mathbb{N}^s$ is used to index elements

Table 2.1: Examples of the structure of multi-modal datasets

As we can see, it is possible and mathematical feasible to express a multi-modal dataset as a tensor[1] $x \in \mathbb{R}^{s \times d}$ with the dimensions s for the spatial extent and d as the extent in numbers of different modalities. The first s dimensions which are most commonly associated with space, are *primal* for the multi-modal data. Everthing is aligned to it.

---

[1] A tensor is a generalized concept of matrices. A tensor of order n consists of several scalar elemets, each of its scalar elements is accessible be using an index $i \in \mathbb{N}^n$. A 2D matrix would be a tensor of order 2. The values contained in a tensor are sometimes called Muxel [PMGC09].

On a broader understanding: multi-modal data does not rely on any spatial reference as *primal* reference. Other referencing systems are possible and in some cases appropriate. It is solely application dependent and does not inflict with the further mathematical modeling of the multi-modal auto-regressive models. The single necessity for the remainder of this paper is, that multi-modal data have to be equally spaced—as shown in Table 2.1.

Weak Stationarity
The definition of the AR models as whitening filters provide the clue for monitoring their adaptation. Indirectly the property of weak stationarity in input data ensures the applicability of the models.

Weak stationarity is a quality of data and derives from the theoretical modeling of an image source as a stochastic process. Each multi-modal image x is a prototype function of this stochastic process. It states two properties that ensures that the data is statistical independent from locations up to the second statistical moment.

$$\mathbb{E}\{x_a\} = \mathbb{E}\{x_{a+d}\} \qquad \forall d \text{ if } a, a + d \text{ are locations within } x$$

$$\text{Cov}\{x_a, x_{a+d}\} = \text{Cov}\{x_b, x_{b+d}\} \quad \forall d \text{ if } a, b, a + d, b + d \text{ are locations within } x$$

These two equations ensure, that the expectation value at a given location is equal in the concerning region and the statistical spatial relation within the region is also independent from the location.

The property of weak stationarity ensures that a model which has been build in only one small region is feasible on the whole data. To make assertions about the stochastic process itself, e.g., pattern-analysis, the property of weak stationarity has to be fulfilled as well as the ergodic hypothesis, nonetheless the ergodicity is not required for the presented results in this paper.

3   Multi-Modal Auto-Regressive Models

The idea behind the usage of auto-regressive models is the explicit adaption of expected structures and subsequently statistical testing. The conducted test is called Null-Hypothesis-Test (H_0-Test). It verifies whether the model is valid for the region it is applied or not. If the model is still valid, the region tested is sufficiently close to the region the model was created for. It is therefore an indicator for the abidance of expectation.

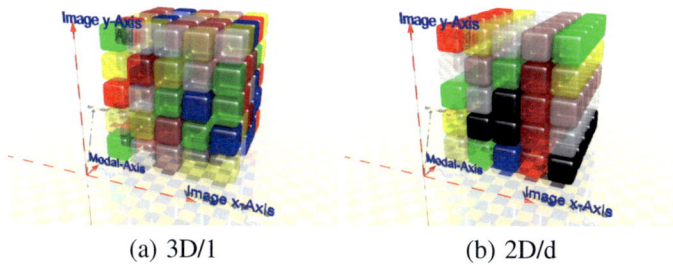

(a) 3D/1   (b) 2D/d

Figure 3.1: This sketch visualize both multi-modal auto-regressive models. The AR coefficients are placed according to their application on the multi-modal data. Same colors indicates same weight or factor.

All AR models are based on the same principle. They are linear, translation-invariant filters and are calculated using a convolution. The estimation of model parameters and filter coefficient is in every model a crucial part and discussed in detail in the following sections. AR models use only a finite number of filter coefficients. They count therefore to the FIR filters (finite impulse responses) and are subject to the issue of stability. The stability of the filters is discussed in the following sections dealing with the process of estimating the filter coefficients.

The following two novel AR models are introduced. The *3D/1 AR model* use statistical information from the multi-modal data in each modality simultaneously for adapting a model to the presented texture. The *2D/d AR model* impose a simplification, which takes advantage of a special constrain on the statisical relation in the data. The simplification results in a less complicated optimization problem, faster calculation and an easier parameterization. Both models are depicted in Fig. 3.1.

3.1 $\mathcal{U}, \mathcal{U}_c, \mathcal{E}$ and Point of Reference

The coefficient model mask $\mathcal{U}$ or $\mathcal{U}_c$

The coefficient model mask $\mathcal{U}$ defines the supporting area which is used for the calculations that lead to the prediction of the point of reference. The mask has great influence on the quality of the prediction and is used in the prediction (see Eqn. (3.1) and (3.4)) as well as in estimation (see Eqn. (3.3) and (3.5)). $\mathcal{U}_c$ defines the data elements that are to be used and may be interpretated as index set.

The design of the mask has to take the statistical properties of the structure into account. This means, that the mask should be designed in such a way that the statistical properties of the data are captured sufficiently.

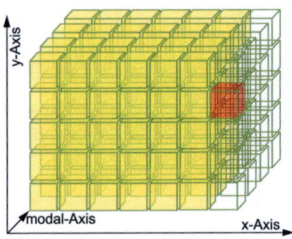

Figure 3.2: The multi-modal image in this paper consists of three axes. The traditional two spatial ones and one axis that indicates the modal dimension. This figure shows a coefficient model mask $\mathcal{U}_c$ of $7 \times 5 \times 4$ size with the point of reference in $c = 1$ and rightmost in $\mathcal{U}_c$.

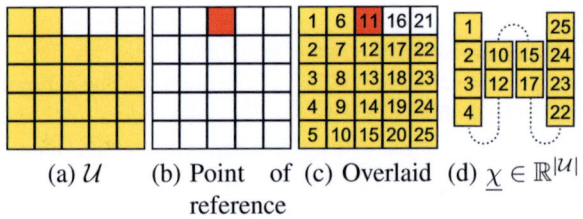

(a) $\mathcal{U}$ (b) Point of reference   (c) Overlaid   (d) $\underline{\chi} \in \mathbb{R}^{|\mathcal{U}|}$

Figure 3.3: The interplay of coefficient model mask, point of reference and the resulting vector $\underline{\chi}$ that is constructed according to Eqn. (3.2).

The AR models are used in a predictive manner. For a true prediction without any influence on the value to be predicted, the *coefficient model mask* may not include the *point of reference*.

A few considerations about the general design of the coefficient model mask besides the statistical ones are also worth mentioning: if the coefficient model mask is *recursive computable*, the associated AR model could be used for texture synthesis. A special case of recursive computable coefficient model masks are the *causal* coefficient model masks that trace back to the ages of the origin of the AR models when they were mostly used in time series analysis.

The estimation region $\mathcal{E}$

The filter coefficients are commonly called *AR coefficients* $\underline{\alpha}$ and are estimated using the coeffiencient model mask $\mathcal{U}$, the *estimation region* $\mathcal{E}$ and a special algorithm for determining the coefficient. The estimation region $\mathcal{E}$ is in most cases restricted to one image. But this restriction is neither necessary nor is it feasible

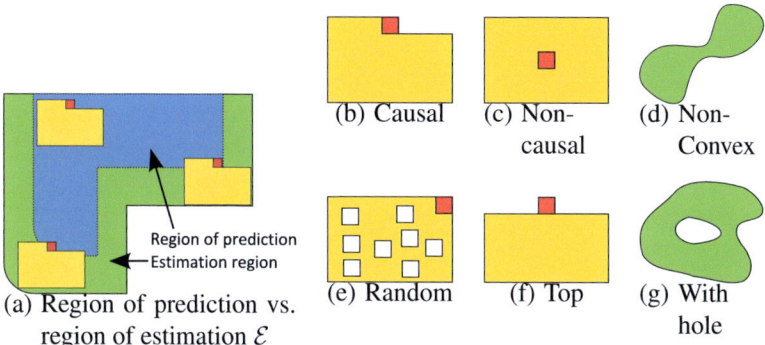

(b) Causal   (c) Non-   (d) Non-
             causal   Convex

(e) Random   (f) Top   (g) With
                        hole

(a) Region of prediction vs.
region of estimation $\mathcal{E}$

Figure 3.4: Figure (a) visualize the difference between the region that is used for collecting information (estimation region $\mathcal{E}$ (green)) and the region that is predicted (light blue). Figures (b), (c), (e) and (f) visualize different possible coefficient model masks (yellow) and points of predictions (red). Figure (d) and (g) shows possible estimation regions that might be appropriate for training the model so that only valid or trustworthy image regions are included.

for each case. If the estimation region is spread over several images, the stochastic process is captured more directly as it would be if the ergodic hypothesis is used.

Point of Reference
The AR models are used to predict the point of reference. This value is calculated by using a surrounding and specially optimized AR coefficients $^{c}\underline{\alpha}$. The surrounding is build according to the coefficient model mask $\mathcal{U}_c$. This predicted value is greatly influenced by the AR coefficients $^{c}\underline{\alpha}$ and the coefficient model mask $\mathcal{U}_c$ as well as the estimation region $\mathcal{E}$. The predicted value plays an important role in the distinction of regions that contain anomalies and regions that did not contain any.

3.2   3D/1

The modalities are treated as ordinary data dimensions exactly like the spatials ones (see Fig. 3.2). This implies, that the pre-condition of AR models must hold and eventually enforced on the whole input data across all modalities.

The naming *3D/1* is based on the organisation of the coefficient model mask and dimension of the prediction. *3D* stands for two spatial and one modal dimension which renders the organisation of the coefficient model mask a three-dimensional artifact. */1* stands for scalar value predicted by this model at the point of reference.

Fig. 3.1(a) visualizes how the coefficients are aligned in the coefficient model mask.

The result of the prediction of the AR model on the data has to be weak stationary. From this requirement by definition follows that the input data x must also be weak stationary (see Sec. 2). Noise $w_{m,n,c} \sim \mathcal{N}(0,1)$ is assumed to be normal, uncorrelated and additive to the image.

After these preliminaries, the elementary mathematical structure of the 3D/1 AR models are defined as follows. Keep in mind, that the 3D/1 AR models are dedicated for the prediction of a scalar value only even in the multi-modal setup.

m, n are used for spatial coordinates and c for the modal coordinate. k, l are used as control variables for spatial coordinates and i for the modal coordinate.

$$\hat{x}_{m,n,c} = \sum_{(k,l,i)\in \mathcal{U}_c} {}^c a_{k,l,i} \cdot x_{m-k,n-l,i} = {}^c\underline{\alpha}^{\mathsf{T}} \underline{\chi}_{m,n} \qquad (3.1)$$

$$x_{m,n,c} = \hat{x}_{m,n,c} + {}^c\sigma^2 w_{m,n,c} = {}^c\underline{\alpha}^{\mathsf{T}} \underline{\chi}_{m,n} + {}^c\sigma^2 w_{m,n,c}$$

$\mathcal{U}_c$ is the coefficient model mask which is specific for channel c (Fig. 3.2). It is possible and in some cases beneficial to use a different coefficient model mask $\mathcal{U}_c$ for each channel, i.e., $\mathcal{U}_{c=1} \neq \mathcal{U}_{c=2} \neq \cdots$. But in most cases, good results are achieved by using equal coefficient model masks for all channels with only small modifications to account for the causality condition.

The difference of the actual value at the point of reference $x_{m,n,c}$ and its prediction $\hat{x}_{m,n,c}$ is called prediction error $e_{m,n,c}$ and is calculated according to:

$$e_{m,n,c} = x_{m,n,c} - \hat{x}_{m,n,c} = -{}^c\underline{\alpha}'^{\mathsf{T}} \underline{\chi}'_{m,n} \quad , \quad e^2_{m,n,c} = {}^c\underline{\alpha}'^{\mathsf{T}} \underline{\chi}'_{m,n} \underline{\chi}'^{\mathsf{T}}_{m,n} {}^c\underline{\alpha}'.$$

Here ${}^c\underline{\alpha}$, ${}^c\underline{\alpha}'$ represents the AR coefficients and $\underline{\chi}$, $\underline{\chi}'$ are the data from a surrounding of a given location are defined according to

$${}^c\underline{\alpha} = \begin{pmatrix} {}^c a_{0,1,1} \\ {}^c a_{0,1,2} \\ \cdots \end{pmatrix} \qquad {}^c\underline{\alpha}' = \begin{pmatrix} -1 \\ {}^c\underline{\alpha} \end{pmatrix} \qquad \underline{\chi}_{m,n} = \begin{pmatrix} x_{m,n-1,1} \\ x_{m,n-2,1} \\ \cdots \\ x_{m,n-1,2} \\ \cdots \end{pmatrix} \qquad \underline{\chi}'_{m,n} = \begin{pmatrix} x_{m,n,c} \\ \underline{\chi}_{m,n} \end{pmatrix}.$$

$\underline{\chi}$ as well as $\underline{\chi}'$ take the coefficient model mask $\mathcal{U}_c$ into account. Its creation is deptied in Fig. 3.3. For determination of a 3D/1 model that is optimally adapted to the multi-modal texture in the estimation region $\mathcal{E}$ on the specimen, the prediction error has to be minimized. This minimization can be performed in different ways. A closed-from solution is proposed here that also provides the advantage that the result is automatically stable [DM84] in BIBO terms (bounded input – bounded output); at least with data similar to those in $\mathcal{E}$.

The structure of the 3D/1 models allows not only a simple minimization of the prediction error, but also minimizing the variance of the predication error which yields much better results.

$$^c\Gamma = \text{Var}\{e\} = \mathbb{E}\{e^2\} - \mathbb{E}\{e\}^2 = \mathbb{E}\{e^2\} \to \min \qquad (3.2)$$

The optimization problem $^c\Gamma$ is minimal and optimal in the least square sense over the estimation region $\mathcal{E}$ if the AR coefficients $^c\underline{\alpha}$ are optimally determined. In Eqn. (3.2) the quality of an optimal approximation is used by assuming the squared prediction error is zero $\mathbb{E}\{e\}^2 = 0$.

The weak stationarity of e (used in Eqn. (3.2)) is needed to provide the statistical justification to prefer the prediction error from only one prototype function (image x) over all other possible realisations of the stochastic process. This methology of using only one prototype function instead of the whole stochastic process is called erodic hypothesis.

One special assumption of the 3D/1 AR models is the space filling coefficent model mask $\mathcal{E}$ in the modal direction c. Therefore the limits of the summation within $^c\Gamma$ varies only over two spatial componentes $(m, n) \in \mathcal{E}$.

$$^c\Gamma' = {}^c\underline{\alpha}'^{\mathsf{T}} \begin{pmatrix} \sum\limits_{m,n} x^2_{m,n,c} & \sum\limits_{m,n} x_{m,n,c}\underline{\chi}^{\mathsf{T}}_{m,n} \\ \sum\limits_{m,n} \underline{\chi}_{m,n} x_{m,n,c} & \sum\limits_{m,n} \underline{\chi}_{m,n}\underline{\chi}^{\mathsf{T}}_{m,n} \end{pmatrix} {}^c\underline{\alpha}'$$

$$= \sum\limits_{m,n} x^2_{m,n,c} - 2{}^c\underline{\alpha}^{\mathsf{T}} \sum\limits_{m,n} \underline{\chi}_{m,n} x_{m,n,c} + {}^c\underline{\alpha}^{\mathsf{T}} \left(\sum\limits_{m,n} \underline{\chi}_{m,n}\underline{\chi}^{\mathsf{T}}_{m,n}\right) {}^c\underline{\alpha}$$

For the minimization of $^c\Gamma'$ which yields also a minimal $^c\Gamma$, it is necessary to derivative $^c\Gamma'$ with respect to the only uncommitted variable $^c\underline{\alpha}$. To be truly minimal the Hessian has to be positive definite which in pratice is always the case according to [Mak75].

$$\frac{\partial ^c\Gamma'}{\partial ^c\underline{\alpha}} = -2\sum\limits_{m,n} \underline{\chi}_{m,n} x_{m,n,c} + 2\sum\limits_{m,n} \underline{\chi}_{m,n}\underline{\chi}^{\mathsf{T}}_{m,n} {}^c\underline{\alpha} = 0$$

$$\Rightarrow {}^c\underline{\alpha} = \left(\sum\limits_{(m,n)\in\mathcal{E}} \underline{\chi}_{m,n}\underline{\chi}^{\mathsf{T}}_{m,n}\right)^{-1} \sum\limits_{(m,n)\in\mathcal{E}} \underline{\chi}_{m,n} x_{m,n,c} \qquad (3.3)$$

$^c\underline{\alpha}$ solves the optimization problem $^c\Gamma$ and forms the coefficients describing the spatial information of the texture. The global information of the texture $^c\sigma^2$ is

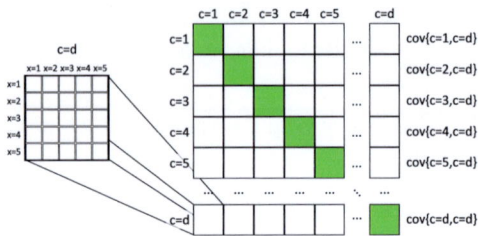

Figure 3.5: This figure shows the block structure of $\underline{\chi}\underline{\chi}^\mathsf{T}$ if $\underline{\chi}$ is defined accordingly. The modalities are plotted horizontally and vertically, each block indicate a correlation between two image regions origined from the labeled modalities.

obtainable by evaluating a simplified $^c\Gamma$. The function $c(\mathcal{E}, \mathcal{U}_c) \in \mathbb{N}$ indicates the number of the coefficient model masks that could be placed within $\mathcal{E}$.

$$^c\sigma = \sqrt{\frac{1}{c(\mathcal{U}_c, \mathcal{E})} \left(\sum_{(m,n)\in\mathcal{E}} x_{m,n,c}^2 - {}^c\underline{\alpha}^\mathsf{T} \sum_{(m,n)\in\mathcal{E}} \underline{\chi}_{m,n} x_{m,n,c} \right)}$$

$d \cdot$ **3D/1**

As we can see from the structure of the 3D/1 model, they can be easily expanded to yield not only one scalar prediction but a vector. Theoretically all parameters ($\mathcal{U}_c$ and $\mathcal{E}$) may be modified in this process.

In the case of very different statistical properties between the modalities which could be easily identified by analysing $\sum \underline{\chi}\underline{\chi}^\mathsf{T}$, it would be worth to identify different sets of parameters especially $\mathcal{U}_c$ or even separate the multi-modal data to be processed by different models.

Classic 2D AR model

The simple two-dimensional AR model is defined on simple scalar valued data that are arranged in two dimensions. If the model is interpreted as an operator on a special multi-modal image, the multi-modal dataset would consists of $s = 2$ and $d = 1$ as dimensions and all the math discussed in the previous section applies.

The 2D(/1) models require only one coefficient model mask, hence the index c may be discarded from $\mathcal{U}_c$ to $\mathcal{U}$ and $^c\underline{\alpha}$ to $\underline{\alpha}$.

Structure of $\sum \underline{\chi}\underline{\chi}^\mathsf{T}$

Within $\underline{\chi}$ the multi-modal image content is encapsulated, sliced according to the coefficient model mask $\mathcal{U}_c$. The axes are systematically varied according to the definition of $\mathcal{U}_c$. This results in block structure of $\underline{\chi}\underline{\chi}^\mathsf{T}$ that is visualised in Fig. 3.5.

From the figure of $\chi\chi^{\mathsf{T}}$, it is clearly visible which blocks correlate among each other. Each block indicates an image region for every modality. On the diagonal all modality blocks are correlated with themselves.

3.3   2D/d

The 2D/d AR models are designed with the assumption, that the characteristical texture is dominated by its spatial relative coordinates. This could easily be visualized in the example of stamped or embossed surfaces. In the process of stamping, a stamp is placed spatially on the surface any suface-surface-interaction (which might be force) occurs. The resulting multi-modal texture is now dominated by the texture imposed be the stamp. In general, this is not a strict functional relation due to diffusion-like processes and special behaviours in the modalities. The 2D/d AR models simplify this assumption to a functional relation. This assumption states that the interchange across the modalities is negligible compared to the statistical relations across the spatial domain. This leads to a coefficient model mask that is arrangeable in spatial dimensions.

One special aspect of stamping or embossing are accidently caused stamps or embossments, which could by related with anomalies or defects, i.e., caused by an accidentally slipped screwdriver.

The naming *2D/d* is based on the organisation of the coefficient model mask and the dimension of the prediction. The coefficient model mask is arrangable in *2D* and the predicted value at the point of reference is *d*-dimensional and contains the predication for all modalities simultaneously.

$$\hat{\underline{x}}_{m,n} = \sum_{(k,l)\in\mathcal{U}} a_{k,l}\underline{x}_{m-k,n-l} = \boldsymbol{\Delta}_{m,n}\underline{\alpha} \tag{3.4}$$

$$\underline{x}_{m,n} = \boldsymbol{\Delta}_{m,n}\underline{\alpha} + \sigma^2\underline{w}_{m,n}, \qquad e_{m,n} = \left\|\underline{x}_{m,n} - \hat{\underline{x}}_{m,n}\right\| = \underline{\alpha}'^{\mathsf{T}}\boldsymbol{\Delta}_{m,n}'^{\mathsf{T}}\boldsymbol{\Delta}_{m,n}'\underline{\alpha}'$$

The structures used are defined as follows:

$$\underline{\alpha} = \begin{pmatrix} a_{0,1} \\ a_{0,2} \\ \cdots \end{pmatrix} \qquad \underline{\alpha}' = \begin{pmatrix} 1 \\ -\underline{\alpha} \end{pmatrix}$$

$$\boldsymbol{\Delta}_{m,n} = \left(\begin{pmatrix} x_{m,n-1,1} \\ x_{m,n-1,2} \\ \cdots \end{pmatrix} \underline{x}_{m,n-2} \cdots \right) \qquad \boldsymbol{\Delta}_{m,n}' = \left(\begin{pmatrix} x_{m,n,1} \\ x_{m,n,2} \\ \cdots \end{pmatrix} \boldsymbol{\Delta}_{m,n} \right)$$

The optimization problem for the determination of an optimal $\underline{\alpha}$ for the given data in the estimation region $\mathcal{E}$ is formulated as:

$$\Gamma = \mathbb{E}\{e_{m,n}\} \to \min \quad \rightsquigarrow \quad \Gamma = \frac{1}{c(\mathcal{E},\mathcal{U})} \sum_{(m,n)\in\mathcal{E}} e_{m,n} \to \min$$

As in the previous section, $c(\mathcal{E},\mathcal{U}) \in \mathbb{N}$ is the number of possible placements of the coefficient model mask $\mathcal{U}$ within the estimation region $\mathcal{E}$. Γ' is derived from Γ by neglecting constant factors irrelevant for the determination of the optimum. Hence, Γ' is given by

$$\Gamma' = \underline{\alpha}'^{\mathsf{T}} \sum_{m,n} \left(\begin{matrix} \underline{x}_{m,n}^{\mathsf{T}}\underline{x}_{m,n} & \underline{x}_{m,n}^{\mathsf{T}}\mathbf{\Delta}_{m,n} \\ \mathbf{\Delta}_{m,n}^{\mathsf{T}}\underline{x}_{m,n} & \mathbf{\Delta}_{m,n}^{\mathsf{T}}\mathbf{\Delta}_{m,n} \end{matrix} \right) \underline{\alpha}'$$

$$= \sum_{m,n} \underline{x}_{m,n}^{\mathsf{T}}\underline{x}_{m,n} - 2\alpha^{\mathsf{T}} \sum_{m,n} \underline{x}_{m,n}^{\mathsf{T}}\mathbf{\Delta}_{m,n} + \underline{\alpha}^{\mathsf{T}} \left(\sum_{m,n} \mathbf{\Delta}_{m,n}^{\mathsf{T}}\mathbf{\Delta}_{m,n} \right) \underline{\alpha}$$

The roots of $\frac{\partial \Gamma'}{\partial \underline{\alpha}} = 0$ yield the minimal Γ' and also the minimal Γ. The determination of $\underline{\alpha}$ from the roots of $\frac{\partial \Gamma'}{\partial \underline{\alpha}}$ yields our optimal AR coefficients in a least squared sence according to:

$$\frac{\partial \Gamma'}{\partial \underline{\alpha}} = -2 \sum_{m,n} \underline{x}_{m,n}^{\mathsf{T}}\mathbf{\Delta}_{m,n} + 2 \left(\sum_{m,n} \mathbf{\Delta}_{m,n}^{\mathsf{T}}\mathbf{\Delta}_{m,n} \right) \underline{\alpha} = 0$$

$$\Rightarrow \underline{\alpha} = \left(\sum_{m,n} \mathbf{\Delta}_{m,n}^{\mathsf{T}}\mathbf{\Delta}_{m,n} \right)^{-1} \sum_{m,n} \underline{x}_{m,n}^{\mathsf{T}}\mathbf{\Delta}_{m,n} \tag{3.5}$$

Structure of $\sum \mathbf{\Delta}^{\mathsf{T}}\mathbf{\Delta}$

For emphasizing the distinction between the 3D/1 and the 2D/d models, we take a closer look at the properties of $\sum \mathbf{\Delta}^{\mathsf{T}}\mathbf{\Delta}$ and compare it with the corresponding matrix $\sum \chi^{\mathsf{T}}\chi$ of the 3D/1 AR model. Within the matrix $\mathbf{\Delta}$ information about the image content in modalities (row-wise) and space (column-wise) is captured. Through the calculation of $\sum \mathbf{\Delta}^{\mathsf{T}}\mathbf{\Delta}$ a statistical analysis of the captured data is done.

For simplification, the following notation is used: $\mathbf{\Delta} = \left(\underline{x}_{0,0} \ \underline{x}_{0,1} \ \cdots \right) \in \mathbb{R}^{d\times\cdot}$ with $\underline{x}_{i_0,i_1}^{\mathsf{T}} = \left({}^1x_{i_0,i_1} \ {}^2x_{i_0,i_1} \ \cdots \right)$ where ${}^c x_{i_0,i_1}$ indicates the scalar value of the modality c at the location (i_0, i_1) ($\underline{x}_{i_0,i_1} \in \mathbb{R}^{d\times 1}$).

	$d \cdot 3D/1$	$2D/d$
Number of AR Coefficients	$\prod_{c=1}^{d} |\mathcal{U}_c|$	$|\mathcal{U}|$
Effort of prediction of one point of reference $\hat{x}_i$	$opd^2 \cdot t_{\mathrm{mul}} +$ $d(opd - 1) \cdot t_{\mathrm{add}}$	$opd \cdot t_{\mathrm{mul}} +$ $d(op - 1) \cdot t_{\mathrm{add}}$

Table 3.1: This table compares the different multi-modal AR models in complexity and numerical issuses. $\mathcal{U}_c$ is assumed to be $o \times p \times d$ in size and $\mathcal{U}$ as $o \times p$.

$$\mathbf{\Delta}^{\mathsf{T}}\mathbf{\Delta} = \underbrace{\begin{pmatrix} {}^0x_{0,0}^2 & {}^0x_{0,0}{}^0x_{0,1} & \cdots \\ {}^0x_{0,0}{}^0x_{0,1} & {}^0x_{0,1}^2 & \cdots \\ & \cdots & \end{pmatrix}}_{\underline{\Delta}_{c=0}\underline{\Delta}_{c=0}^{\mathsf{T}}=\mathrm{Cov}\{\underline{\Delta}_{c=0},\underline{\Delta}_{c=0}\}} + \underbrace{\begin{pmatrix} {}^1x_{0,0}^2 & {}^1x_{0,0}{}^1x_{0,1} & \cdots \\ {}^1x_{0,0}{}^1x_{0,1} & {}^1x_{0,1}^2 & \cdots \\ & \cdots & \end{pmatrix}}_{\underline{\Delta}_{c=1}\underline{\Delta}_{c=1}^{\mathsf{T}}=\mathrm{Cov}\{\underline{\Delta}_{c=1},\underline{\Delta}_{c=1}\}} + \cdots$$

$$= \sum_i^d \mathrm{Cov}\{\underline{\Delta}_{c=i}, \underline{\Delta}_{c=i}\} \tag{3.6}$$

The vector $\underline{\Delta}_{c=i} \in \mathbb{R}^{d \times 1}$ represents all information of one modality across all spatial location within $\mathcal{U}$, this is similar to $\underline{\chi}$. In Equation (3.6) it is clearly visible, that $\mathbf{\Delta}^{\mathsf{T}}\mathbf{\Delta}$ is the sum of covariance matrices for each spatial relation in each modality. Through this equation we can easily see, that the 2D/d models are robust against weak correlation between modalities and therefore preferable in situations where the modalities in multi-modal data are weakly correlated. These models nevertheless enforce the interrelation between the modalities.

Table 3.1 provides a short comparison between the $d \cdot 3D/1$ and 2D/d AR models.

4 Inspection Framework

Input
As stated before, the data processed by an AR model has to be weak stationary. The reasons and exact preconditions are stated in section 2. The first step is to check for weak stationarity and eventually enforcing it. It could be enforced in different ways, e.g., removing prevouisly known structures that destroy the condition. [BL98] propose a method, that is able to remove random lines from an image.

Structual output
For compability reasons, the two multi-modal AR models have to produce the

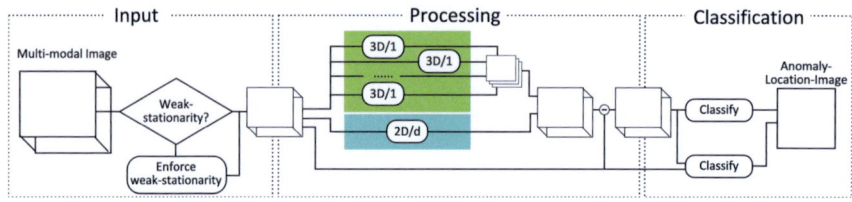

Figure 4.1: Scheme of the framework described in Section 4.

same structural data as result of their filtering. The 3D/1 is not compatible with the 2D/d models, as the 3D/1 models predict only a scalar value, while 2D/d predict a vector. To derive a compatible output, the 3D/1 is repeated d times with appropiate modifications such as that each model is responsable for the prediction of only one modality. The resulting model is called $d \cdot 3D/1$. Subsequently the $d \cdot 3D/1$ must have d different coefficient model masks $\mathcal{U}_c$ and points of reference.

One simple method to achieve this, is building a special series of coefficient model masks that do not take any data on the *non*-primal dimension of the point of reference (see Fig. 3.2) into account. The resulting coefficient model masks are therefore the same. Only the point of reference, which also have to be modified, differs between those models. Nonetheless, if the coefficient model masks are equal $\mathcal{U}_{c=1} = \mathcal{U}_{c=2} = \ldots$, the $\underline{\chi}$-vectors of each model is equal.

Classification

After the structure of the output is comparable, the output has to be classified to yield an indicator that qualify a region whether it is free of anomalies or not. The literature name many different methods to achieve this distinction. For instance neuronal networks, support-vector-machine or support-vector-data-description [Tax01].

In [TQD86] a method named *CFAR* (Constant False Alarm Rate) is proposed that squares the prediction error, divide it by the local variance and apply a threshold to the resulting value. The threshold is derived from a region known to be free of anomalies.

A different approach employs the ability of more advanced classifiers for distinguishing not only one single feature vector but also combinations of feature vectors. The output of the AR filtering may also be combined with other feature generating filters or the AR filter output is used as input for feature generating processes.

The framework discussed here is depicted in Fig. 4.1.

Figure 5.1: This figure shows the $\sum \chi\chi^{\mathsf{T}}$ from real world data. The different correlations within one modality and between them is clearly visible in the figure. Brigther color indicates a better correlation. The yellow line on the diagonal visualize the autovariance. We can easily see, that the correlative information between the first five modalities are not negligible.

5 Experimental Results

The experiments were conducted on a small part of a cylinder barrel of a combustion engine. The multi-modal data were generated by using a variation of deflectory[2]. [WMHB09] provide a complete introduction into deflectometry including some insights into the problems and geometric reconstruction. The multi-modal data derived here contain nine modalites.

The coefficient model mask $\mathcal{U}_c$ used for the calculation of $\sum \chi\chi^{\mathsf{T}}$ is enfigured in Fig. 3.3. $\sum \chi\chi^{\mathsf{T}}$ is visualized in Fig. 5.1. It shows that not all modalities correlate well with each other. In fact the figure shows that the autocorrelation in weakly correlated modalities is smaller than the autocorrelation of modalities that correlate well with some other modalities.

The $d \cdot 3\mathrm{D}/1$ AR models can cope with these data. Nevertheless the optimization problem has high dimension and may be numerically unstable. The 2D/d AR models takes advantage of the weakly correlated blocks shown in Fig. 5.1, but they discard information in non-autocorrelated blocks. The data may be split with respect to the statistical nature and processed separately optimally in each fragment by one $d \cdot 3\mathrm{D}/1$-Model or 2D/d AR model. The visible difference in the prediction error of both models are negligible.

---

[2]Deflectometry is done on highly specular surfaces. Typical information gained from deflectometric measurements are for example: synthetic grayvalue and hints for the surface inclination.

6 Conclusion and Future Work

We presented two AR models that are specially designed for multi-modal setups, which gain more influence in the visual inspection. In the automated visual inspection as well as in every image based algorithm, regions which are known to be less trustworthy has to be explicitly respected in the calculation. Nonetheless, methods that indicates which model has to be used, would be helpful.

Bibliography

[BL98]   Jürgen Beyerer and Fernando Puente León. Adaptive Separation of Random Lines and Background. In *Optical Engineering*, volume 37, pages 2733–2741, 1998.

[DM84]   Dan E. Dugeon and Russel M. Mersereau. *Multidimensional Digital Signal Processing*. Prentice-Hall, 1984.

[KP02]   Ajay Kumar and Grantham K. H. Pang. Defect Detection in textured Materials using Gabor Filters. *Industry Applications, IEEE Transactions on*, 38(2):425–440, Mar/Apr 2002.

[Mak75]   John Makhoul. Linear prediction: A tutorial review. *Proceedings of the IEEE*, 63(4):561–580, April 1975.

[PMGC09] Sebastian Pfeiffer, Michael Mai, Wolfgang Globke, and Jan Calliess. On Generalized Separation and the Speedup of local Operators on Multi-Dimensional Signals. In *Multidimensional (nD) Systems, 2009. nDS 2009. International Workshop on*, 29 2009-July 1 2009.

[PP01]   Daniel Peña and Francisco J. Prieto. Multivariate Outlier Detection and Robust Covariance Matrix Estimation. In *Technometrics, Special Tukey Memorial Issue.*, volume 43, pages 286–300. American Statistical Association, 2001.

[Tax01]   David Martinus Johannes Tax. *One-class Classification*. PhD thesis, Technische Universiteit Delft, 2001.

[TQD86]   Charles W. Therrien, Thomas F. Quatieri, and Dan E. Dudgeon. Statistical model-based algorithms for image analysis. *Proceedings of the IEEE*, 74(4):532–551, April 1986.

[WMHB09] Stefan Werling, Michael Mai, Michael Heizmann, and Jürgen Beyerer. Inspection of Specular and Partially Specular Surfaces. *Metrology and Measurement Systems*, XVI, 2009.

[ZPY01]   Yang Xue Zhi, Grantham K. H. Pang, and Nelson H. C. Yung. Fabric defect detection using adaptive wavelet. In *Acoustics, Speech, and Signal Processing, 2001. Proceedings. (ICASSP '01). 2001 IEEE International Conference on*, volume 6, pages 3697–3700 vol.6, 2001.

Shape from Specular Reflection – Remarks on Shape Reconstruction and Experimental Design

Stefan Werling

Vision and Fusion Laboratory
Institute for Anthropomatics
Karlsruhe Institute of Technology (KIT), Germany
stefan.werling@kit.edu

Technical Report IES-2009-10

Abstract: The main principle of shape from specular surface acquisition is to use a highly controllable environment, where a screen on which a well-defined pattern is presented is observed via the specular reflecting surface. Knowing that pattern, it is possible—at least with certain additional knowledge—to reconstruct the surface under test. In this paper, we discuss two aspects of this principle: first, a new iterative algorithm for shape reconstruction using surface normal data is introduced, and second, some rules of thumb for the experimental design of inspection systems are derived from the investigation of the normal field induced by measurement.

1 Introduction

Let us consider our knowledge about object surfaces from a technical and visual perspective. There are two aspects we can distinguish: the reflectance and the shape.

Once the bidirectional reflectance distribution function (BRDF) for every point of the surface is known, all information about the reflectance properties of the surface is available. The BRDF as a function of the geometric arrangements of the illumination and the observation relative to the surface normal. It describes how bright the surface will appear in proportion to a given irradiance. Many types of automated visual inspection methods for industrial surfaces employ the knowledge of the BRDF implicitly.

Other surface properties that can be evaluated are geometric properties, which ultimately describe the object's shape. The knowledge about this aspect is usually represented through an object model. The simplest form of such a model is a 3D point cloud, which consists of the raw data,i.e., 3D points of the objects's surface, that are obtained directly through the measurement process. The problem of finding a more appropriate model for given raw data is one of the fundamental problems for the reconstruction of 3D objects in computer graphics [Rem03, Hop94]. In the context of industrial automated visual inspection systems, we can stress at least two inspection tasks considering object shape—first: how well fits the global geometry of the object under test into its designed shape, and second: is there a local object deformation.

How do these aspects appear in the context of the considered inspection task, the inspection of specular surfaces? The at least partially specular nature of the objects under test implies the validity of the law of geometric optic reflection. This knowledge is the only assumptions we will take into account. Hence, for specular surfaces, the BRDF is well known. For partially specular surfaces, it is possible to model the reflection through a specular and a diffuse component. For many types of practically relevant surfaces, it is sufficient for the automated visual inspection to employ the well known *Phong shading model*, which assumes a perfectly diffuse reflection component and a specular component that decays polynomially from the ideal specular direction [Pho75]. In either case, it is assumed that it is possible to determine the direction of the specular reflection.

For the shape from specular reflection problem, we will assume that the reflectance properties of the objects under test are known and we will focus on the determination of the object shape. The main challenge in the field of automated visual inspection of specular surfaces can be stated as follows: how can we gather information about a surface only by assuming its specular property? With *deflectometry* we denote the family of such methods, evaluating reflected images of a priori known patterns, for specular shape information retrieval. According to this definition, *shape from specular reflection* is a special case of deflectometry, focusing only on 3D-shape reconstruction, whereas other aspects of deflectometry, like the estimation of surface deviations, are ignored.

The basic deflectometric principle can be described as follows: a presumably distorted (deflected) image of a well known and calibrated scene or light source L is captured with an image acquisition device C such that the light path includes the unknown specular surface S, cf. Figure 1.1. Knowing the intrinsic and extrinsic parameters of the camera, the light source, and the image acquisition constellation, it is possible to obtain normals of the unknown surface. Thereby the mapping l_r from sight ray to scene point—the deflectometric measurement—is usually done

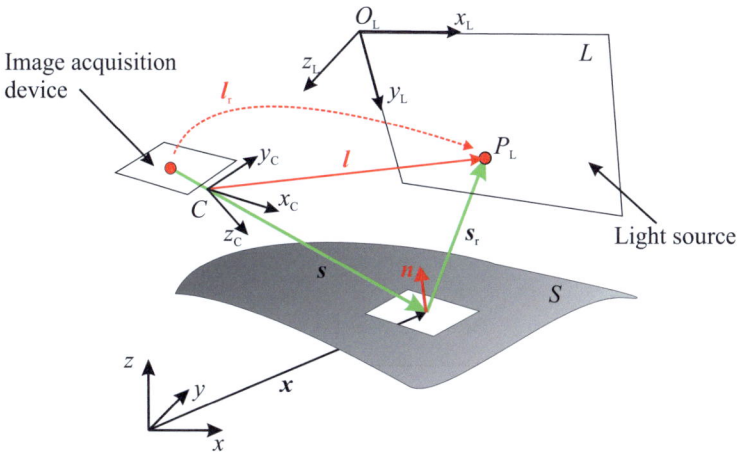

Figure 1.1: General geometric setup for deflectometric inspection.

by a unique coding of the scene positions. It is well known that the shape from specular reflection problem for such a simple setup is mathematically ill-posed and additional knowledge for the regularization of this problem is required [Bal08].

1.1   Contributions and Structure

There are two main contributions, which structure the report at hand:

1. A novel approach for the reconstruction problem for specular surfaces is given in Section 2. Solving a nonlinear Poisson equation iteratively, by means of finite element methods, yields a robust and fast converging method for industrial inspection tasks.

2. It is well known, that observing specular surfaces in the deflectometric manner yields to normal-fields [Bal08]. Examing those fields is fruitful for the experimental design of specular inspection systems. The answer to the question, where to place the camera and the screen in such a setup, is given in Section 3.

2 Shape from Specular Reflection

Because of the assumption that the reflection law holds for each surface point, the following relation

$$n = \frac{s}{\|s\|} - \frac{s_r}{\|s_r\|} = \hat{s} - \hat{s}_r$$

between the sight ray s to the surface S, the reflected ray s_r, and the local surface normal n holds (vectors of unit length are marked by an additional hat, i.e. $\|\hat{x}\| = 1$). With $s_r = l - s$ (see Figure 1.1), from equation 2 follows the relation 2.1 between possible surface normals [1] n_m due to the measurement and the measurement $l(u)$ itself, with $u \in U \subset \mathbb{R}^2$ for all $x \in \Omega$ with $\Omega = \{x | x \in \mathbb{R}^3 \wedge P(x) \subseteq U\}$:

$$n_m(x) = \hat{x} - \widehat{l - x} = \frac{x}{\|x\|} - \frac{l(P(x)) - x}{\|l(P(x)) - x\|} =: m(x, l(P(x))). \quad (2.1)$$

Here $P : \mathbb{R}^3 \to \mathbb{R}^2$ denotes the projection $P(x) := (\frac{x_1}{x_3}, \frac{x_2}{x_3})^\top$, $x = (x_1, x_2, x_3)^\top$, u points in the image plane of the camera, and Ω describes the cameras sight cone.

Note that for all $x \in S$ and for all undisturbed measurement,

$$\hat{n}(x) = \hat{n}_m(x) \quad (2.2)$$

must hold. For all $\tilde{x} \in \Omega \backslash S$, $\hat{n}_m(\tilde{x})$ is a possible surface normal to a hypothetical surface $\tilde{S}$ in the sense that $\tilde{S}$ would lead to the same deflectometric measurement $l(u)$ as S, cf. Figure 2.

We can summarize: the deflectometric measurement establishes a normal field $\hat{n}_m(x)$ so that the *shape from specular reflection* problem reads as: find the very surface which fits into this measured normal field.

2.1 Shape Reconstruction for Surface Graph Representations

The surface S can be described as graph of a function $f : (x, y) \to f(x, y)$, $\mathbb{R}^2 \supset \Omega_{xy} \mapsto \mathbb{R}$ using the parametrization

$$S = \{(x, y, z)^\top | z = f(x, y)\}, \quad \hat{n} = \frac{1}{\sqrt{(\partial_x f)^2 + (\partial_y f)^2 + 1}} \begin{pmatrix} -\partial_x f \\ -\partial_y f \\ 1 \end{pmatrix}. \quad (2.3)$$

---

[1] The induced normal field

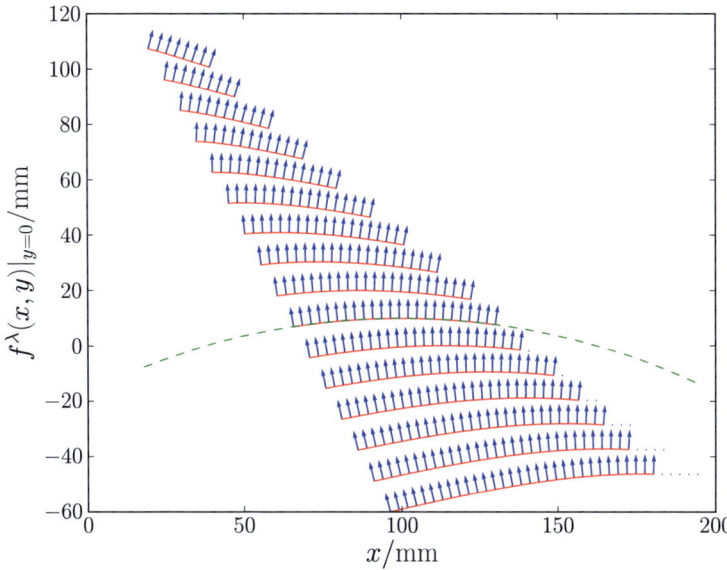

Figure 2.1: Example of solution manifold: hypothetical surfaces $\tilde{S}$ (solid lines) and real surface S (dashed line) are presented as family of function graphs f^λ.

For each surface point, Equation (2.2) must hold. This leads to the nonlinear deflectometric partial differential equation (PDE)

$$-\nabla f(x,y) = \begin{pmatrix} \hat{n}_{\mathrm{m},1}/\hat{n}_{\mathrm{m},3} \\ \hat{n}_{\mathrm{m},2}/\hat{n}_{\mathrm{m},3} \end{pmatrix} =: \boldsymbol{q}(x,y,f) = \begin{pmatrix} q_1(x,y,f(x,y)) \\ q_2(x,y,f(x,y)) \end{pmatrix}. \qquad (2.4)$$

Many deflectometric reconstruction approaches use a linear variant of this equation, see for example Massig [Mas01], which implicitly leeds to some regularization for selecting the *correct* normals $\hat{\boldsymbol{n}}_{\mathrm{s}}$ to the real surface out of the normal field $\hat{\boldsymbol{n}}_{\mathrm{m}}$ [2]:

$$\zeta : (x,y)^\top \mapsto \hat{\boldsymbol{n}}_{\mathrm{s}}, \quad \mathbb{R}^2 \to \mathbb{R}^3, \quad \hat{\boldsymbol{n}}_{\mathrm{s}}(x_0,y_0) \in \{\hat{\boldsymbol{n}}_{\mathrm{m}}(x,y,z) \mid x = x_0, y = y_0\}.$$

---

[2]Selecting the correct normals in this sense is commonly done by a stereo approach [KKH04, PT04], which therefore can be thought of as a linearizion process due to the elemination of the $f(x,y)$ dependency of the projected normal field $\boldsymbol{q}(x,y,f)$.

With the surface representation of Equation (2.3), this mapping yields the linear variant of problem (2.4) according to

$$-\nabla f(x,y) = \tilde{q}(x,y)\,.$$

Here we have to point out, that first selecting the normals $\hat{n}_s$ is not sufficient for reconstructing the unknown surface, since we need initial and/or border values to solve the reconstruction problem [WBB07]. Furthermore, the normal field is not necessarily curl free, which implies that a potential f might not exist and only an approximative solution can be obtained.

In [WMHB09] the author of this report gives a short overview on commonly used approaches for normal field integration methods in the context of deflectometry.

It is possible to directly utilize the nonlinear problem (2.4), which can be transformed into a scalar PDE by applying the divergence operator according to

$$-\Delta f(x,y) = \operatorname{div} \boldsymbol{q}(x,y,f)\,. \tag{2.5}$$

In the following, an iterative solution approach for this equation is presented. For common inspection problems one can observe that the right hand side of equation (2.5) shows a weak dependancy on $f(x,y)$. In Section 3 the vector gradient of the normal field in a given direction is further analyzed. To eliminate the dependancy on $f(x,y)$ in the divergence term, one can choose an estimate for the surface. This can be done in several ways. First: model driven, because in industrial inspection tasks we always know the object we are inspecting and one is mainly interested in shape deviations. Second: it is possible to linearize the problem by approximating the surface $f(x,y)$ with a plane; in an upcoming paper we will show that with a well-designed inspection setup, the plane cut through the normal field leads to a negligible error for visual inspection tasks. Third: a linearization of problem (2.5) could be achieved by successive solving the following linear *Neumann* problems for $i > 0$:

$$
\begin{aligned}
-\Delta f_i(x,y) &= \operatorname{div} \boldsymbol{q}(x,y,f_{i-1})\,, & (x,y) &\in \Omega_{xy}\,, \\
\langle \nabla f_i(x,y) \mid \hat{o} \rangle &= \langle -\boldsymbol{q}(x,y,f_{i-1}) \mid \hat{o} \rangle\,, & (x,y) &\in \partial\Omega_{xy}\,,
\end{aligned}
\tag{2.6}
$$

with the initial surface

$$f_0(x,y) = c(x,y)\,,$$

where $c(x,y)$ could be chosen as constant function $c(x,y) = const$ and $\hat{o}$ denotes the outer normal to Ω_{xy}, $(\langle \nabla f_i \mid \hat{o} \rangle = \partial f_i/\partial \hat{o})$ whith the scalar product $\langle \cdot \mid \cdot \rangle$.

From the theory of partial differential equations, it is well known that a variational formulation for the problem (2.6) exists [BL05], which allows weak solutions. This means, instead of directly solving (2.4), one is looking for a solution

$f_i(x, y) \in \mathrm{H}^1(\Omega_{xy})$ of the equivalent variational problem [Ste08]

$$a(f_i, \nu) = Q(\nu), \quad \forall \nu \in V_0, \tag{2.7}$$

with the bilinear form

$$a(f_i, \nu) = \int_{\Omega_{xy}} \langle \nabla f_i \mid \nabla \nu \rangle \, \mathrm{d}\boldsymbol{x}, \tag{2.8}$$

and the linear form

$$Q(\nu) = \int_{\Omega_{xy}} \mathrm{div}(\boldsymbol{q}) \, \nu \, \mathrm{d}\boldsymbol{x} - \int_{\partial\Omega_{xy}} \langle \boldsymbol{q} \mid \hat{\boldsymbol{o}} \rangle \, \nu \, \mathrm{d}o. \tag{2.9}$$

Here $\mathrm{H}^1(\Omega_{xy})$ denotes the Sobolev H^1 space over Ω_{xy}, V_0 the space of test functions, and $\mathrm{d}\boldsymbol{o} = \hat{\boldsymbol{o}} \, \mathrm{d}o$ an element on $\partial\Omega_{xy}$.

For symmetric and positive bilinear forms, like equation (2.8), the variational problem (2.7) is equivalent to the following minimum problem:

$$J(f_i) = \inf_{g \in \mathrm{H}^1} J(g), \quad f_i \in \mathrm{H}^1(\Omega_{xy}),$$

with the *Ritz* energy functional

$$J(g) = \frac{1}{2} a(g, g) - Q(g).$$

Inserting equations (2.8) and (2.9) in the energy functional yields

$$J(g) = \frac{1}{2} \int_{\Omega_{xy}} \langle \nabla g \mid \nabla g \rangle \, \mathrm{d}\boldsymbol{x} - \int_{\Omega_{xy}} \mathrm{div}(\boldsymbol{q}) \, g \, \mathrm{d}\boldsymbol{x} + \int_{\partial\Omega_{xy}} \langle \boldsymbol{q} \mid \hat{\boldsymbol{o}} \rangle \, g \, \mathrm{d}o.$$

With integration by parts of the divergence term according to

$$-\int_{\Omega_{xy}} \mathrm{div}(\boldsymbol{q}) \, g \, \mathrm{d}\boldsymbol{x} = \int_{\Omega_{xy}} \langle \boldsymbol{q} \mid \nabla g \rangle \, \mathrm{d}\boldsymbol{x} - \int_{\partial\Omega_{xy}} \langle \boldsymbol{q} \mid \hat{\boldsymbol{o}} \rangle \, g \, \mathrm{d}o,$$

the functional becomes

$$J(g) = \int_{\Omega_{xy}} \frac{1}{2} \|\nabla g\|^2 + \langle \nabla g \mid \boldsymbol{q} \rangle \, \mathrm{d}\boldsymbol{x}.$$

Adding the positive constant term $\frac{1}{2} \int_{\Omega_{xy}} \|\boldsymbol{q}\|^2 \, \mathrm{d}\boldsymbol{x}$ leads to the final result [3]

$$J(g) = \frac{1}{2} \int_{\Omega_{xy}} \|-\nabla g - \boldsymbol{q}\|^2 \, \mathrm{d}\boldsymbol{x}. \tag{2.10}$$

---

[3]This will not change the minimum of the functional $J(g)$; the integral depends only on the measurement $\hat{\boldsymbol{n}}_{\mathrm{m}}$.

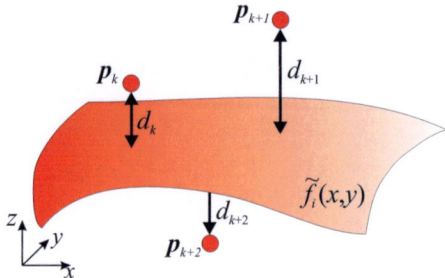

Figure 2.2: Adjusting the surface $\tilde{f}_i$ according to minimal distances to given points.

Solving the variational formulation (2.7) of the Neumann problem yields a normal adaption problem: find the function $f_i \in \{g \mid g \in \mathrm{H}^1\}$ so that the normals to its graph fits best to the given measurement. This is the deeper justification for applying the divergence operator in equation (2.5). A second justification follows from the *Hodge* decomposition of a vector field $\boldsymbol{F} = \nabla\varphi + \nabla \times \boldsymbol{A} + \boldsymbol{H}$, which deconstructs the field $\boldsymbol{F}$ in a rotational free part φ (the scalar potential), a divergence free part $\boldsymbol{A}$ (the vector potential) and a harmonic component $\boldsymbol{H}$, cf. [TLHD03]. Applying the decomposition to the measurement dependend field $\boldsymbol{q}$, one can interpret Equation (2.5) as a normalization of the vector field $\boldsymbol{q}$ to ensure integrability, that is the existence of the scalar potential f.

For solving problem (2.6) we propose finite-element-methods (FEM) [Sol06] due to the following reasons:

1. By solving the corresponding variational problem (2.7), weak solutions can be obtained, which allows the reconstruction of surfaces that are not necessarily differentiable in a classical sense.

2. FEM implies a triangulation of the region of interest Ω_{xy}, so that irregular borders and regions, where the determination of the normal-field fails, can be managed.

3. FEM is a computational efficient method due to ansatz functions with local support.

4. Adaptive mesh refinement methods can be employed.

5. For further computation speed up, multigrid methods can be applied.

6. FEM is an industrial standard for solving PDEs, so that robust software packages do exist.

Because the deflectometric reconstruction problem for a monocular setup is ill-conditioned in a mathematical sense, further information is required. This means initial and/or border values are needed. Some common regularization procedures are described in [WMHB09]. Having additional surface points, its possible to combine this information with the solution of equation 2.6 in an optimal manner for the selection of the correct surface out of the solution manifold. The surface f_i is a solution of a linear problem, therefore $\tilde{f}_i = f_i + const$ will also solve the Neumann problem (2.6). Hence, it is possible to place the surface $\tilde{f}_i$ so that the following distances $d_k = \left\| z_k - \tilde{f}_i(x_k, y_k) \right\|$ from points $p_k = (x_k, y_k, z_k)^\top$ to the surface $\tilde{f}_i$ are minimal, cf. Figure 2.2:

$$\frac{1}{2} \sum_k d_k{}^2 = \frac{1}{2} \sum_k \left\| p_{k,z} - \tilde{f}_i(x_k, y_k) \right\|^2 \rightarrow \min . \tag{2.11}$$

This leads to an optimal solution in a twofold sense: first, regarding the surface normals, the normals to the solution surface fit optimally to the measured normal field $\hat{n}_m$, cf. equation (2.10), second regarding position dependent information, the surface itself has minimal distance to measured surface points p_k, cf. Equation (2.11). This approach allows the combination of surface gradient with position sensitive methods.

Finally, we summarize our approach for the shape reconstruction problem in Algorithm 2.1.

In Figure 2.1 the solution of Equation (2.7) for partially specular objects is shown. Here the initial solution f_0 was a plane. Shown are the reconstructed surfaces f_4 after the fourth iteration according to Algorithm 2.1. Even in strong convex and concave regions a clear solution is obtainted, e.g., the fork rakes.

3   Experimental Design

In Section 2, the connection of deflectometric measurement and its induced normal field is derived, cf. (2.1). The question is still open: which is an optimal geometric setup for deflectometric measurement with regard to normal field characteristics. Some of the characteristics are presented by simulating a realistic example, like the inspection of truck side mirrors.

The example surface is the following sphere:

$$S = \{(x, y, z)^\top \mid z = \sqrt{200^2 - (x - 100)^2 - y^2} + 190\} .$$

Algorithm 2.1 Iterative specular shape reconstruction.

1: Given: a region of interest $\Omega \subset \mathbb{R}^3$, the induced normal field $\hat{\boldsymbol{n}}_{\mathrm{m}}(\Omega)$ and a non-empty set of points $\{\boldsymbol{p}_k \,|\, \boldsymbol{p}_k \in \Omega\} \neq \emptyset$.

2: Select $f_1 = const.$ // Information about the measurement setup can be used.

3: Select termination condition ϵ.

4: Setup the FEM system (integrating scheme, linear solver, basis functions).

5: **repeat**

6:    $f_{i-1} \leftarrow f_i$

7:    Generate a mesh M on $\Omega \cap f_{i-1} \rightarrow (\Omega_{\mathrm{xy}}, M)$.

8:    Calculate $\mathrm{div}\, \boldsymbol{q}$ at the nodes of M.

9:    Calculate $\boldsymbol{q}$ at the edge nodes of M.

10:    Solve problem (2.6) with FEM on $M \rightarrow f_i$.

11:    Solve problem (2.11) for f_i and $\{\boldsymbol{p}_k\} \rightarrow f_i$.

12: **until** $\|f_i - f_{i-1}\| < \epsilon$

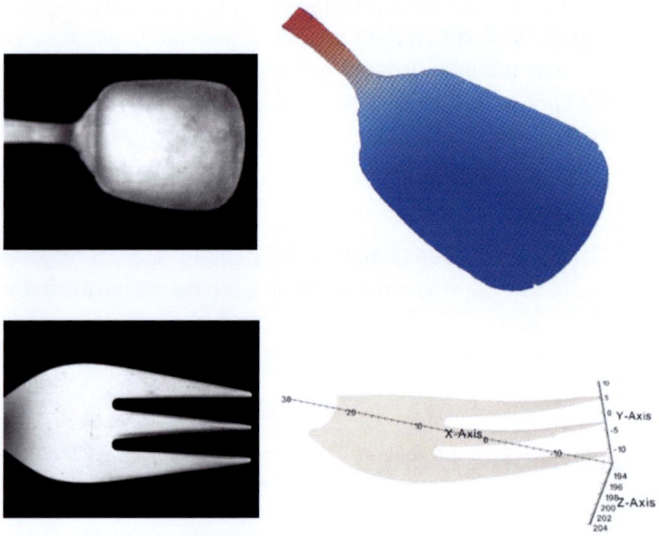

Figure 2.3: Real world examples (left column) and corresponding FEM solutions of Equation (2.5) (right column).

Image acquistion device: camera with focallength $= 30\,\mathrm{mm}$, pixelsize $= 6\,\mu\mathrm{m}$, resolution $= 1000 \times 1000$ pixel. The camera is located at $(0, 0, 150)^\top\mathrm{mm}$ and looks at $(150, 0, 0)\mathrm{mm}$.

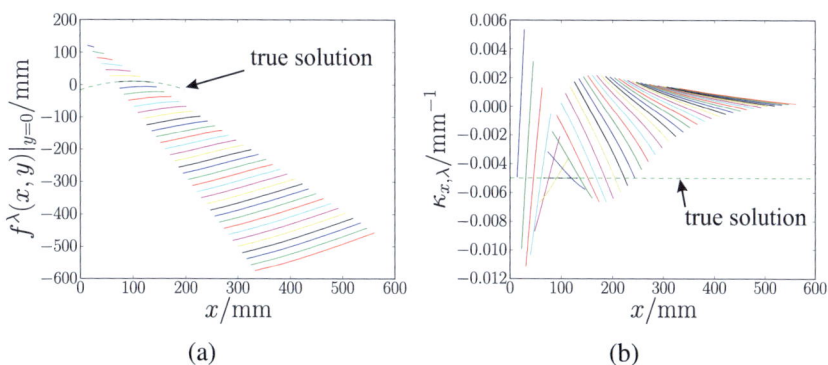

Figure 3.1: Example of a solution manifold (a) and the corresponding curvature (b), all solving the problem of Equation (2.5).

Light source: LCD with pixelsize $= 0.294\,\mathrm{mm}$, resolution $= 1024 \times 768\,\mathrm{pixel}$.

For this setup, examples of the solution manifold are shown in Figure 3.1(a). The family of solutions $\{f^\lambda\}$ can be obtained with several runs of Algorithm 2.1 with distinct regularization points p_λ. In Figure 3.1(b) the principal curvature in x-direction $\kappa_{x,\lambda}$ for these solutions f^λ are shown.

We can observe:

- All solutions are located in the sight cone Ω of the camera. Corresponding points at different surfaces f^λ are connected via camera sight rays, in other words, there exists a scaling.

- Due to the LC-Display being located at a finite position, the solutions get rotated while traveling along a sight ray.

- The shape, i.e., the surface curvature changes along the sight rays. Along a sight ray, points with equal local curvature do not exist. Thus all solutions have different shape. This observation is important when dealing with the uniqueness of the stereo based normal estimation problem.

- At infinity, all solutions converge to an ellipsoid with infinite radius, i.e., if we place our object under test far enough away from the inspecting system, selecting the correct surface is an easy task due to the small change of the surface shape with distance. This can be described as regularization by approximation.

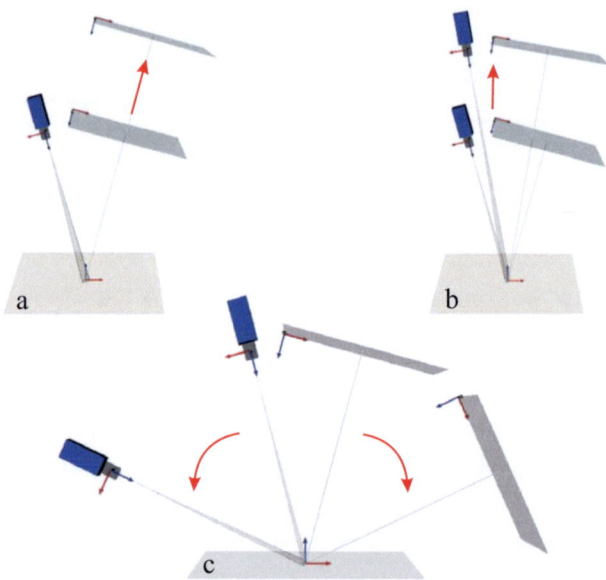

Figure 3.2: Inspection setup. Shown are three sets of parameter variation, see text.

The dependency of the solution manifold from geometrical setup can be evaluated by looking at the vector gradient of the normal field in a given direction v

$$V = J_n(\hat{n}_m) \cdot v \,,$$

with the Jacobi matrix J_n of the normal field.

We will evaluate the norm of V for three parameter sets of the geometrical inspection setup, cf. Figure 3.2.

In the first setup, the position of the LC-Display changes, whereas the position of camera and object remained fixed. The camera's distance to the xy-plane is 500mm. In Figure 3.3, the norm of the vector gradient in direction of the optical camera axis $\|J_n[\hat{n}_m] \cdot \hat{e}_z\|$ is shown for three positions of the LCD, thereby z_{LCD} denotes the distance of the LCD center to the xy-plane and z_c the distance from the optical camera center along the optical axis in camera coordinates, cf. Figure 3.2(a).

With increasing distance of the LCD from the object plane, the change of the normal field decreases. The norm of the vector gradient converges to the same value for all LCD positions. This normal field characteristic is shown in Figure 3.1(b)

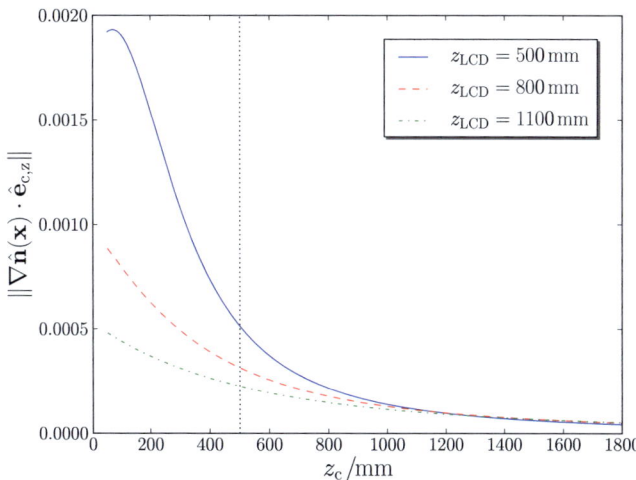

Figure 3.3: Norm of vector gradient of the normal field against distance from optical camera center along a sight ray for different LCD positions, for the setup depicted in Figure 3.2(a).

by means of principal curvature. The larger the distance of the LCD to the object, the smaller the change of the normal field along a sight ray.

In Figure 3.4 the norm of the vector gradient in direction of the optical camera axis is shown for three distances of the whole sensor to the object, z_0 denotes thereby the sensor distance, cf. Figure 3.2(b). The norm of the vector gradient does not differ significantly for the three sensor positions, but dereases with increase of z_0.

Finally in Figure 3.5 the norm of the vector gradient in direction of the optical camera axis is shown for several polar angles ϑ, cf. Figure 3.2(c). With increasing polar angle the maximum of the normal field change moves to greater values of z_c. If one want a maximal change in the normal field, e.g., for determining surface points with a stereo approach, a medium polar angle like $45°$ leads to good results. In opposite, if one needs a very small normal change, the smallest possible polar angel should be selected. Small changes are favored in cases like the regularization by approximaten approach. With a plane cut through the normal field, only litte errors with respect to the *correct* normals are made in that case.

Following rules of thumbs for the experimental design of inspection systems for specular surfaces can be given:

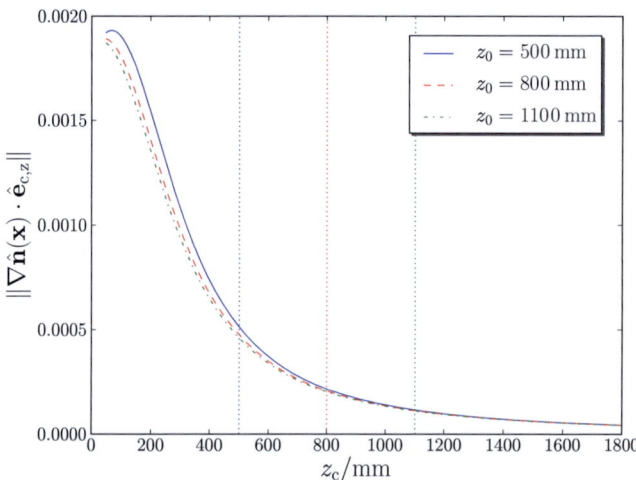

Figure 3.4: Norm of vector gradient of the normal field against distance from optical camera center along a sight ray for different sensor positions, for the setup depicted in Figure 3.2(b).

1. Determining surface points with a stereo setup, e.g., for the regularization of the shape from specular reflection problem, needs strong varying normal fields along search rays. The stereo method imply the determination of normal disparities like $\|\hat{n}_{\mathrm{m}}^1 - \hat{n}_{\mathrm{m}}^2\|$ for the normals of the two measurements. For further details see [WI93, BS03, KKH04, PT04]. Large disparities can be achieved through:

   - Small camera to object and small LCD to object distances.
   - Angle between camera / LCD axis and mean object normal about $45°$.

2. Determining surface normals with high precision is supported through small changes in the normal field. This allows approximation approaches for the selection of the correct normals, even through plan cuts. To achieve small changes one can select:

   - Large system to object distances.
   - Large LCD to object distances.
   - Small angles between camera / LCD axis and mean object normal.

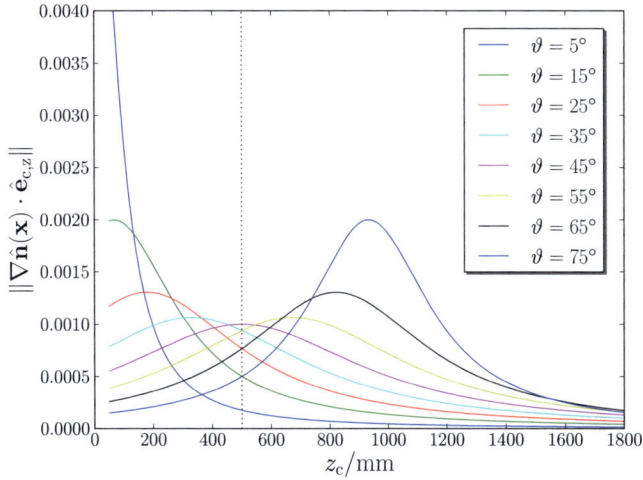

Figure 3.5: Norm of vector gradient of the normal field against distance from optical camera center along a sight ray for different polar angles, for the setup depicted in Figure 3.2(c).

4   Conclusions and Further Work

In this report we presented a new approach for shape reconstruction using surface normal data. It is shown, that an optimal reconstruction can be achieved due to the implicit employment of two minimizing problems. The normals to the reconstructed surface fits best to the measured normals and the surface has minimal distance to given regularization points. This allows the combination of surface gradient with position sensitive methods, especially by the inspection of partially specular surfaces. Furthermore, the proposed approach is insensitive to unbiased disturbances of normal and position data.

Two main aspects regarding normal field sensitivity for the system setup for automated inspection of specular surfaces can be considered: first, determining points on specular surfaces needs strong varying normal fields along search directions, and second, surface normals can be estimated with high precision in regions with small changes. For both inspection tasks, some rules of thumb for the experimental design of the inspection systems are given. This insight can be achieved by the investigation of the changes in the normal field induced by measurement.

In an upcoming publication we present an extension of our proposed algorithm to the inspection of complex surfaces, which requires the combination of several measurements from distinct positions.

The characteristics of the induced normal field will be further investigated, above all with regard to the global uniqueness problem of specular stereo regularization.

Bibliography

[Bal08]   Jonathan Balzer. *Regularisierung des Deflektometrieproblems – Grundlagen und Anwendung*. PhD thesis, Universität Karlsruhe (TH), 2008.

[BL05]   Pavel Bochev and R. B. Lehoucq. On the Finite Element Solution of the Pure Neumann Problem. *SIAM Rev.*, 47:50–66, 2005.

[BS03]   Thomas Bonfort and Peter Sturm. Voxel Carving for Specular Surfaces. In *Proc. ICCV*, pages 591–596, 2003.

[Hop94]   Hugues Hoppe. *Surface Reconstruction from Unorganized Points*. PhD thesis, Dept. of Computer Science and Engineering, University of Washington, 1994.

[KKH04]   Markus Knauer, Jürgen Kaminski, and Gerd Häusler. Phase Measuring Deflectometry: a new approch to measure specular free-form surfaces. In Wolfgang Osten and Mitsuo Takeda, editors, *Optical Metrology in Production Engineering*, volume 5457, pages 366–376, Strasbourg, France, 2004. Proc. SPIE.

[Mas01]   Jürgen H. Massig. Deformation measurement on specular surfaces by simple means. *Optical Engineering*, 40(10):2315–2318, 2001.

[Pho75]   Bui Tuong Phong. Illumination for Computer Generated Pictures. *Communications of the ACM*, 18(6):311–317, 1975.

[PT04]   Marcus Petz and Rainer Tutsch. Rasterreflexions-Photogrammetrie zur Messung spiegelnder Oberflächen. *Technisches Messen*, 71:389–397, 2004.

[Rem03]   Fabio Remondino. From point cloud to surface: the modeling and visualization problem. In *International Archives of Photogrammetry, Remote Sensing and Spatial Information Sciences, Vol. XXXIV-5/W10*, 2003.

[Sol06]   Pavel Solin. *Partial Differential Equations and the Finite Element Method*. Pure and applied mathematics. Wiley-Interscience, 2006.

[Ste08]   Olaf Steinbach. *Numerical Approximation Methods for Elliptic Boundary Value Problems: Finite and Boundary Elements*. Springer, New York, 2008.

[TLHD03]   Yiying Tong, Santiago Lombeyda, Anil N. Hirani, and Mathieu Desbrun. Discrete Multiscale Vector Field Decomposition. In *SIGGRAPH '03: ACM SIGGRAPH 2003 Papers*, pages 445–452. ACM, 2003.

[WBB07]   Stefan Werling, Jonathan Balzer, and Jürgen Beyerer. Initial Value Estimation for Robust Deflectometric Reconstruction. In *Proceedings of 8th International Conference on Optical 3-D Measurement Techniques, Zürich*, 2007.

[WI93]   Zengfu Wang and Seiji Inokuchi. Determining Shape of Specular Surfaces. In *The 8th Scandinavian Conference on Image Analysis*, pages 1187–1194, 1993.

[WMHB09]   Stefan Werling, Michael Mai, Michael Heizmann, and Jürgen Beyerer. Inspection of Specular and Partially Specular Surfaces. *Metrology and Measurement Systems*, 16(3):415–431, 2009.

Feature-Based Probabilistic Data Association and Tracking - A Novel Approach Capable of Tracking Objects under Splits, Merges and Occlusions

Michael Grinberg

Vision and Fusion Laboratory
Institute for Anthropomatics
Karlsruhe Institute of Technology (KIT), Germany
michael.grinberg@ies.uka.de

Technical Report IES-2009-11

Abstract: Uncertainties in the sensor data such as measurement noise, false detections caused by clutter, as well as merged, split, incomplete or missed detections due to a sensor malfunction or occlusions (both due to the limited sensor field of view and objects in the scene) make multi-target tracking a very complicated task. Thus one of the big challenges is track management and correct data association between detections and tracks. In this contribution we present an algorithm for visual detection and tracking of multiple extended targets under occlusions and split and merge effects. Unlike most of the state-of-the-art approaches we utilize low-level information integrating it in a unified approach based on a threshold-free probabilistic conception. The introduced scheme makes it possible to utilize information about composition of the measurements gained through tracking of dedicated feature points in the image and resolves data association ambiguities in a soft decision using a globally optimal probabilistic data association approach. Beside existence evolution consideration we also exploit the spatial and temporal relationship between stably tracked points and tracked objects, which along with observability analysis, allows us for reconstruction of compatible measurements and thus correct track update even in cases of splits, merges and partial occlusions of the tracked targets.

1 Introduction

Most of the vision-based vehicle detection and tracking systems presented in the field of driver assistance systems in the last few decades were focusing on the front-looking applications and particularly on highway driving applications. Many of them make use of various presumptions and restrictions regarding possible objects' motion profiles and their lateral position (e.g. relative to the tracked lane markings), as well as assumptions about symmetrical appearance, shadows etc. In many other applications such as intersection assistance systems or side-looking pre-crash systems, most of those restrictions and assumptions do not apply any more. Many different object orientations have to be taken into account. Combined with a large variety of object types and large region of interest, this makes it extremely challenging to detect and track objects based on their appearance in real time. For the realization of such applications that are capable of a robust and reliable object detection, a generic approach has to be chosen. Object hypotheses are often generated from the range data that are the result of binocular stereo or motion stereo processing. Finding corresponding structures in two video images and reconstructing their depth using knowledge of mutual orientation of both viewpoints, delivers range data, the so-called depth maps. After extracting a depth map, road location is estimated and points belonging to the ground plane are removed. Spatial clustering of the remaining three-dimensional points delivers point clouds which are used as an input in the data association step.

Due to the noisy range estimation process, combined with the well known problems of stereo vision systems such as difficulties of depth estimation in homogeneous image regions and gross depth errors in regions with regular patterns, the results of clustering may vary from frame to frame leading to incomplete, split, merged or missing object measurements as well as to phantom objects. Further problem are incomplete measurements due to partial occlusions and limitations of the field of view (FoV) of the sensors. Visible dimensions of objects entering or leaving FoV or becoming occluded may change rapidly, which combined with a centroid-based object tracking approach leads to strongly biased object position and dynamics estimation.

The basic idea of this contribution is depicted in Figure 1.1. Instead of "blind" association between detections and tracks a novel detection-by-tracking algorithm is proposed which allows for a correct reconstruction of appropriate detection based on a feature-based probabilistic data association scheme. It utilizes information gained by tracking object points in the image (and in 3D space) for creation of point-to-track affiliation information. This information is then used for reconstruction of appropriate measurements and allows for a correct update of the object's position and dynamics in spite of partial occlusions, splits and merges.

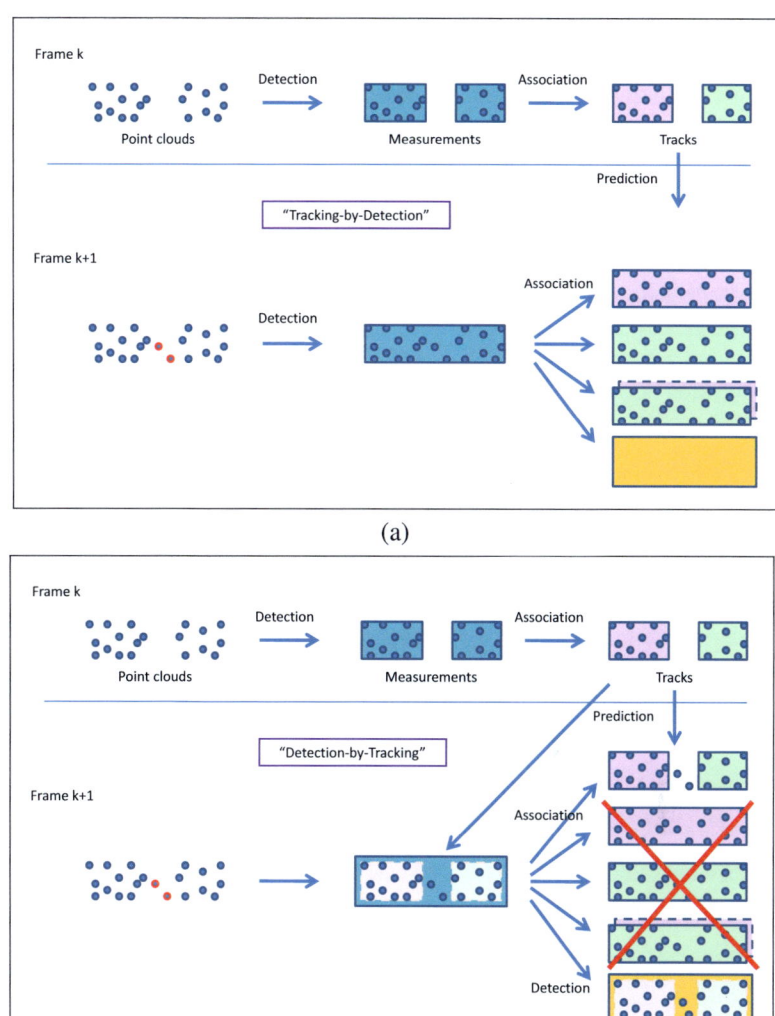

(a)

(b)

Figure 1.1: (a) Wrong data association in standard tracking-by-detection approach in case of a clutter-based cluster merge. (b) Basic idea of the FBPDA: utilization of the information about point-to-track affiliation for "reconstruction" of appropriate measurements for the tracking (detection-by-tracking).

Track initialization and termination as well as data association are done using a globally optimal probabilistic approach which takes into account object existence and observability probability and implements a track-before-detect approach. Additionally, we propose an observability treatment scheme utilizing a grid-based object representation with occupancy and occlusion modeling for each cell. This allows for a dedicated observability and occlusion handling.

The proposed Feature Based Probabilistic Data Association and Tracking Algorithm (FBPDA) consists of four major steps: time forward prediction, association between detections and tracks, reconstruction of composite measurements from associated point clouds and innovation. These four steps are described in Sections 3, 4, 5 and 6 respectively. The overall framework for visual object tracking is introduced in Section 2.

2   Overall system description

The overall video-based object tracking framework used in this work is depicted in Figure 2.1. It has been built in the course of the EU funded project APROSYS

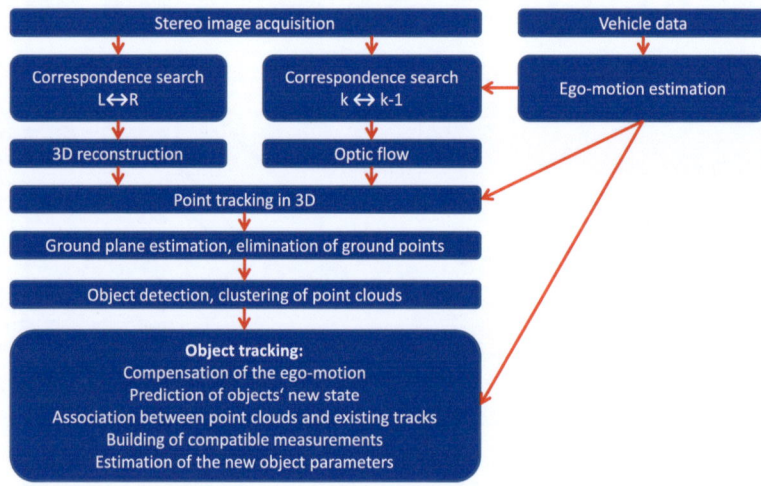

Figure 2.1: Overall framework for visual object detection and tracking

[APR]. The goal was detection of imminent side collisions to enable timely activation of novel occupant protection systems [TZM+08]. The sensor system under consideration here is a side-looking stereo video camera [TWG07]. Ego-motion estimation and compensation is done using vehicle odometry data which was shown to deliver sufficient accuracy even for the structure-from-motion task [WPGW07]. Detection and tracking of the feature points is realized similar to the system proposed in [FRBG05]. Up to 3000 feature points are tracked simultaneously in 3-D space using Kalman Filters. Their six-dimensional state vectors $[x, y, z, v_x, v_y, v_z]^T$ are estimated from the stereo depth measurements as well as from their displacement in the image between consecutive frames (optic flow). The measurement vector is thus $[u, v, d]^T$ with image coordinates (u, v) and feature depth d.

After elimination of the ground points, the remaining points are clustered to the point clouds that give measurements for object tracking. Object parameters are estimated using an Extended Kalman Filter. Internally, objects are modeled as cuboids with a centroid (x, y, z), dimensions (l, w, h), geometrical orientation ϕ, motion orientation φ, speed v, acceleration a and yaw rate $\dot{\varphi}$. This corresponds to the Constant Yaw Rate Model with Acceleration, which has proved to deliver the best performance in the case of a side-looking system [RGW08]. Due to the fact that often only a part of an object is visible to the sensors, orientation of the object's motion may differ from the estimated geometrical orientation. Object's geometric orientation and dimensions are updated taking into account the occlusion information as described in Section 5.

For performing the association between the point clouds and the tracks and for the track state propagation we propose to use the Feature-Based Probabilistic Data Association and Tracking Algorithm (FBPDA) which is described in the following sections. For effective noise handling as well as for handling of split and merged point clouds FBPDA provides affiliation probabilities of each point to the current tracks. These affiliation probabilities are exploited in the course of the data association as well as for updating tracks' position, dynamics and dimensions.

For handling of occlusions we explicitly model and propagate targets' observability probability thus decoupling existence and visibility of the targets. Contrary to other approaches ([MES94], [MSL$^+$08]), we do not bundle two of the three possible states (○: "object existent and observable", ∅: "object existent but not observable" and P: "object non-existent" ("phantom track")) but model the object observability by means of a separate Markov chain with the states "object observable" and "object not observable" as depicted in Fig. 2.2(d). This leads to object state propagation scheme with three cross-coupled Markov chains as depicted in Fig. 2.3. One of the Markov chains is responsible for object existence propagation and implements an JIPDA scheme [ME02], the second one models dynamic object state propagation which is done using an Extended Kalman-Filter, and the third one is used for object observability modeling.

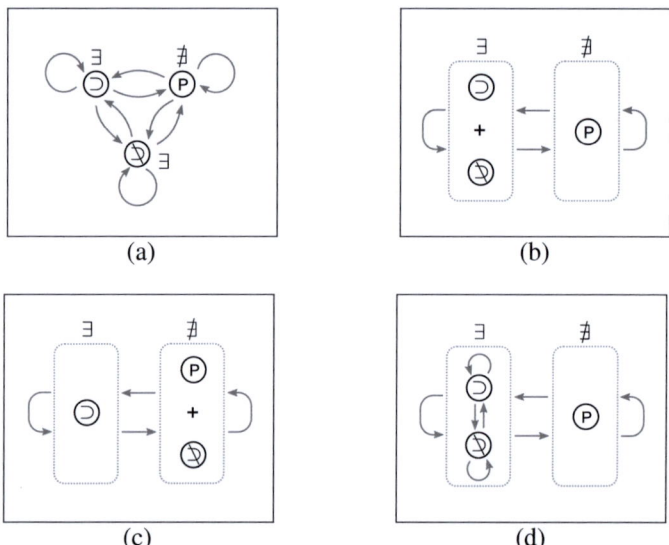

Figure 2.2: Markov chain based modeling of object existence and observability (a). The three possible track states ⊃, ⊅ and P (object existent and observable, object existent but not observable and object non-existent (phantom track)) can be bundled in different ways. One possibility is to bundle the two first states to the umbrella states "object existent" and "object non-existent" (∃ and ∄) as done in [MES94] (b). Another possibility is to model occluded objects as non-existent as done in [MSL⁺08] (c). This leads to existence-based track termination of occluded targets. FBPDA decouples existence and observability modeling object observability as a separate Markov chain (d).

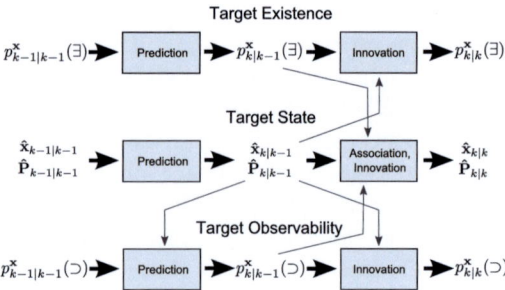

Figure 2.3: Three cross-coupled Markov chains used in the FBPDA

3 Time forward prediction

At each time step, after having performed the ego-motion compensation, we start by predicting the new track attributes. This includes prediction of the track's dynamic state as well as prediction of it's existence and observability probabilities. The FBPDA state prediction of a track is identical to the common Extended Kalman Filter prediction. The time forward prediction equations for the existence and non-existence probabilities $p^{\mathbf{x}}_{k|k-1}(\exists)$ and $p^{\mathbf{x}}_{k|k-1}(\nexists)$ of a track $\mathbf{x}$ are:

$$p^{\mathbf{x}}_{k|k-1}(\exists) = p^{\mathbf{x}}(\exists \to \exists) \cdot p^{\mathbf{x}}_{k-1|k-1}(\exists) + p^{\mathbf{x}}(\nexists \to \exists) \cdot p^{\mathbf{x}}_{k-1|k-1}(\nexists)$$

$$p^{\mathbf{x}}_{k|k-1}(\nexists) = 1 - p^{\mathbf{x}}_{k|k-1}(\exists)$$

with $p^{\mathbf{x}}_{k-1|k-1}(\exists)$ being the a-posteriori existence probability from the last frame and $p^{\mathbf{x}}(\exists \to \exists)$ and $p^{\mathbf{x}}(\nexists \to \exists)$ denoting the persistence and the birth probabilities of a track $\mathbf{x}$. The last two factors are used for modeling the spatial distribution of the target birth and death probabilities. This makes it possible to account e.g. for the fact that at the borders of the field of view and at far distances the birth probability is higher than right in front of the sensors.

For the computation of the observability probability and for the reconstruction of occluded measurements we use a grid-based 3-D representation of the targets. For each track $\mathbf{x}_i$, we define a 3-D grid with the origin at its centroid. The orientation of the grid is aligned with the track's orientation (cf. Fig. 3.1 (a)). Using this representation of predicted objects it is possible to calculate their appearance masks in the camera image $M^{\mathbf{x}_i}_A(u, v) \in \{0, 1\}$ by projecting the occupied grid cells into the image. The Appearance Probability Mask $M^{\mathbf{x}_i}_{p(A)}(u, v)$ for each track is given by

$$M^{\mathbf{x}_i}_{p(A)}(u, v) = p(A^{\mathbf{x}_i}(u, v)) = M^{\mathbf{x}_i}_A(u, v) \cdot p^{\mathbf{x}_i}_{k|k-1}(\exists)$$

where $A^{\mathbf{x}_i}(u, v)$ is the event of the track $\mathbf{x}_i$ appearing at the image position (u, v) and $p^{\mathbf{x}_i}_{k|k-1}(\exists)$ is the predicted existence probability of the track $\mathbf{x}_i$. By overlaying the appearance probability masks of all the objects lying in front of the object $\mathbf{x}_i$ we get the occlusion probability map for the respective object in the new frame (cf. Fig. 3.1 (b)). The occlusion probability $p^{\mathbf{x}_i}(\not\exists, u, v)$ at each pixel (u, v) is calculated as

$$p^{\mathbf{x}_i}(\not\exists, u, v) = p(\bigcup_{\mathbf{x}_r \in X^i_O} A^{\mathbf{x}_r}(u, v))$$

with X^i_O being set of the objects lying at the pixel position (u, v) in front of the object $\mathbf{x}_i$. After the occlusion probability map for an object is built, we can estimate the occlusion probability $p^{\mathbf{x}_i}(\not\exists, c)$ of the object's grid cells. This is done by

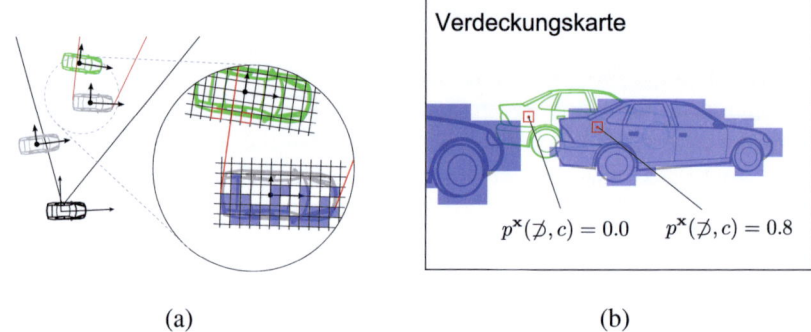

(a)   (b)

Figure 3.1: Grid-based object representation (a) and occlusion probability estimation for grid cells using occlusion map (b)

projecting the cell centers into the image and grabbing the corresponding value of the occlusion probability map as shown in the Fig. 3.1 (b).

Based on these probabilities we can calculate the observability transition probabilities $p^{\mathbf{x}_i}(\supset \to \supset)$, $p^{\mathbf{x}_i}(\supset \to \not\supset)$, $p^{\mathbf{x}_i}(\not\supset \to \supset)$ and $p^{\mathbf{x}_i}(\not\supset \to \not\supset)$ of a track and predict its observability probability and occlusion probability in the new frame:

$$p^{\mathbf{x}}_{k|k-1}(\supset) = p^{\mathbf{x}}(\supset \to \supset) \cdot p^{\mathbf{x}}_{k-1|k-1}(\supset) + p^{\mathbf{x}}(\not\supset \to \supset) \cdot p^{\mathbf{x}}_{k-1|k-1}(\not\supset)$$
$$p^{\mathbf{x}}_{k|k-1}(\not\supset) = 1 - p^{\mathbf{x}}_{k|k-1}(\supset) \,.$$

4 Data association between detections and tracks

Given multiple active tracks and multiple detections, there are often several assignment possibilities being more or less probable. Unlike other methods such as GNN, FBPDA does not choose one of these hypotheses for the innovation of a track, but considers all assignment possibilities in a soft decision. For this aim we define the set $X=\{X', \mathbf{x}_B, \copyright\}$ as the aggregation $X'=\{\mathbf{x}_1, \mathbf{x}_2, ..., \mathbf{x}_n\}$ of the n current tracks plus two special elements $\mathbf{x}_B$ representing a so far not known object and $\copyright$ representing a clutter source and the set $Z=\{Z', \mathbf{z}_\varnothing, \mathbf{z}_{\not\supset}, \mathbf{z}_\sharp\}$ as the aggregation $Z'=\{\mathbf{z}_1, \mathbf{z}_2, ..., \mathbf{z}_m\}$ of the m current point clouds plus three special elements $\mathbf{z}_\varnothing$, $\mathbf{z}_{\not\supset}$ and $\mathbf{z}_\sharp$. The element $\mathbf{z}_\varnothing$ stands for erroneously missed detection caused by sensor failure, $\mathbf{z}_{\not\supset}$ represents the correct absence of a detection because of occlusion of the target and $\mathbf{z}_\sharp$ the correct absence of a detection because of the target non-existence (death). The association between point clouds and tracks is modeled as a bipartite graph with edges $e : (\mathbf{x} \in X \mapsto \mathbf{z} \in Z)$ between elements of X and elements of Z. Assignments between two special elements are prohibited. A valid assignment hypothesis can thus contain six types of edges e:

- $\mathbf{x}_i \mapsto \mathbf{z}_j$: assumption that point cloud $\mathbf{z}_j$ has been caused by the track $\mathbf{x}_i$

- $\mathbf{x}_B \mapsto \mathbf{z}_j$: point cloud $\mathbf{z}_j$ has been caused by a so far not known object

- $\copyright \mapsto \mathbf{z}_j$: assumption that point cloud $\mathbf{z}_j$ has been caused by clutter

- $\mathbf{x}_i \mapsto \mathbf{z}_{\not\supset}$: track $\mathbf{x}_i$ did not cause a point cloud because it is not observable

- $\mathbf{x}_i \mapsto \mathbf{z}_{\not\ni}$: track $\mathbf{x}_i$ did not cause a point cloud because it does not exist

- $\mathbf{x}_i \mapsto \mathbf{z}_\varnothing$: track $\mathbf{x}_i$ did not cause a point cloud because of a sensing error

Fig. 4.1 illustrates four valid assignment hypotheses for the case of $n = 2$ tracks and $m = 2$ point clouds.

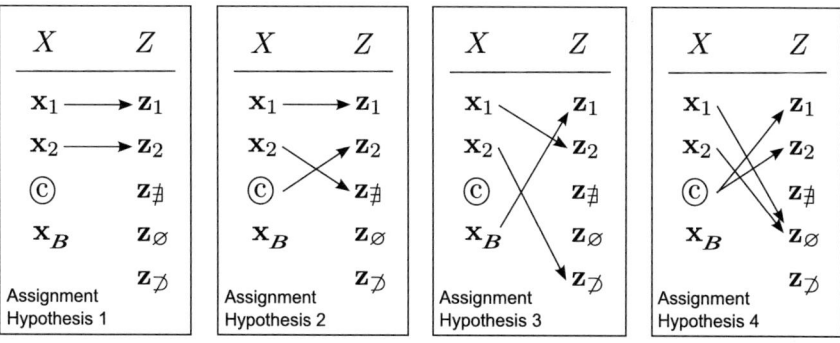

Figure 4.1: Examples of valid assignment hypotheses

The probabilities of the six edge types are calculated in analogy to [MSL$^+$08]:

$$p(e =(\mathbf{x}_i \mapsto \mathbf{z}_j)) = p_{k|k-1}^{\mathbf{x}_i}(\exists) \cdot p_{k|k-1}^{\mathbf{x}_i}(\supset) \cdot p^{\mathbf{z}_j}(TP|\mathbf{x}_i) \cdot (1 - p^{\mathbf{z}_j}(FP))$$

$$p(e =(\mathbf{x}_i \mapsto \mathbf{z}_{\not\supset})) = p_{k|k-1}^{\mathbf{x}_i}(\exists) \cdot (1 - p_{k|k-1}^{\mathbf{x}_i}(\supset))$$

$$p(e =(\mathbf{x}_i \mapsto \mathbf{z}_\varnothing)) = p_{k|k-1}^{\mathbf{x}_i}(\exists) \cdot p_{k|k-1}^{\mathbf{x}_i}(\supset) \cdot p^{\mathbf{x}_i}(FN)$$

$$p(e =(\mathbf{x}_i \mapsto \mathbf{z}_{\not\ni})) = (1 - p_{k|k-1}^{\mathbf{x}_i}(\exists)) \cdot p_{k|k-1}^{\mathbf{x}_i}(\supset) \cdot (1 - p^{\mathbf{x}_i}(FN))$$

$$p(e =(\mathbf{x}_B \mapsto \mathbf{z}_j)) = (1 - \sum_i p^{\mathbf{z}_j}(TP|\mathbf{x}_i)) \cdot (1 - p^{\mathbf{z}_j}(FP))$$

$$p(e =(\copyright \mapsto \mathbf{z}_j)) = (1 - \sum_i p^{\mathbf{z}_j}(TP|\mathbf{x}_i)) \cdot p^{\mathbf{z}_j}(FP) \tag{4.1}$$

with $p^{\mathbf{z}_j}(FP)$ being the probability that a clutter-caused point cloud appears at the position of $\mathbf{z}_j$, $p^{\mathbf{x}_i}(FN)$ the false negative probability for the track $\mathbf{x}_i$ and $p^{\mathbf{z}_j}(TP|\mathbf{x}_i)$ being the likelihood function obtained from the Kalman filter.

With edge probabilities in (4.1) it is now possible to calculate the probability of an assignment hypothesis $E = \{e_1, .., e_q\}$ by:

$$p(E) = \prod_{a=1}^{q} p(e_a)$$

The association probabilities $\beta^{\mathbf{x}_i}_{\mathbf{z}_j}$ are calculated as the sum of all assignment hypothesis probabilities including the edge $e = (\mathbf{x}_i \mapsto \mathbf{z}_j)$ divided by the sum of the probabilities of all assignment hypotheses assuming track $\mathbf{x}_i$ as existent:

$$\beta^{\mathbf{x}_i}_{\mathbf{z}_j} = \frac{\sum_{\{E|e=(\mathbf{x}_i \mapsto \mathbf{z}_j) \in E\}} p(E)}{\sum_{\{E|e=(\mathbf{x}_i \mapsto \mathbf{z}_{\sharp}) \notin E\}} p(E)} . \tag{4.2}$$

$\beta^{\mathbf{x}_i}_{\mathbf{z}_0}$ is the probability of the event that no point cloud originated from track $\mathbf{x}_i$. It is calculated analogously to (4.2).

5   Handling of split and merge effects and reconstruction of compatible object measurements

For the handling of the possibility of split and merge events in the course of data association, one option is to allow the assignment of a set of point clouds to one track or a set of tracks to one point cloud, respectively [KRSW06]. This would make it possible to identify splits and merges but would not allow to make an appropriate update since there is a one-to-one association necessary for doing so. Another possibility would be to create virtual measurements from the original measurements by splitting and merging them using predicted states of the tracked objects as proposed in [GOM04]. This approach would maintain one-to-one matchings between objects and associated point clouds and would allow to update the track's state after creation of compatible state measurement. The disadvantages of the method are ambiguous partitioning of original measurements in case of merging targets and exploding number of feasible associations. Furthermore, when using a centroid-based tracking approach, in the case of split and merged targets the resulting measurement's center of gravity (CoG) might not lie inside the gating ellipse of the targets' tracks. Another problematic case is the position update of a target which is partially occluded (due to either other objects in the scene or restricted field of view of the sensors). If target position is updated based on the CoG of the point cloud, it will cause a shift of the track's centroid and induce an impulse which will introduce bias to the estimated track's state.

To avoid such problems we reconstruct for each detection-to-track association the track's centroid and orientation using stably tracked points. We hereby utilize information about the affiliation of the tracked points to the tracks independently of the currently occurred splits and merges. The reconstructed centroids can then be used instead of the CoGs of the corresponding point clouds for the computation of the state measurement for each track.

5.1   Determination of the point-to-track affiliation probabilities

The affiliation probability $p(\mathbf{x}_i \mapsto \mathbf{p}_q)$ of a point $\mathbf{p}_q$ to a tracked object $\mathbf{x}_i$ is determined based on the association probability $\beta_{\mathbf{z}}^{\mathbf{x}_i}$ of the point cloud $\mathbf{z}$ containing $\mathbf{p}_q$ to that object. For the realization of a memory effect we filter the affiliation probabilities using a gain constant $g \in [0,1]$:

$$p_k(\mathbf{x}_i \mapsto \mathbf{p}_q) = g \cdot \beta_{\mathbf{z}}^{\mathbf{x}_i} + (1-g) \cdot p_{k-1}(\mathbf{x}_i \mapsto \mathbf{p}_q).$$

5.2   Point cloud based reconstruction of the track's position and orientation

For the reconstruction of the track centroid $\mathbf{p}_O$ from an associated point cloud we first calculate the CoG $\mathbf{p}_{CoG}$ of the stably tracked points of this point cloud both in the current and previous frame. Hereby we are weighting the points' 3-D positions with their track affiliation probability (known from the previous frame). Having computed $\mathbf{p}_{CoG}$ in both current and previous frames, we can for each tracked point $\mathbf{p}_q$ reconstruct the vector $(\overrightarrow{\mathbf{p}_{CoG}\mathbf{p}_O})_q$ pointing from the $\mathbf{p}_{CoG}$ to the object centroid $\mathbf{p}_O$ in the current frame using knowledge about the relative orientation of this vector regarding the vector $\overrightarrow{\mathbf{p}_{CoG}\mathbf{p}_q}$ in the previous frame (cf. Fig. 5.1). Building a weighted sum of the resulting vectors $(\overrightarrow{\mathbf{p}_{CoG}\mathbf{p}_O})_q$ according to the affiliation probability of the respective points $\mathbf{p}_q$ we get the new position of the track's centroid with respect to the considered point cloud. The track's new orientation can be obtained in the same way. Together those parameters form the reconstructed measurement of the point cloud. All these measurements weighted according to the association probabilities of the corresponding point clouds build a composed measurement which is then used for the innovation of the Kalman Filter responsible for the track's dynamics.

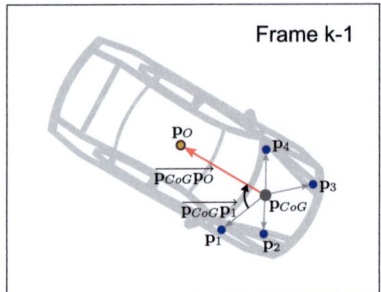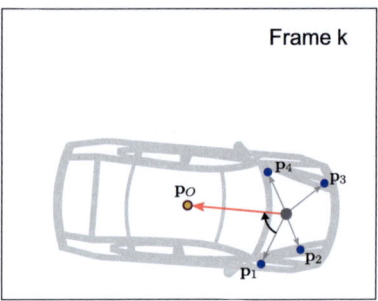

Figure 5.1: Object position reconstruction based on spatial relationship to stably tracked points

5.3   Grid-based reconstruction of the track's extent

The extent of a track is obtained in a similar way. We create one composite measurement from all point clouds associated to the track. This is done using the grid representation of the track which is aligned according to its new position and orientation gained through the innovation of the track's dynamics. The points of each associated point cloud are sorted into the grid. Thereby points of a point cloud contribute to the occupancy value of the grid cell according to their affiliation probability to the track and the association probability of the point cloud. For each cell c its current occupancy value o at time step k with respect to the track $\mathbf{x}_i$ is computed according to

$$o_k^{\mathbf{x}_i}(c) = \sum_{j=1}^{m} \left(\beta_{\mathbf{z}_j}^{\mathbf{x}_i} \cdot \sum_{q=1}^{l} p(\mathbf{x}_i \mapsto \mathbf{p}_q) \right)$$

with m being current number of point clouds and l being the number of points $\mathbf{p}_q$ belonging to the point cloud $\mathbf{z}_j$ and falling into the cell c. The grid is updated using this occupancy values. To avoid an update of the occupancy value of an occluded cell with 0, we filter the occupancy values of the cells using their occlusion probability. This process is visualized in Fig. 5.2. For each cell c its filtered occupancy value $\bar{o}_k(c)$ at time step k is given by

$$\bar{o}_k^{\mathbf{x}_i}(c) = p_k^{\mathbf{x}_i}(\supset, c) \cdot o_k^{\mathbf{x}_i}(c) + p_k^{\mathbf{x}_i}(\not\supset, c) \cdot \bar{o}_{k-1}^{\mathbf{x}_i}(c)$$

with $p^{\mathbf{x}_i}(\supset, c) = 1 - p^{\mathbf{x}_i}(\not\supset, c)$.

Object's geometric orientation and dimensions are obtained using a RANSAC based estimation of the main visible object surface in the top view and fitting

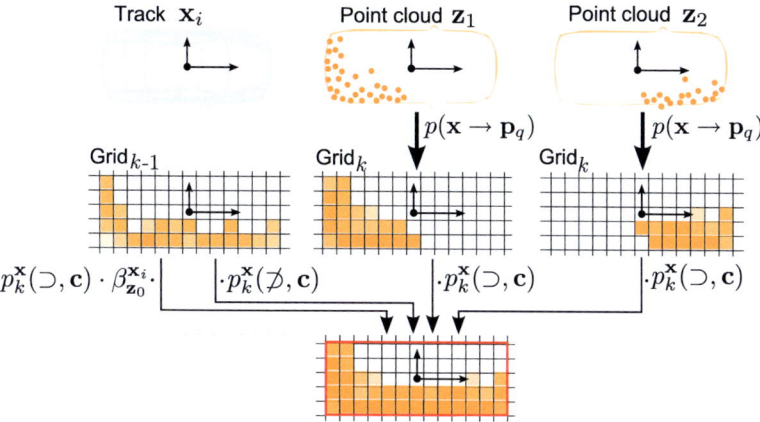

Figure 5.2: Process of grid-based measurement composition for object extent

a rectangle with this orientation into the ground projection of the occupied grid cells. Together, these parameters form the resulting composite measurement which is then used for the innovation of the track's geometric orientation and its dimensions.

6   State, existence and observability innovation

In the innovation step, all three Markov chains are updated. The innovation of the target's physical attributes corresponds to the standard Extended Kalman Filter innovation. For maintaining the centroid position obtained from the grid based object extent computation as the reference point to be tracked, we switch to this point as a new reference point at the end of each frame. This prevents the object dimensions from jittering due to the one-sided changes of the visible object extent (e.g. in the case of a target entering the field of view). The a-posteriori probability of the track existence is calculated as the sum of the probabilities of all assignment hypotheses assuming track $\mathbf{x}_i$ as existent divided by the sum of the probabilities of all possible hypotheses:

$$p_{k|k}^{\mathbf{x}_i}(\exists) = \frac{\sum_{\{E|e=(\mathbf{x}_i \mapsto \mathbf{z}_{\not\exists}) \notin E\}} p(E)}{\sum_{\{E\}} p(E)} \; .$$

The observability update is done analogously to the existence innovation.

7 Experimental results

The algorithm has been validated with both simulated and real data. For our simulations we used a tool which generated point clouds with pre-defined parameters and behavior. We modeled several scenarios that caused problems for the standard approach such as splitting and merging point clouds, objects entering and leaving the FoV and occlusion scenarios. Compared to the standard association and tracking scheme which lead to considerable corruption of the position and velocity estimation and even to the termination and re-initialization of the tracks, FBPDA managed to correctly update tracks' parameters through multiple merges, splits and occlusions.

8 Conclusion

In this contribution we have presented an algorithm for visual detection and tracking of multiple extended targets which is capable of coping with noisy, split, merged, incomplete and missed detections. The proposed approach resolves data association ambiguities in a soft decision based not only on target state prediction but also on the existence and observability estimation modeled as two additional Markov Chains. For the correct estimation of the desired object parameters, low-level information about measurement composition is utilized which is gained through tracking dedicated feature points in the image and 3D space. Along with the occlusion analysis, spatial and temporal relationship between the set of stably tracked points and the object's centroid is exploited which allows for the reconstruction of the desired object characteristics from the data even in case of detection errors due to limited FoV, occlusions, noise and sensor malfunction. For tracking applications that have to cope with the ebove-mentioned efects, our algorithm offers a much-needed enhancement which has the potential to greatly increase detetction and tracking performance and overall system robustness.

Bibliography

[APR]   APROSYS - Advanced PROtection SYStems: An Integrative Project in the 6th Framework Programme, online at http://www.aprosys.com.

[FRBG05]   Uwe Franke, Clemens Rabe, Hernán Badino, and Stefan Gehrig. 6D Vision: Fusion of Motion and Stereo for Robust Environment Perception. In *DAGM Symposium 2005*, Pattern Recognition, pages 216–223. 2005.

[GOM04]   Auguste Genovesio and Jean-Christophe Olivo-Marin. Split and Merge Data Asso-
           ciation Filter for Dense Multi-Target Tracking. In *Proceedings of 17th International
           Conference on Pattern Recognition*, 2004.

[KRSW06]   Pankaj Kumar, Surendra Ranganath, Kuntal Sengupta, and Huang Weimin. Co-
           operative Multitarget Tracking With Efficient Split and Merge Handling. In *IEEE
           Transactions on Circuits and Systems for Video Technology*, volume 16, 2006.

[ME02]   Darko Mušicki and Rob Evans. Joint Integrated Probabilistic Data Association -
           JIPDA. In *Proceedings of the 5th International Conference on Information Fusion*,
           pages 1120–1125, 2002.

[MES94]   Darko Mušicki, Rob Evans, and S. Stankovic. Integrated Probabilistic Data Associa-
           tion. In *IEEE Transactions on Automatic Control*, volume 39, 1994.

[MSL+08]   Mirko Mählisch, Magdalena Szcot, Otto Löhlein, Michael Munz, and Klaus Dietmayer.
           Simultaneous Processing of Multitarget State Measurements and Object Individual
           Sensory Existence Evidence with the Joint Integrated Probabilistic Data Association
           Filter. In *Proceedings of the 5th International Workshop on Intelligent Transportation
           (WIT2008)*, 2008.

[RGW08]   Steffen Rühl, Michael Grinberg, and Dieter Willersinn. Empirical evaluation of mo-
           tion models for a side-looking driver assistance system. In *Proceedings of the 5th
           International Workshop on Intelligent Transportation (WIT2008)*, 2008.

[TWG07]   Joachim Tandler, Dieter Willersinn, and Michael Grinberg. Data Analysis of the
           APROSYS Side Pre-Crash Sensing System. In *Proceedings of Intellligent Vehicles
           Symposium*, pages 926–930, 2007.

[TZM+08]   Joachim Tandler, Eric Zimmerman, Vlad Muntean, Björn Seipel, Thorsten Koch, Di-
           eter Willersinn, Michael Grinberg, Christian Mayer, and Monica Diez. A new pre-
           crash system for side impact protection. *International Journal of Crashworthiness*,
           13(6):679–692, 2008.

[WPGW07]   Philipp Woock, Frank Pagel, Michael Grinberg, and Dieter Willersinn. Odometry-
           Based Structure from Motion. In *Proceedings of Intellligent Vehicles Symposium*, pages
           1112–1117, 2007.

A First Approach to Trellis-Based Classification

Martin Grafmüller

Vision and Fusion Laboratory
Institute for Anthropomatics
Karlsruhe Institute of Technology (KIT), Germany
grafmueller@kit.de

Technical Report IES-2009-12

Abstract: The current state-of-the-art in pattern and character classification still reveals many unsolved problems, e.g., a robust classifier with respect to noise or other distortions in the character images is one of them. It is desirable that a classifier is easy to train and on the other hand very robust to any possible errors in the character images. Furthermore, the classification procedure should be real-time capable. In this technical report we introduce a new classifier that is based on trellis diagrams. It basically works like a Viterbi decoder known from communication systems. The fundamentals of the training and classification procedure are discussed in detail. In addition, we show the performance of the classifier on data with and without additive noise of different levels.

1 Introduction

In this report we introduce a new classifier, which is based on trellis diagrams. The performance of this classifier is demonstrated on an example in optical character recognition (OCR), which has a quite long history. The first patent on OCR was filed in the year 1929 in Germany by Tauscheck, whose system is based on optical and mechanical template matching. In the United States, Handel applied for the first patent on OCR in 1933. However, OCR was not satisfactorily applicable until the 1950s when the first digital computers and improved scanning devices were introduced. In 1955 the first commercial OCR system was installed at Reader Digest, and since 1965 the US Postal Service has been using OCR for sorting mail. Nowadays, since memory and computational power has become cheap, OCR is applicable in several fields, like readers for the blind, automatic data entry of bank account information, and process automation.

In recent years many different systems have been developed. Most of them are based on statistical methods, artificial neural networks, support vector machines, or ensemble methods that cascade several weak learners to one powerful classifier. These methods are well known and have been investigated in detail. However, there are still a lot of not adequately solved problems, e.g., if there are any changes in font, font size, or distortions in the images the performance of the classifiers significantly decreases. A detailed documentation about the advances and the remaining problems of common classifiers can be found in [LF08]. For more information about OCR the reader is referred to [MSY92, GS90, Man86].

1.1 Contributions

The application of the classifier we introduce in this report is on reading single printed numerals on different kind of materials, sometimes under severe environmental conditions. Furthermore, the numerals are variable in size and font, which requires a classifier with a good generalization ability with respect to different fonts and font sizes. Since the classification task changes depending on the application we need a classifier that can be easily augmented with additional classes or by new training data. The different materials the characters are printed on can additionally cause errors in the character images, which can be interpreted as noise. Hence, the classifier has to be robust to noise occurring in the character images as well.

The classifier we introduce in this report is based on trellis diagrams, where each diagram represents one model corresponding to one class. The models consist of states and weights, which are obtained in the training procedure. Basically, one model is similar to a Markov model except that the number of states be variable. The number changes with respect to the pixel position in the character image. Furthermore, the transitions from state to state are weighted, which is similar to the transition probabilities known from Markov models.

For classification the "shortest" path through the trellis diagrams is determined with respect to a given test vector. The winning class is finally the model with the "shortest" path. Basically, the classification procedure is similar to signal detection of discrete time signals as known from many communication systems. For this reason we use the Viterbi algorithm for the evaluation of the trellis diagrams, i.e., for classification.

In this report we point out the training procedure, which allows an easy augmentation of the classifier by new training data or even new classes. Furthermore, we want to show how the performance of the classifier is influenced by noise in the character images.

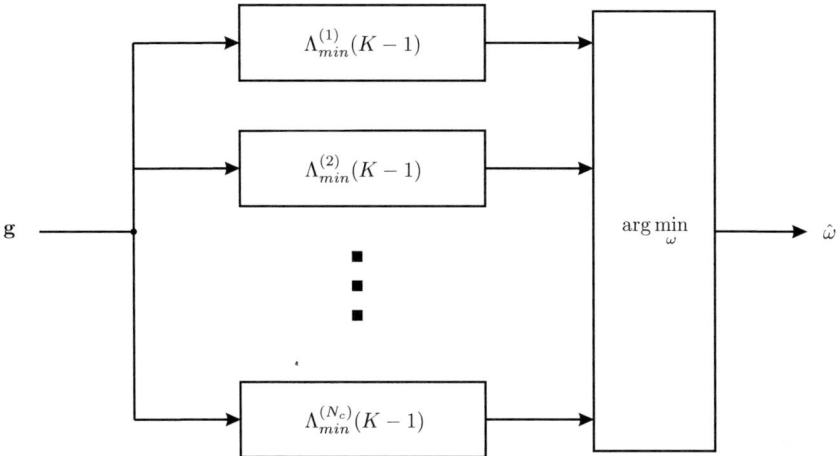

Figure 2.1: Block diagram of the entire classifier that discriminates between N_c classes.

1.2 Structure

The technical report is organized as follows. The training of the classifier is discussed in Section 2. Section 3 is devoted to the fundamentals of the classification procedure. In Section 4 we demonstrate the performance of the classifier. Finally, we give a conclusion and some remarks for future work in Section 5.

2 Training of the Classifier

The classifier we introduce is based on one model for each class, where each model is built according to the available training data. Thus, the entire classifier consists of N_c models for classification of N_c classes. The structure is shown in Figure 2.1. To keep the derivation of the training and classification procedure easy we only consider a one class classifier. Thus, the superscripts indicating the class are neglected in the following. Before the training procedure of the trellis-based classifier is introduced we want to start with some assumptions.

The character image $\mathbf{G} \in \mathbb{B}^{M \times N}$ with M columns, N rows, and gray values in $\mathbb{B} = \{0, 1, \ldots, 255\} \subset \mathbb{N}_0$ is represented by the column vector $\mathbf{g} \in \mathbb{B}^K$ of dimension $K = M \cdot N$. This allows the interpretation of an image as signal sequence similar to a received discrete signal transmitted over a communication channel.

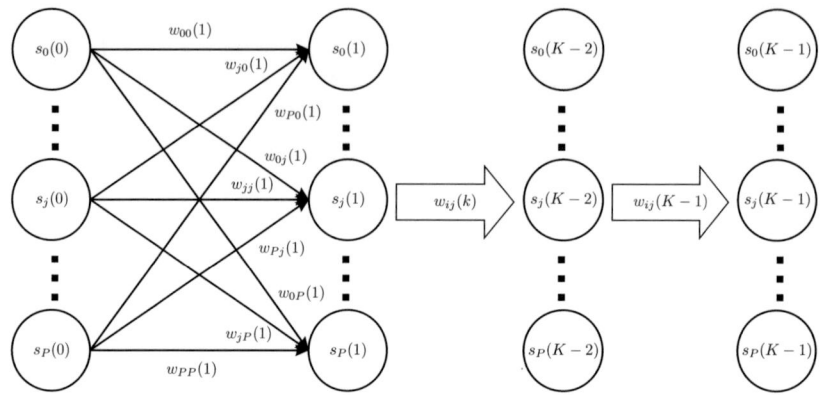

Figure 2.2: Basic idea of a part of a model representing one class.

During the training we determine a model for each class, which consists of vertexes $s_j(k)$ representing gray values that are called states in the following, and edges assigned with weights $w_{ij}(k)$. The weights can be interpreted as the cost of the transition from state $s_i(k-1)$ to state $s_j(k)$, where k denotes the pixel position of the image in the vector $\mathbf{g}$. This is analog to the transition probabilities in hidden Markov models. The structure of one model is illustrated in Figure 2.2, where the transitions from state to state are indicated by arrows. The big arrows are for simplification. They are indicating the transitions like the arrows on the left hand side. Formally, the states in Figure 2.2 can be represented by matrix

$$\mathbf{S} := \begin{bmatrix} \mathbf{g}_1 & \mathbf{g}_2 & \cdots & \mathbf{g}_P \end{bmatrix}^{\mathrm{T}} = \begin{bmatrix} s_0(0) & \cdots & s_0(K-1) \\ \vdots & \ddots & \vdots \\ s_P(0) & \cdots & s_P(K-1) \end{bmatrix},$$

in which the P given training samples of one class are arranged line-by-line. Matrix $\mathbf{S}$ contains the different states $s_j(k)$ line-by-line whereas the columns denote the pixel position k. In most cases the same gray value at position k appears multiple times. But those have to be evaluated only once since they yield in classification to the same result. This is the reason why they can be merged to one state with the corresponding gray value. Hence, every possible state is contained only once in a column. This enables the alignment of the obtained valid states at the beginning of each column k. Now, in every column are equal to or less than P elements. To keep the matrix structure the remaining elements of matrix $\mathbf{S}$ are filled with -1. Thus, the corresponding transition weights can be neglected as well, i.e., they are set to infinity. For the model, the remaining weights $w_{ij}(k) \in (0,1]$ are determined according to

$$w_{ij}(k) = \frac{1}{1 + |e_{ij}(k)|} , \qquad k = 1, \ldots, K - 1 , \qquad (2.1)$$

where $|e_{ij}(k)|$ denotes the number of transitions from state $s_i(k - 1)$ to $s_j(k)$ for all training samples of one class. This favors transitions that occur more frequently in the training data, i.e., those paths are more likely.

This procedure has to be performed N_c times since we need N_c models for the discrimination of N_c classes. The computational complexity of the training procedure is kept within a reasonable limit since the procedure is quite simple. This results in further advantages. One of them is the easy augmentation of the classifier by a new class, since just a model for that class has to be added to the already existing classifier models. Another one is that the existing classifier models can be easily augmented by new training data without a re-considering of the old data. For new training data, only the non-existing states and the corresponding weights have to be added to the model. If the state already exists only the corresponding weights have to be adapted.

3 Classification

For classification the evaluation of all models is necessary. This is done by determining the path of minimal cost—shortest path—for every model of the different classes. According to the *principle of optimality* [Ber05] we can apply dynamic programming since the path can be recursively determined. Dynamic programming reduces the computational complexity of the determination of the shortest path through a trellis diagram. For this reason and the fact that this classifier is similar to signal detection in communication systems the Viterbi algorithm is used.

3.1 Viterbi Algorithm

Andrew Viterbi [Vit67] introduced the Viterbi algorithm in 1967. This algorithm is a so-called forward dynamic programming algorithm, which can be used for the determination of the shortest path through a trellis diagram. The advantage of the Viterbi algorithm is that it reduces the computational effort of the evaluation of one trellis from a product

$$O \left(\prod_{k=1}^{K-1} B(k - 1)B(k) \right)$$

to a sum

$$O\left(\sum_{k=1}^{K-1} B(k-1)B(k)\right) ,$$

where K is the length of the image vector **g**. Here, the number of states in the trellis diagram at position k are denoted by $B(k)$.

The determination of the shortest path through the trellis diagram starts at image position $k = 0$ and recursively proceeds to the last $k = K - 1$. For all positions k, the squared difference is calculated between g_k and all given states $s_j(k)$ of the trellis diagram. g_k indicates the element of vector **g**—representing an image to be classified—at position k. Formally, this can be expressed as

$$\lambda_j(k) = (g_k - s_j(k))^2 , \qquad k = 0, \ldots, K - 1 .$$

In the next step the shortest distance leading to state $s_j(k)$ at position k is calculated. At position $k = 0$ it is just equal to the squared difference

$$\Lambda_j(0) = \lambda_j(0) .$$

If $k > 0$ then the metric is given by

$$\Lambda_j(k) = \min_i \{\Lambda_i(k-1) + w_{ij}(k)\lambda_j(k)\} ,$$
$$k = 1, \ldots, K - 1 .$$

The metric is the minimum of the sum of the shortest distance in state $s_i(k-1)$ and the weighted squared difference $\lambda_j(k)$ over all states i at position $k - 1$. If the last pixel $k = K - 1$ of the image is reached, the algorithm ends and the shortest path can be determined by

$$\Lambda_{min}(K-1) = \min_j \Lambda_j(K-1) \qquad (3.1)$$

The algorithm that has been described so far is related to the evaluation of one model. Hence, this has to be repeated N_c times if the classifier is trained with N_c models to discriminate between N_c classes. In the next section, the entire classifier that consists of N_c models is described in detail. Further information concerning the Viterbi algorithm can be found in [Vit67, For73, Ber05, MS00].

3.2 The Classifier

In this section we discuss the entire classifier that consists of N_c models. The models are necessary for the discrimination of N_c classes. The evaluation of each model is done by the Viterbi algorithm as described in the previous section. Hence, the computational effort of the entire classifier increases N_c times to

$$O\left(N_c \sum_{k=1}^{K-1} B(k-1)B(k)\right) .$$

According to Equation (3.1) the shortest path of one model is determined, which is the basis of the decision. The winning class $\hat{\omega}$ is finally given by the minimal cost over all N_c shortest paths

$$\hat{\omega} = \arg\min_{\omega} \Lambda_{min}^{(\omega)}(K-1) .$$

For simplification of the derivation superscript ω—indicating the class—has been neglected in Section 2, but now it is reintroduced since the classification task has more than one class. In Figure 2.1 the block diagram of the entire classifier is given.

4 Experiments

In this section the experimental results of the trellis-based classifier are discussed. For that purpose a character dataset was created and randomly split into a training and a test set. Additionally, the test set was affected by different noise levels to show the robustness of this classifier.

4.1 Character Image Dataset

For the character database, numbers from zero to nine were printed in several fonts and different sizes, see Table 4.1. The variation of the appearance is important as the classification task introduced in Section 1.1 requires a certain robustness against such changes. For digitalization, the printed pages were captured with an industrial camera. Additionally, the single characters were separated such that each image contains only one character. Finally, to get a consistent size of all characters they were scaled to $[24 \times 24]$ pixel images. Due to the fact that two disjoint datasets are needed for training and classification the character dataset was randomly divided. The training set contains 5014 and the test set 1256 samples, where all classes are almost equally distributed in both sets. For equalization in illumination and contrast of the single character images, they were normalized with respect to mean and variance of the gray values in each image.

Fonts	Arial, Bookman-Old-Style, Book-Antiqua, Century, Courier-New, Garamond, Lucida-Console, Lucida-Sans-Unicode, MS-Serif, Tahoma, Times-New-Roman, Verdana
Types	normal, bold, italic, italic-bold
Sizes	10, 12, 14, 16, 18

Table 4.1: All fonts contained in the character dataset.

4.2   Experimental Results

The training with the introduced training set results in a classifier with ten models, which has 85 states per pixel on average. Additionally, $5 \cdot 10^6$ transition weights are approximately determined during training for every model on average.

Firstly, the classifier is tested on the training set on which it classifies all characters correctly. Next, we determine the error rate on the test set containing 1256 samples. Again, all characters are classified correctly on this set, which indicates that no overfitting has been occurred. Figure 4.1 shows a so-called boxplot, where the minimal values $\Lambda_{min}^{(\omega)}(K-1)$ of all images containing number seven are plotted

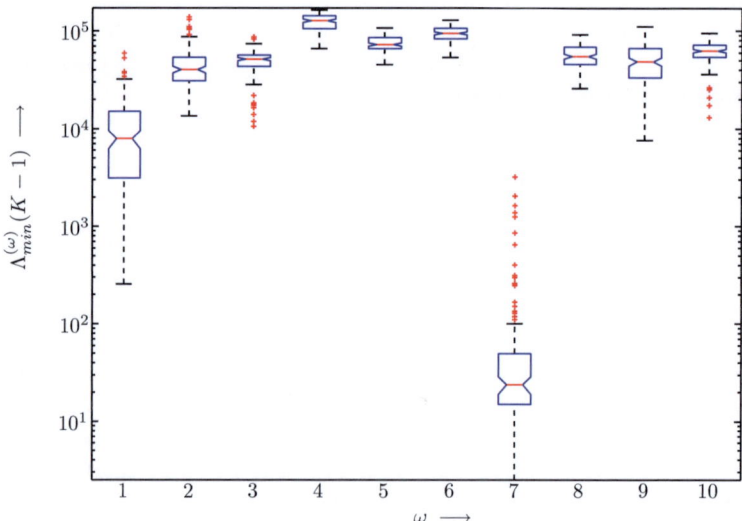

Figure 4.1: Boxplot of $\Lambda_{min}^{(\omega)}(K-1)$ for all images of class 7 contained in the test dataset.

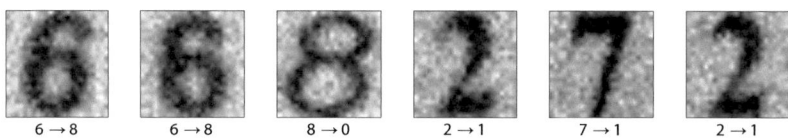

$6 \rightarrow 8$ $6 \rightarrow 8$ $8 \rightarrow 0$ $2 \rightarrow 1$ $7 \rightarrow 1$ $2 \rightarrow 1$

Figure 4.2: All misclassified numbers of the test set affected by zero-mean white Gaussian noise with $\sigma = 25.5$.

against all classes. In the plot one can see that the values $\Lambda_{min}^{(7)}(K-1)$ of model seven are significantly—about two orders of magnitude—lower than the values $\Lambda_{min}^{(\omega)}(K-1)$ of the other models. Due to the fact that number one and seven are similar, the values $\Lambda_{min}^{(1)}(K-1)$ of model one show the second lowest values. In spite of many outliers for model seven the discrimination of all sevens is correct.

In the case of errors in the character images the values $\Lambda_{min}^{(\omega)}(K-1)$ of all models are increased and move closer to each other, i.e., the values $\Lambda_{min}^{(7)}(K-1)$ are not two orders of magnitude smaller anymore. For example, if noise is added to the character images of all sevens, the values $\Lambda_{min}^{(\omega)}(K-1)$ in Figure 4.1 are increased. Especially, the values $\Lambda_{min}^{(7)}(K-1)$ are dramatically increased, which makes the discrimination of the classes more challenging.

To show the performance of the trellis-based classifier, we perform another experiment. For this experiment, the test set is affected by additive zero-mean Gaussian noise with standard deviation $\sigma = 25.5$. This causes a slight increase of the error rate to 0.48%. This corresponds to six misclassified characters that are shown in Figure 4.2. As one can see, most of the misclassified numbers are similar to the numbers assigned by the classifier, e.g., six looks similar to eight, or eight looks similar to zero, which is additionally amplified by the noise. The numbers underneath the characters (on the left hand side of the arrows) indicate the actual class and (on the right hand side) the class assigned by the classifier. Furthermore, the figure shows the noisy images in which we can see how the noise influences the characters.

For the next experiment we increase the standard deviation to $\sigma = 44.2$. In this experiment the trellis-based classifier shows an error rate of 2.79%, which is acceptable considering the errors due to the additive noise. All misclassified characters can be found in Figure 4.3. Analog to the result of the previous experiment, most of the misclassified numbers look similar to the assigned numbers. It is conspicuous in Figure 4.3 that many twos are classified as ones, in spite of the two characters do not have significant similarities.

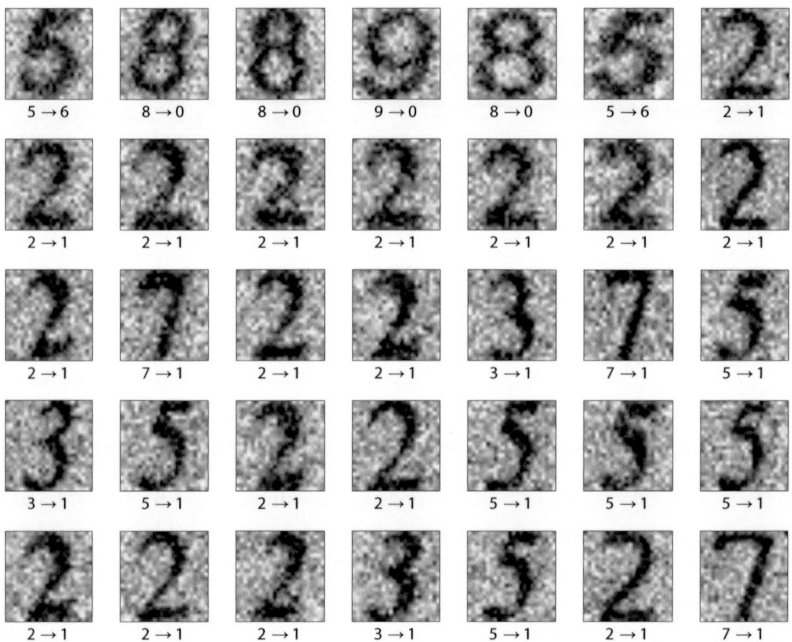

Figure 4.3: All misclassified numbers of the test set affected by zero-mean white Gaussian noise with $\sigma = 44.2$.

4.3 Discussion

Finally, we can summarize that this new kind of classifier is very easy to train. Hence, the classifier models can be easily augmented by new training data or new models can be added if the new training data contains new classes. The results of the experiment show that the performance even on noise affected character images decreases as expected, but it is still appropriate. One main drawback is that a lot of weights have to be stored and processed during classification, which mainly influences classification speed. Furthermore, the weights are determined according to equation (2.1), which is not an appropriate approach. It will probably be a better way to determine the weights adaptively during training, i.e., similar to the determination of the weights in neural networks. We assume that this will improve the models of the classifier, since they will probably be better adapted to the training data of course under the consideration that overfitting is avoided. Hence, we can assume that the performance of classification will be improved, too.

5   Conclusion

We have shown the fundamentals of the classifier that is based on the evaluation of trellis diagrams using the Viterbi algorithm. The training procedure has been discussed in detail and the simplicity of training has been pointed out. This implies the simple augmentation of the classifier by new training data or even a new class.

Finally, the performance of the classifier has been demonstrated on the example of character recognition. Furthermore, we have shown the performance on a character dataset affected by noise of different levels. As expected the error rate increases with a higher standard deviation of the noise, but it still remains low.

In future we will work on an adaptive determination of the transition weights during the training procedure. Additionally, we will investigate whether a reduction of the number of states is possible without a significant loss of classification performance. This will lower the computational complexity and thus, speed up classification.

Bibliography

[Ber05]   Dimitri P. Bertsekas. *Dynamic Programming and Optimal Control*, volume 1. Athena Scientific, Belmont, Mass., 3. edition, 2005.

[For73]   G. David Forney. The Viterbi Algorithm. *Proceedings of the IEEE*, 61(3):268–278, 1973.

[GS90]   V. K. Govindan and A. P. Shivaprasad. Character Recognition—A Review. *Pattern Recognition*, 23:671–683, 1990.

[LF08]   Cheng-Lin Liu and Hiromichi Fujisawa. Classification and Learning Methods for Character Recognition: Advances and Remaining Problems. In *Machine Learning in Document Analysis and Recognition*, volume 90/2008 of *Studies in Computational Intelligence*, pages 131–161, 2008.

[Man86]   J. Mantas. An Overview of Character Recognition Methodologies. *Pattern Recognition*, 19:425–430, 1986.

[MS00]   Todd K. Moon and Wynn C. Stirling. *Mathematical Methods and Algorithms for Signal Processing*. Prentice Hall, Upper Saddle River, NJ, 2000.

[MSY92]   Shunji Mori, Ching Y. Suen, and Kazuhiko Yamamoto. Historical Review of OCR Research and Development. *Proceedings of the IEEE*, 80:1029–1058, 1992.

[Vit67]   Andrew J. Viterbi. Error Bounds for Convolutional Codes and an Asymptotically Optimum Decoding Algorithm. *IEEE Transactions on Information Theory*, 13(2):260–269, 1967.

Cooperative Motion Planning using Branch and Bound Methods

Christian Frese

Vision and Fusion Laboratory
Institute for Anthropomatics
Karlsruhe Institute of Technology (KIT), Germany
frese@ies.uni-karlsruhe.de

Technical Report IES-2009-13

Abstract: Automated cooperative maneuvers could help to avoid or mitigate accidents in road traffic. This report presents a tree search approach for cooperative motion planning. Different branch and bound methods relying on precomputation and pruning are explored. Simulation results show that successful collision avoidance in intersection scenarios is achievable with acceptable computation times.

1 Introduction

Advances in communication technology enable wireless vehicle-to-vehicle communication. This capability may be used to increase road safety. Until now, research has focused on warning systems [MS06] and on vehicle platoons [Var93]. However, cooperative maneuvers offer a large potential for collision avoidance and mitigation that has not yet been exploited. By negotiating a cooperative motion plan using wireless communication, vehicles might automatically intervene in dangerous situations and prevent accidents more effective than a driver could do on his own. Scenarios where the gain of cooperative actions becomes evident include overtaking, obstacle avoidance and intersection situations [FBB08]. This report describes a method to plan a cooperative maneuver for the vehicles within a cooperative group [FBWB08].

Previous approaches to motion planning for multiple vehicles or robots usually make certain assumptions which simplify the problem. Common simplifications are motion planning in a fixed order of priority [ELP87, vdBO05] and decoupling of path planning and velocity planning [KZ86]. These assumptions narrow the space of possible solutions, especially in the present context of vehicles with significant dynamics and high velocities [FBB09]. Therefore, cooperative motion planning without those assumptions is pursued in this report. While it is rather straightforward to formulate the planning problem in the composite configuration space [LaV06], this approach has rarely been applied in practice due to its computational complexity. In this report, methods to alleviate the complexity are investigated. Especially, it is shown that precomputation of certain information enables a more efficient search.

The paper is organized as follows. Section 2 formulates the problem of cooperative motion planning. In Section 3, a loss functional and models of the vehicles and their actions are presented. Section 4 proposes different algorithms to solve the cooperative planning problem using branch and bound search. Results are discussed in Section 5. Finally, conclusions are presented in Section 6.

2 Problem Formulation

The following problem is considered in this report: given the initial positions $\mathbf{x}_0$ and velocities $\mathbf{v}_0$ of the m vehicles within a cooperative group and a time interval $[0, t_{\max}]$, plan a cooperative maneuver $\mathbf{x}(t)$ that optimizes certain criteria encompassing collision avoidance. In contrast to most work on motion planning, the goal positions are not predefined. As this method is only applied to circumvent dangerous traffic situations, they can be optimized by the planning algorithm in order to achieve the best collision-free cooperative motion.

Positions, states, capabilites, and geometric properties of the vehicles are assumed to be known from the common relevant picture of the cooperative group [FBB08]. The resulting cooperative maneuver is transmitted to all members of the group. Each vehicle performs a detailed planning within the tolerances determined by the cooperative plan and executes its part of the maneuver. These steps are outside the scope of this report.

3 Modeling

The planning algorithm described in this report has the advantage of explicitly specifying the vehicle model, the vehicle actions, and the loss functional. This allows to trace back effects observed in the resulting plans to the model assumptions, and hence a systematic design of the models. The models currently used are presented in the remainder of this section.

3.1 Vehicle Model

The configuration of the ith vehicle is denoted by $\mathbf{x}_i = (x_i, y_i, \phi_i)^{\text{T}}$, where $(x_i, y_i)^{\text{T}}$ is its position in the road plane and ϕ_i is its orientation. The linear velocity v_i is regarded as an additional state variable. The control variables are longitudinal acceleration acc_i and steering angle α_i.

This yields the following vehicle model:

$$
\begin{pmatrix} \dot{x}_i \\ \dot{y}_i \\ \dot{\phi}_i \\ \dot{v}_i \end{pmatrix} = \begin{pmatrix} v_i \cos \phi_i \\ v_i \sin \phi_i \\ 0 \\ 0 \end{pmatrix} + \begin{pmatrix} 0 \\ 0 \\ v_i \frac{\tan \alpha_i}{l_i} \\ acc_i \end{pmatrix} , \tag{3.1}
$$

where l_i is the wheelbase of the vehicle.

The abstraction from slip angles and tire friction coefficients seems to be admissible as such effects can be considered during the detailed planning performed subsequently by each vehicle. However, the presented algorithm is not restricted to this particular model. The model can be replaced by a more accurate one if necessary.

3.2 Actions

To allow a finite search, both time and the continuous control space are discretized. Time is divided in equidistant intervals of duration Δt. The planning horizon consists of T such intervals: $t_{\max} = T \cdot \Delta t$. Decisions are made at the points in time $t = 0, \Delta t, \ldots, (T-1)\Delta t$ and the corresponding actions are executed for the next time interval.

An action of the ith vehicle is denoted by a_i, the set of all considered actions of the vehicle by $\mathcal{A}_i$. A cooperative action of m vehicles is a vector $\mathbf{a} = (a_1, \ldots, a_m)^{\text{T}} \in \mathcal{A}$ with $a_i \in \mathcal{A}_i$. For simplicity of the analysis, we sometimes assume that all vehicles have identical action sets $\mathcal{A}_0$. In this case, $\mathcal{A} = \mathcal{A}_0^m$.

The action a_i can be expressed in terms of the control inputs acc_i, α_i. Its execution is simulated by numerically integrating the vehicle model (3.1) for the time interval Δt. The resulting trajectory $\mathbf{x}_i : [j\Delta t, (j+1)\Delta t] \rightarrow \mathbb{R}^3$ is denoted by $f(\mathbf{x}_i(j\Delta t), v_i(j\Delta t), a_i, \Delta t)$, where $\mathbf{x}_i(j\Delta t)$ and $v_i(j\Delta t)$ are position and velocity, respectively, of the ith vehicle at the beginning of the time interval. Analogously, $f(\mathbf{x}(j\Delta t), \mathbf{v}(j\Delta t), \mathbf{a}, \Delta t)$ are the trajectories $\mathbf{x} : [j\Delta t, (j+1)\Delta t] \rightarrow \mathbb{R}^{3m}$ of a cooperative motion.

In this work, the modeled action alternatives consist of

- turning sharp left, going straight, turning sharp right,

- hard braking, driving with constant speed, accelerating,

and combinations thereof. This choice has been inspired by the emergency maneuvers commonly considered for a single vehicle [SOB06].

3.3 Loss Functional

A loss functional L is used to evaluate a cooperative trajectory $\mathbf{x}(t)$. The loss functional can be considered the negative of a utility functional. Different aspects including collisions, road departure, and control energy are incorporated by a sum of several terms:

$$L\{\mathbf{x}(t)\} := L_{\text{coll}}\{\mathbf{x}(t)\} + L_{\text{obst}}\{\mathbf{x}(t)\} + L_{\text{road}}\{\mathbf{x}(t)\} + L_{\text{control}}\{\mathbf{x}(t)\}$$

For example, a simple approach to penalize collisions is as follows:

$$L_{\text{coll}}\{\mathbf{x}(t)\} := \int_0^{t_{\max}} \sum_{i=1}^{m} \sum_{j=i+1}^{m} \lambda_{\text{coll}} \delta_{ij}(\mathbf{x}_i(t), \mathbf{x}_j(t)) \mathrm{d}t$$

with the penalty factor $\lambda_{\text{coll}} \gg 0$ and

$$\delta_{ij}(\mathbf{x}_i, \mathbf{x}_j) := \begin{cases} 1 & \text{if vehicle } i \text{ in configuration } \mathbf{x}_i \text{ and vehicle } j \text{ in} \\ & \quad \text{configuration } \mathbf{x}_j \text{ are in geometric collision} \\ 0 & \text{otherwise} \end{cases}.$$

A more sophisticated loss functional could use information on the collision momentum to estimate the risk of injury [MH00, WW02].

The terms L_{obst} for collisions with obstacles and L_{road} for road departure can be defined in a similar way. Obstacles may be stationary or moving on a known (resp. predicted) trajectory.

The control term L_{control} penalizes longitudinal and lateral accelerations which cause energy consumption and passenger discomfort.

4   Branch and Bound Search

4.1   Tree Structure

Considering the possible decisions of one vehicle over time, a tree of possible action sequences is obtained (Figure 4.1). At each node, a decision among $|\mathcal{A}_0|$

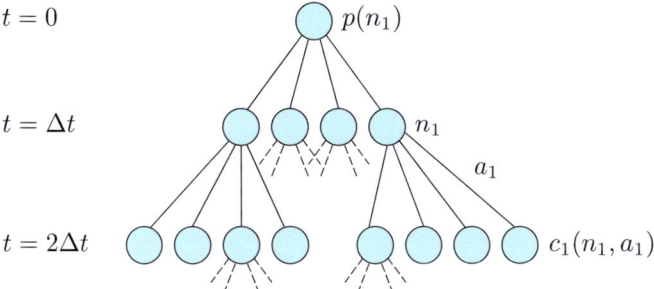

Figure 4.1: Tree structure of one vehicle's decisions.

different actions is performed. A level of the tree corresponds to a point in time. The tree has $|\mathcal{A}_0|^T$ leaves, each representing a distinct action sequence.

For m vehicles, the different approaches of decoupled and cooperative planning can be demonstrated in the tree structures: decoupled planning yields m separate trees with a total of $m|\mathcal{A}_0|^T$ leaves, while cooperative planning results in one tree having $|\mathcal{A}_0|^{mT}$ leaves. A node of the cooperative tree has $|\mathcal{A}| = |\mathcal{A}_0|^m$ children corresponding to all possible combinations of the vehicles' actions at one point in time.

In order to find the best sequence of actions, it is not necessary to construct the entire tree. Instead, the algorithm only stores the path corresponding to the action sequence currently under consideration. Additionally, the best path found so far and its loss value L^* are memorized.

A naïve depth-first search for the best solution can become computationally intensive, as indicated by the exponential number of leaves. Therefore methods for reducing computation time without affecting the quality of the solution have been investigated. In principle, two approaches are possible:

1. Reduce the number of nodes expanded during search

2. Reduce the processing time per node

Both approaches will be detailed below, after the necessary notation has been introduced.

4.2 Notation

A node of a tree is denoted by n, its parent node by $p(n)$. The child node of n obtained after executing the action $\mathbf{a}$ is given by the function $c_m(n, \mathbf{a})$. The position vector of the vehicles and the previously executed action vector are annotated to a node n by $\mathbf{x}(n)$ and $\mathbf{a}(n)$, respectively, yielding $\mathbf{a}(c_m(n, \mathbf{a}_0)) = \mathbf{a}_0$. The loss functional and its components can be applied to node n as follows:

$$L(n) := \begin{cases} 0 & \text{if } n \text{ is the root} \\ L(p(n)) + L\{f(\mathbf{x}(p(n)), \mathbf{v}(p(n)), \mathbf{a}(n), \Delta t)\} dt & \text{otherwise} \end{cases}$$

If the tree consists only of the decisions of vehicle i or of vehicles i, j, the nodes are labeled n_i or n_{ij}, respectively. The function $n_k(n, i_1, \ldots, i_k)$ returns the node of the k-vehicle tree which corresponds to n.

4.3 Branch and Bound

Branch and bound search is a standard method for eliminating irrelevant nodes from the search. A node and all of its descendants can be pruned if it is known that it cannot be contained in the optimal solution path. Let $L(n)$ be the loss value accumulated on the path from the root to node n, and L^* the loss value of the best solution known so far, identified by leaf node n^*. Then, the loss value of any solution containing n must be greater than $L(n)$ because the loss functional is additive over time and non-negative. This means that n can be pruned if

$$L(n) > L^* .$$

Standard branch and bound can reduce the number of visited nodes considerably in many cases, however, a further reduction is desirable. This will require a more informed pruning criterion, i.e., the incorporation of knowledge on the subtree under consideration. If a lower bound $h(n)$ for the minimal loss value of any path in the subtree can be obtained, the pruning can be improved as follows (see Figure 4.2): the subtree can be eliminated if

$$L(n) + h(n) > L^* .$$

The resulting general branch and bound search method is presented in Algorithm 4.1.

The tighter the bound $h(n)$, the better the pruning. However, the complexity of computing the criterion has to be traded off against the gain resulting from the more effective pruning.

Algorithm 4.1 General branch and bound method for cooperative motion planning

---

1: **procedure** SEARCH(t, n)
2:     **for all** $\mathbf{a} \in \mathcal{A}$ **do**
3:         $n_c \leftarrow c_m(n, \mathbf{a})$
4:         Compute $\mathbf{x}(n_c)$ and $L(n_c)$
5:         **if** $L(n_c) + h(n_c) < L^*$ **then**
6:             **if** $t + \Delta t < t_{\max}$ **then**
7:                 SEARCH$(t + \Delta t, n_c)$
8:             **else**
9:                 $L^* \leftarrow L(n_c)$
10:                $n^* \leftarrow n_c$
11:            **end if**
12:        **end if**
13:    **end for**
14: **end procedure**
15: **procedure** PLAN$(\mathbf{x}_0, \mathbf{v}_0)$
16:     Perform precomputation
17:     $L^* \leftarrow \infty$
18:     $L(root) \leftarrow 0$
19:     $\mathbf{x}(root) \leftarrow \mathbf{x}_0$
20:     $\mathbf{v}(root) \leftarrow \mathbf{v}_0$
21:     SEARCH$(0, root)$
22:     **return** n^*
23: **end procedure**

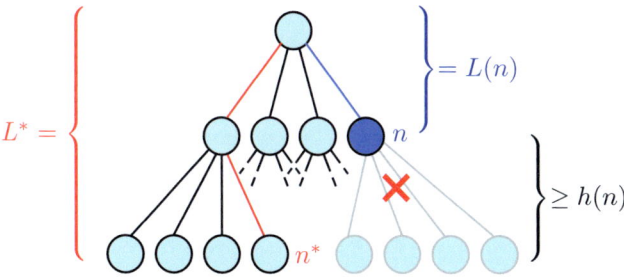

Figure 4.2: Criterion to prune a subtree.

4.4   Precomputation of Single Vehicle Information

A key to the derivation of a first lower bound $h_1(n)$ for a subtree is the observation that several terms of the loss functional only depend on a single vehicle's actions. This means that these terms can be computed within the single vehicle trees without requiring expontential complexity in the number of vehicles.

In the precomputation phase, the vehicle position $\mathbf{x}_i(n_i)$ and the following loss value is computed for each node n_i:

$$L_1(n_i) := L_{\text{road}}(n_i) + L_{\text{obst}}(n_i) + L_{\text{control}}(n_i)$$

When ascending in the single vehicle tree, a lower bound $h_1(n_i)$ for the subtree rooted at n_i is obtained as follows:

$$h_1(n_i) := \begin{cases} 0 & \text{if } n_i \text{ is a leaf} \\ L_1(n_i) - L_1(p(n_i)) + \min_{a_i \in \mathcal{A}_i} h_1(c_1(n_i, a_i)) & \text{otherwise} \end{cases}$$

The gain resulting from this precomputation is twofold:

1. A node n and its subtree can be pruned from the cooperative search if

$$L(n) + h_1(n) > L^* \qquad (4.1)$$

   with

$$h_1(n) := \sum_{i=1}^{m} h_1(n_1(n, i)) \,.$$

2. The precomputed vehicle positions $\mathbf{x}_i(n_i)$ and loss values $L_1(n_i)$ are used during cooperative search. Thereby, the processing time per node is reduced drastically, as redundant computations are eliminated. This is possible because the position $\mathbf{x}_i$ of a vehicle is determined solely by its own actions, while the composite state $\mathbf{x}$ depends on the decisions of all vehicles.

4.5   Precomputation of Collision Information

As long as follow-up collisions are not considered, the collision loss L_{coll} only depends on the decisions of two vehicles [LH98]. Therefore, the idea from the previous subsection can be pursued one step further: the collision information can be precomputed by constructing every two-vehicle tree in advance, yielding

$L_2(n_{ij}) := L_{\text{coll}}(n_{ij})$. A lower bound $h_2(n_{ij})$ for the collision loss in a subtree of a two-vehicle tree can be computed as follows:

$$
h_2(n_{ij}) := \begin{cases} 0 & \text{if } n_{ij} \text{ is a leaf} \\ L_2(n_{ij}) - L_2(p(n_{ij})) \\ \quad + \min_{a_i \in \mathcal{A}_i,\, a_j \in \mathcal{A}_j} h_2(c_2(n_{ij}, a_i, a_j)) & \text{otherwise} \end{cases}
$$

These lower bounds improve the pruning criterion for the cooperative search:

$$
L(n) + h_1(n) + h_2(n) > L^* \tag{4.2}
$$

with

$$
h_2(n) := \sum_{i=1}^{m} \sum_{j=i+1}^{m} h_2(n_2(n, i, j)) .
$$

5 Results

5.1 Collision Avoidance

The proposed algorithms have been evaluated on different intersection scenarios involving two to four vehicles. Figure 5.1 shows some examples of successful collision avoidance. The scenarios have been generated using the traffic simulator described in [VNB+07].

5.2 Planning Time

In Figure 5.2, the runtime of the different algorithms is plotted with logarithmic time axis scale. For a better comparison of the more efficient algorithms, Figure 5.3 shows the range below a runtime of 3 seconds with linear scale. The portions below the black line are for precomputation, the remainder for the branch and bound search. Each time shown is a mean value for more than a hundred different intersection scenarios with m vehicles and T decision points. The variants of the algorithm are specified as follows:

branch-bound: Standard branch and bound without precomputation (Algorithm 4.1 with $h(n) = 0$).

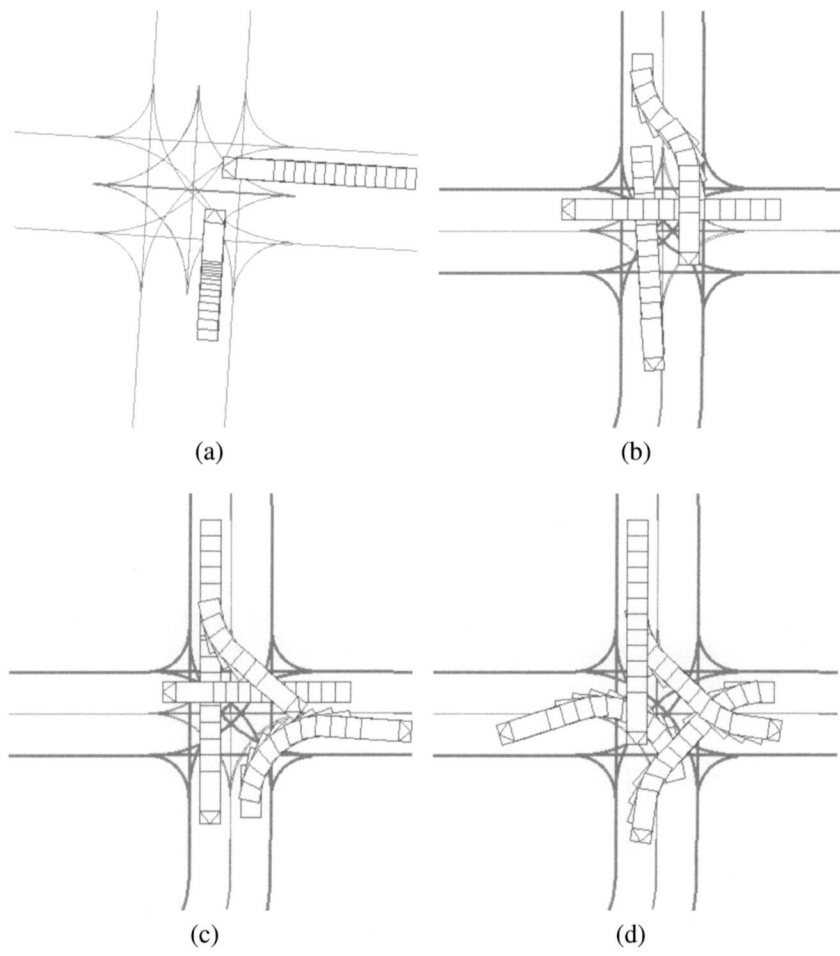

(a)

(b)

(c)

(d)

Figure 5.1: Visualization of planned cooperative maneuvers involving two to four vehicles in intersection scenarios.

algorithm	precomputation	total time	expanded nodes
branch-bound	0.00 ± 0.00	533.36 ± 779.23	1100454 ± 1620584
precomp L1	0.22 ± 0.02	1.73 ± 1.86	1100442 ± 1620703
pruning h1	0.23 ± 0.01	0.23 ± 0.02	734 ± 2486
pruning h2	0.53 ± 0.18	0.53 ± 0.18	112 ± 307

Table 5.1: Mean and standard deviation of precomputation time, total runtime and number of expanded nodes for 150 simulation scenarios with $m = 3$ and $T = 3$ (all times in seconds).

precomp L1: Precomputation of the single vehicle information (positions $\mathbf{x}_i(n_i)$ and loss value $L_1(n_i)$), but standard pruning ($h(n) = 0$). This variant is shown to distinguish the gain resulting by avoiding redundant computations from the additional gain by more effective pruning.

pruning h1: Precomputation of the single vehicle information $L_1(n_i)$, $\mathbf{x}_i(n_i)$, $h_1(n_i)$ and pruning with criterion (4.1).

pruning h2: Additional precomputation of the collision information $L_2(n_{ij})$, $h_2(n_{ij})$ and pruning with criterion (4.2).

The precomputation results in a substantial performance improvement. The pruning reduces the number of expanded nodes by several orders of magnitude (Figure 5.4). The variance of the runtime also decreases, as the precomputation effort is less dependent on the particular scenario (Table 5.1). However, the precomputation of the collision information is advantageous only in rare cases because the precomputation effort often outweighs the pruning gain.

5.3 Search Strategy

It is interesting to compare the described depth first branch and bound strategy with the A* search strategy [RN03]. Preliminary results on this issue show no clear preference in the average case. However, some scenarios that seem to be rather easy for the branch and bound method are quite difficult to solve for A* and vice versa. The avoidance of redundant computations as presented in this report is crucial also for the efficiency of the A* strategy.

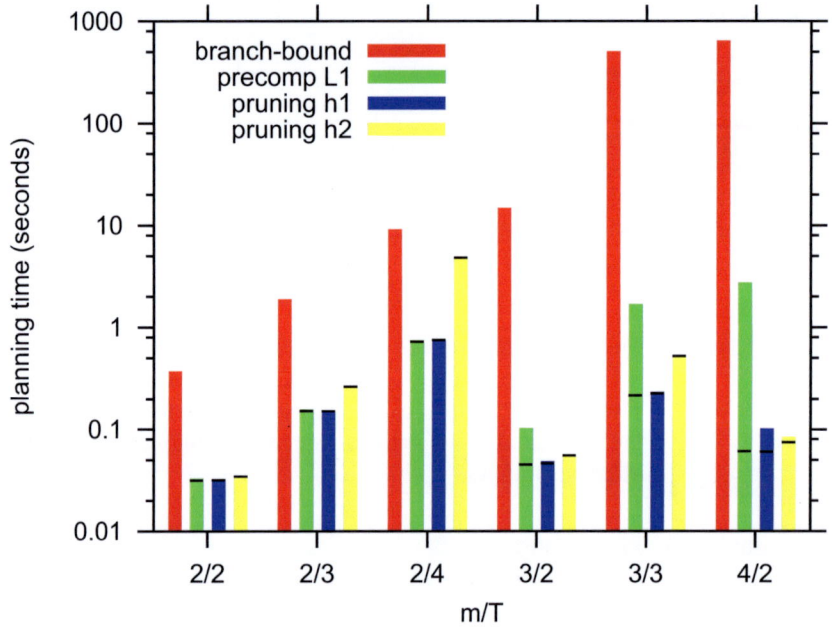

Figure 5.2: Runtime of the algorithms (logarithmic scale).

6 Conclusion

A tree search method for cooperative motion planning has been presented. Acceptable computation times can be achieved by using precomputation and pruning.

Further studies are necessary to evaluate the performance of the proposed algorithm in other scenarios, e.g., obstacle avoidance and overtaking maneuvers. Changes in the action models and discretization parameters might be required in order to solve these problems.

Acknowledgements

The author gratefully acknowledges support of this work by Deutsche Forschungs-gemeinschaft (German Research Foundation) within the Transregional Collaborative Research Center 28 "Cognitive Automobiles". Furthermore, the author would

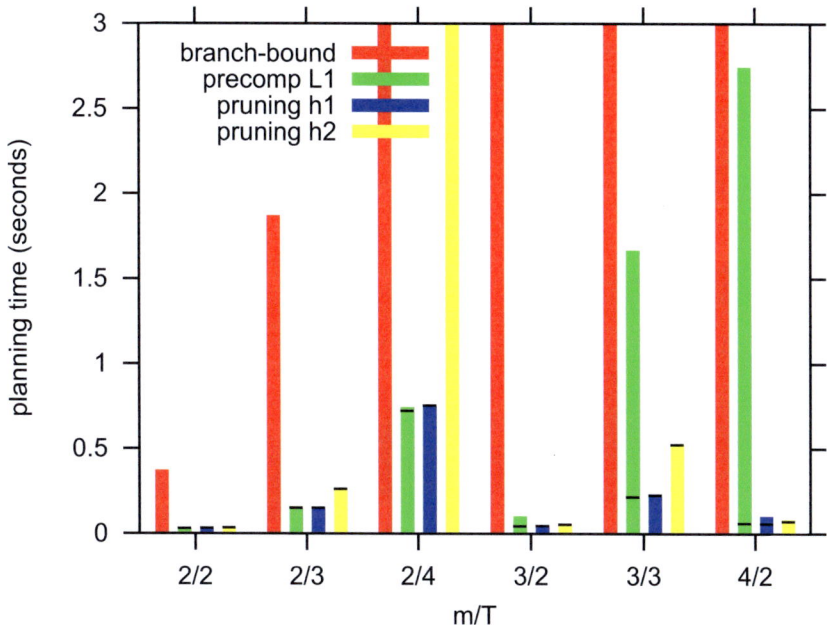

Figure 5.3: Runtime of the algorithms (linear scale).

like to thank all project partners participating in the development of the simulation system.

Bibliography

[ELP87]   Michael Erdmann and Tomás Lozano-Pérez. On multiple moving objects. *Algorithmica*, 2:477–521, 1987.

[FBB08]   Christian Frese, Thomas Batz, and Jürgen Beyerer. Cooperative behavior of groups of cognitive automobiles based on a common relevant picture. *at – Automatisierungstechnik*, 56(12):644–652, December 2008.

[FBB09]   Christian Frese, Thomas Batz, and Jürgen Beyerer. Kooperative Bewegungsplanung zur Unfallvermeidung im Straßenverkehr mit der Methode der elastischen Bänder. In *Autonome Mobile Systeme*. Springer, December 2009. Accepted for publication.

[FBWB08] Christian Frese, Thomas Batz, Martin Wieser, and Jürgen Beyerer. Life cycle management for cooperative groups of cognitive automobiles in a distributed environment. In *Proc. IEEE Intelligent Vehicles Symposium*, Eindhoven, June 2008.

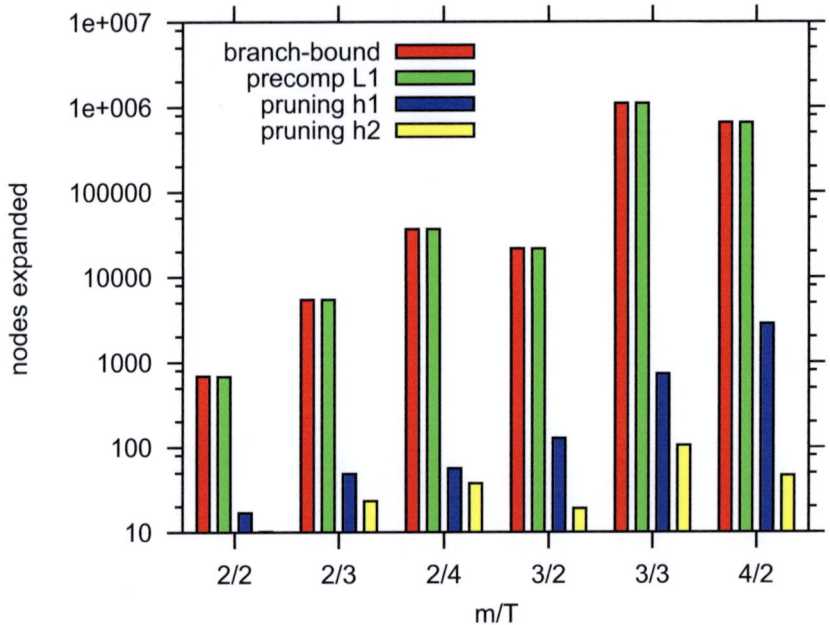

Figure 5.4: Nodes expanded by the different algorithms (logarithmic scale).

[KZ86]   Kamal Kant and Steven Zucker. Toward efficient trajectory planning: The path-velocity decomposition. *Journal of Robotics Research*, 5(3):72–89, 1986.

[LaV06]   Steven LaValle. *Planning Algorithms*. Cambridge University Press, 1st edition, 2006.

[LH98]   Steven LaValle and Seth Hutchinson. Optimal motion planning for multiple robots having independent goals. *IEEE Transactions on Robotics and Automation*, 14(6):912–925, December 1998.

[MH00]   H. Mooi and J. Huibers. Simple and effective lumped mass models for determining kinetics and dynamics of car-to-car crashes. *Journal of Crashworthiness*, 5(1), 2000.

[MS06]   James Misener and Steven Shladover. PATH investigations in vehicle-roadside cooperation and safety: A foundation for safety and vehicle-infrastructure integration research. In *Proc. IEEE Intelligent Transportation Systems Conf.*, pages 9–16, September 2006.

[RN03]   Stuart Russell and Peter Norvig. *Artificial Intelligence: A Modern Approach*. Prentice Hall, 2nd edition, 2003.

[SOB06]   Christian Schmidt, Fred Oechsle, and Wolfgang Branz. Research on trajectory planning in emergency situations with multiple objects. In *Proc. IEEE Intelligent Transportation Systems Conf.*, pages 988–992, September 2006.

[Var93]   Pravin Varaiya. Smart cars on smart roads: Problems of control. *IEEE Transactions on Automatic Control*, 38(2):195–207, February 1993.

[vdBO05]   Jur van den Berg and Mark Overmars. Prioritized motion planning for multiple robots. In *Conf. Intelligent Robots and Systems*, 2005.

[VNB+07]   Stefan Vacek, Robert Nagel, Thomas Batz, Frank Moosmann, and Rüdiger Dillmann. An integrated simulation framework for cognitive automobiles. In *Proc. IEEE Intelligent Vehicles Symposium*, pages 221–226, June 2007.

[WW02]   Denis Wood and D. Walsh. Car to car interaction in frontal collisions: A model for the behaviour of the car population and options for improved crashworthiness. *Journal of Crashworthiness*, 7(1), 2002.

On Situation Modeling and Recognition

Yvonne Fischer

Vision and Fusion Laboratory
Institute for Anthropomatics
Karlsruhe Institute of Technology (KIT), Germany
yvonne.fischer@kit.edu

Technical Report IES-2009-14

Abstract: This paper gives an overview of the components that have to be taken into account for automatic situation recognition. Automatic situation recognition in complex situations enhances situation awareness of decision makers. The technical basis for achieving human situation awareness is provided through data fusion. Because of this connection, there exist unified models which combine both situation awareness and data fusion. One of these unified models is reviewed here. We also explain our interpretation of the term situation recognition and conclude that the first challenge is to find a suitable formalization of the term situation. Then, the basic requirements of a formalized description of a situation are extracted from general definitions of a situation. A possible formalization of a situation, which recently appeared in literature and covers the requirements extracted before, is reviewed.

1 Introduction

Currently, the need for intelligent decision support systems in the surveillance domain increases. In existing systems, the signal processing aspects like detecting, identifying, and tracking objects in the observed area are usually well developed. The next challenge is to analyze the large amount of data, which can be generated in a surveillance system, automatically. The general question is therefore, how a situation, especially a threat situation, can be recognized. Essentially for human beings for recognizing a critical situation is to be aware of the situation. In the literature, the term *(human) situation awareness* is used to describe this. Methods and algorithms for analyzing complex situations by the use of data from several sources are developed by the data fusion community. Because of this, data fusion can be interpreted as the technical basis for achieving human situation awareness. In this article, we give an overview of the frequently used expressions situation awareness, situation assessment, and data fusion. Especially, we describe how these terms are interpreted in literature. We explain our interpretation of term situation recognition. By our analysis, we come to the conclusion that the first challenge in situation recognition is to find a formal description of a situation. The requirements for a formalized description of a situation are then extracted from various definitions of the term situation. We finally highlight one formal description of a situation in literature that covers the requirements extracted before.

The paper is structured as follows. Section 2 gives an overview of the expressions situation awareness, situation assessment, and data fusion in literature and the connections between them. Section 3 deals with situation recognition in general. Here, the essential components of how a situation can be recognized are pointed out. We extract the requirements for a formalized description of a situation from general definitions and highlight a formalized description of a situation that recently appeared in literature. In Section 4, we summarize this report and give an outlook to future work.

2   Situation Awareness

2.1   Human Situation Awareness

A commonly accepted definition of the term situation awareness of human beings has been introduced by Endlsey, see for example [End95]:

> "Situation Awareness is the perception of the elements in the environment within a volume of time and space, the comprehension of their meaning, and the projection of their status in the near future."

In [End95], Endsley also points out the difference between situation awareness and situation assessment. According to Endsley, situation awareness can be seen as a state of knowledge whereas situation assessment is the process of achieving, acquiring or maintaining situation awareness. The meaning of these terms is equivalently used in Niklasson [NRJ$^+$08]. But there also exist some other interpretations in literature, for example Lambert [Lam01] defines situation assessment as a stored representation of relations between objects and denotes the associated process with the term situation fusion. But at least the interpretation of the term situation awareness as a mental model of the environment according to Endsley is almost accepted throughout the literature. Based on Endsley's definition, situation awareness can be described through three different hierarchical levels:

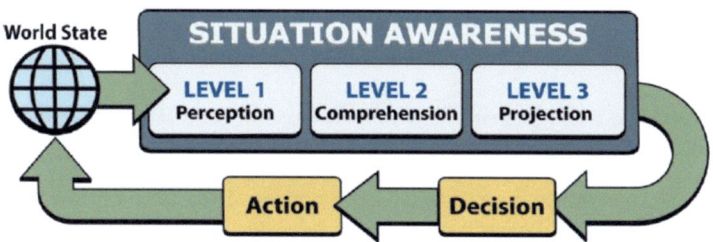

Figure 2.1: Situation Awareness (taken from Endsley [EC08]).

- **Level 1:** Perception of status, attributes, and dynamics of relevant elements in the environment, for example through sensory detection.

- **Level 2:** Comprehension of the current situation based on knowledge of level 1 elements. In this level, the decision maker understands the significance of objects and events in relation to the operator's goals.

- **Level 3:** The ability to project the future actions of the elements in the environment based on the knowledge of level 1 and 2. Level 3 consists of extrapolating information forward in time to determine how it will affect future states.

A simplified illustration of these levels is depicted in Figure 2.1. It should be noted that the three different levels are not processed successively but rather parallel by human beings and all of them are contributing to the operator's situation awareness. Endsley [End95] showed that the decision process of an operator is strongly determined by his situation awareness of the environment. Therefore, a good decision can only be made if the situation awareness is sufficient. Endsley [End95] developed a model of decision making that takes situation awareness into account. The model addresses the impact of critical factors like attention, working memory, design features, workload, stress, system complexity, and automation on the operator's situation awareness and the model can therefore be used to generate design implications in complex systems. Based on the decision of an operator, an action is performed that changes the state of the environment, see Figure 2.1. This state change influences again the situation awareness of an operator and therefore, the whole process can be described as a closed loop.

2.2   The JDL Data Fusion Model

In [SBW99], the following definition of the term data fusion has been given:

> "Data fusion is the process of combining data to refine state estimates and predictions."

The aim of data fusion is to improve the estimate of the state of an observed environment. This can be achieved by using synergistic differences of overlapping information to determine relationships between multiple data from possibly different sources. As a result, data fusion allows improved estimation of situations and therefore, improved responses to situations. The most widely accepted model of the data fusion process is the JDL (Joint Directories of Laboratories) data fusion model [SBW99]. The model was first developed with focus on the military domain but is now well established as a general architecture model for system description, design, and development. Because of this, there exist several revisions of the original model and in this article we refer to the more general version of [SBW99]. The JDL data fusion model is divided into different fusion levels that can be interpreted as a technical categorization of data fusion-related methods. The different levels of the model are depicted in Figure 2.2 and can be described as follows:

- **Level 0 - Sub-Object Assessment:** the process of estimation and prediction of signal states.

- **Level 1 - Object Assessment:** the process of estimation and prediction of entity states. In this level, sensor data is combined to obtain reliable, consistent and accurate estimates of an entity's attributes (e.g., identity, location, velocity, heading)

- **Level 2 - Situation Assessment:** the process of estimation and prediction of relations among entities. These can be entity-to-entity relations but also entity-to-environment relations (e.g., close to, on top of, greater than)

- **Level 3 - Impact Assessment:** the process of estimation and prediction of effects on situations of planned or predicted actions.

- **Level 4 - Process Refinement:** the process of adaptive data acquisition and processing to support mission objectives.

Level 4 can be interpreted as a process that is concerned with monitoring and optimizing the overall data fusion process. In the literature, level 0 and 1 are often called low-level data fusion whereas level 2 and 3 are called high-level data fusion, or even information fusion, which is motivated through the use of interpreted data as input.

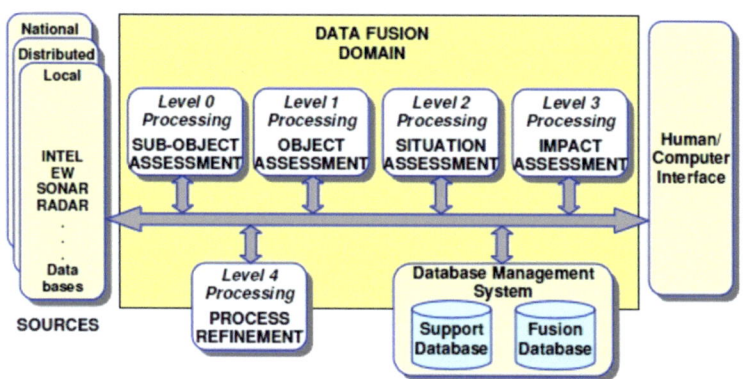

Figure 2.2: JDL Data Fusion Model (taken from Steinberg [SB04]).

2.3   A Unified Model

Obviously there is a correlation between the human situation awareness levels and the JDL data fusion levels proposed in Section 2.1 and Section 2.2, respectively. Lambert [Lam01] associates the data fusion levels of the JDL model with the situation awareness levels of Endsleys mental/human model as follows:

Data Fusion Level:		Situation Awareness Level:
sub-object and object assessment	↔	perception
situation assessment	↔	comprehension
impact assessment	↔	projection

Level 4 of the JDL data fusion model influences all data fusion levels and is skipped here for simplicity. Associated to human situation awareness, the process refinement level can be interpreted as organizing and classifying the information in mind. The JDL Data fusion model can therefore be seen as the technical basis for achieving human situation awareness. The connection proposed by Lambert [Lam01] is quite evident and often used in literature. Niklasson [NRJ+08] used this connection to introduce a unified situation analysis model that allows the combination of automatic and human interaction at different levels. He argues that within the near future, the high-level data fusion tasks (such as impact assessment) cannot be fully automated and will mainly be performed manually. Therefore, he proposed a descriptive model for integrating automatic, manual, and semi-automatic decision support, which is depicted in Figure 2.3. In this model, situation analysis implies the collection and processing of relevant information, the knowledge of the relations between the different information and how the information influences future decisions. In Figure 2.3, human situation analysis can be seen on the right-hand side and machine situation analysis on the left-hand side. Important in that model is the possibility to combine the analysis processes by the use of interaction channels. The central human computer interaction channel allows interaction between human and machine situation analysis and the inter level interaction channels allow interaction between different levels of human and machine situation analysis. In this model, situation awareness is interpreted as a result of human or machine situation analysis and it can be an output of one level as well as an input to another level of situation analysis. Therefore, the interaction channels allow the transportation of situation awareness between different levels and between humans and machines.

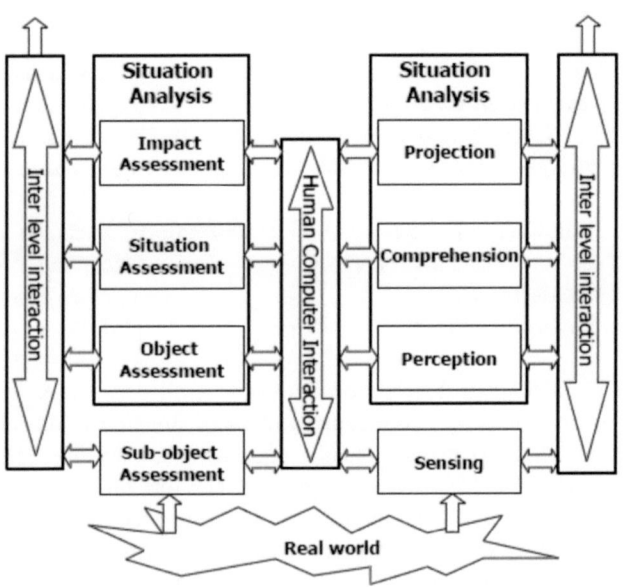

Figure 2.3: A Unified Model (taken from Niklasson [NRJ+08])

3 Situation Recognition

3.1 Situation Recognition in General

Based on the information in Section 2, we can state that human decision making is a complex task and that the main aspect of making a good decision is the achievement of sufficient situation awareness of the decision maker. It is known that complex situations can easily lead to insufficient situation awareness, which is the main cause of human mistakes and accidents (see for example [EC08]). Hence, in complex systems, an automatic assistance for enhancing situation awareness of the human decision maker is required. But on the other hand, as pointed out in [NRJ$^+$08], the situation awareness of a human decision maker might become worse if the system processes too many tasks automatically. These facts have always to be taken into account when a decision support system has to be designed.

In today's decision support systems, automation of the lower levels of the JDL data fusion model like object detection, identification, and tracking is present. But there is still a need for approaches in high-level data fusion like the automatic recognition of specific and complex situations. Generally, automatic situation recognition has to deal with the following problems:

- relevant features of the reality have to be observed and stored over time,

- observations of the reality usually imply uncertainties (sensorial uncertainties caused for example by noise),

- formalized descriptions of situations that have to be recognized are necessary (the system have to know what situations have to be recognized), and

- situations are often not accurately describable (different configurations of observed features may imply the same situation).

Automatic situation recognition addresses the problem of how to match the observed reality with predefined situations under uncertainties, hence situation recognition is a typical classification problem. The main problem is that complex situations are typically not accurately describable and also that the relevant observed features are typically afflicted with uncertainties. The connection of automatic situation recognition with the JDL data fusion model and the human situation awareness model of Endsley is depicted in Figure 3.1. The top layer shows the situation awareness levels introduced by Endsley and the middle layer shows the data fusion levels of the JDL model. The bottom layer shows a possible technical

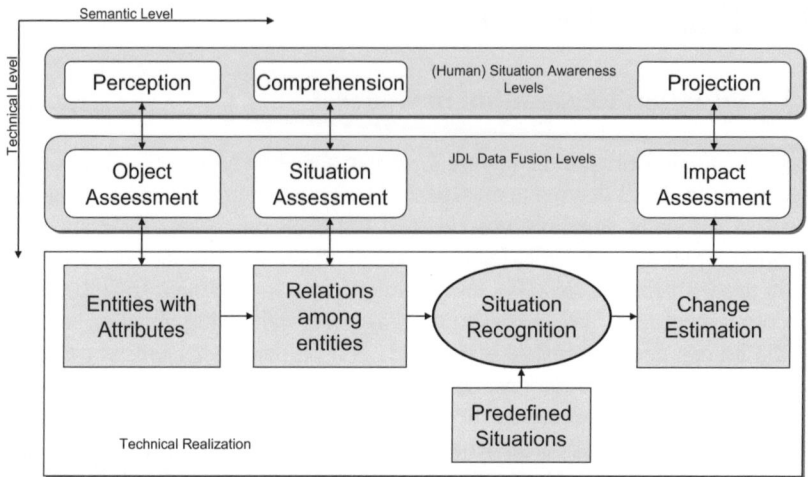

Figure 3.1: The connection of Situation Recognition with Situation Awareness and Data Fusion.

realization of the upper layers, whereas the components of the technical realization are adopted from the description of the data fusion levels in the JDL model. The predefined situations, which are matched with the observed reality, are illustrated as an input for situation recognition We argue that the situation recognition part should be inserted after determining the relations among entities, because situation recognition is an interpretation of the entities and its relations. Based on the results of the situation recognition, the state changes based on different actions can be estimated.

Actually, the first challenge in situation recognition is to provide a formal description of a situation. In the following section, the main components of different definitions of the term situation are investigated.

3.2   Requirements on a Description of a Situation

On different online-dictionaries, the following definitions of the term situation are given:

- "The way in which something is placed in relation to its surroundings" ([Mer])

- "The set of things that are happening and the conditions that exist at a particular time and place" ([Cam])

- "The general state of things; the combination of circumstances at a given time" ([Wor])

All definitions include objects and how they can be characterized ("state of things"). The characterization of objects can be described by associated relevant attributes. Also the relations between different objects is highlighted in these definitions. It has to be noted that it is not clear, whether a situation occurs at a specific point of time or whether a situation is defined over a time interval.

At this point we can state the following requirements for a formal description of a situation:

- objects are an important part of a situation,

- objects are characterized by attributes,

- time or time intervals should be considered, and

- temporal, spatial, and attributive relations between objects are important.

These basic requirements are illustrated by the following simplified example. Imagine the problem of recognizing the transport of illegal immigrants over sea, let us say from Lybia to the island Lampedusa in Italy. The situation can be described by a small, but fast boat that crosses the maritime border and approaches the island. The objects that are part of the situation are the boat, but also the maritime border and the island. In this example, the situation is also characterized by spatial relations. Therefore, the spatial positions of the objects are mandatory attributes to describe the situation. In case of the boat, the position is a dynamic attribute whereas in case of the maritime border and the island, the position is a static attribute, respectively. Further attributes of the boat are a mixture of static or dynamic types. Necessary attributes of the boat for the description of the situation are the size, the velocity, and the heading of the boat. Considered relations are the distance of the boat to the maritime border and the distance of the boat to the island.

This example is quite simple, because only few objects, especially only one moving object, are considered and only a few attributes are necessary to describe the situation. However, although the situation seems to be quite simple, there are more problems to consider. One problem is the classification of the attributes. That means especially when is the velocity of a boat considered as fast? Or at which size is a boat considered as small? Another point concerns the inclusion of uncertainties into the description of a situation because the situation is not accurately describable. In our example, this could be the trajectory of the boat, which is not included in our example. So the boat could make a detour and will not heading directly to the island. The interpretation of the situation is then the same but attributes like the heading of the boat can have different values.

3.3   A Formalized Description of a Situation

In literature, a formalized notation of situation is not clearly defined. One general formalization has been presented by Jakobson in [JBL07], which should be outlined in the following. Jakobson states that the modeling of a situation can be divided into three components: the structural, dynamic, and representational component. The structural component defines the topology of the represented situation. Structural objects are entities, attributes of the entities, classes of entities, and relations between entities. The dynamic component includes the behavior of the entities over time and the representational component concerns the utilities by which the situation can be described. This is usually a set of languages, for example the Web Ontology Language, see [OWL], or the Unified Modeling Language, see [UML].

In the structural component, the main elements are entities $e \in E$, where $E \subseteq U$ is a subclass of all entities of the universe U. Each entity e is characterized by its set of attributes $\{a_1, \ldots, a_p\}$, where each attribute is a collection of attribute properties like name, type, value, default value, etc. The attribute property value is represented as a triplet containing the actual value, uncertainty estimation and time t. The value-triplet of an entity is defined during the existence of the entity and is denoted by $a(t), t \in \delta$. δ denotes the time interval $\delta = (t', t'')$ whereas t' is the creation time and t'' the clear time of the entity. A relation is mathematically defined as a subset of entities $R \subseteq E_1 \times \ldots \times E_m$ with $E_i \subseteq U$ for $i = 1, \ldots, m$. Similar to entities, a relation can be characterized by a set of attributes $\{b_1, \ldots, b_h\}$ and the attribute value of the relation is also only defined during the existence of the relation and is denoted by $b(t)$ with $t \in \delta \subseteq \bigcap_{i=1}^{m} \delta_i$. In case of a binary relationship, the notation $e_i R e_j$ is used. The lifespan δ of a binary relation is then $\delta \subseteq \delta_i \cap \delta_j$.

In the dynamic component, Jakobson [JBL07] distinguishes three types of situations. An *entity-based situation* $S_e(d)$ of an entity e over a time interval $d \subseteq \delta$ is defined as the collection of specific attributes $a_1(t), \ldots, a_m(t)$ of the entity e that have the same value during the time interval d. So for all $t, t' \in d$ the equality

$a_i(t) = a_i(t')$ $(i = 1, \ldots, m)$ holds. We will denote this by

$$S_e(d) = < a_1(t), \ldots, a_m(t) >_d . \tag{3.1}$$

Equivalently, a *relational entity-based situation* of a relation R over a time interval $d \subseteq \delta$ is defined as the collection of specific relational attributes $b_1(t), \ldots, b_h(t)$ of the relation R that have the same value during the time interval d. So for all $(t, t') \in d$ the fact $b_i(t) = b_i(t')$ $(i = 1, \ldots, h)$ holds. We will denote this by

$$S_R(d) = < b_1(t), \ldots, b_h(t) >_d . \tag{3.2}$$

The last situation type, the *relational situation*, considers only the relational aspect of the situation and is not concerned about the attribute values of the relation or the entities. In case of a binary relation, the relational situation over a time interval $d \subseteq \delta_i \cap \delta_j$ can be denoted by

$$S_{(e_i, e_j)}(d) = e_i R e_j. \tag{3.3}$$

More complex situations can now be described with the three basic situations (3.1), (3.2), and (3.3) by using a kind of set-theoretical union and intersection operations. If $S_1(d_1)$ and $S_2(d_2)$ are two basic situations of the above types, a new situation S with the lifespan $d = d_1 \cap d_2$ can be defined through

$$S(d) = S_1(d_1) \cup S_2(d_2)$$

or

$$S(d) = S_1(d_1) \cap S_2(d_2).$$

This formalization of a situation by Jakobson [JBL07] is quite general but also powerful because it allows to describe a lot of complex situations. But one critical point is that no kinds of uncertainties are considered in the situation description. We argue that, for example, a specific situation does not imply that the relevant entity has to hold the same attribute values during a time interval. This point was also highlighted in our example in the previous section where the heading of the boat can be different but the interpretation of the situation is the same. But on the other hand, the formalization fulfills the requirements on a formalization of the term situation that have been stated in the previous section. Objects are in Jakobson's formalization represented by entities with associated attributes and also time intervals are included. The relations in Jakobson's formalization can also be of temporal, spatial, and attributive types. If the description is useful for situation recognition has not been investigated by Jakobson. Therefore, this question may be a topic in further research.

4 Summary and Outlook

In this article, an overview of the terms situation awareness, situation assessment, and data fusion is presented. Especially, the connections between these terms are highlighted. Situation awareness is the key factor in making good decisions, but complex situations may easily lead to insufficient situation awareness of a human decision maker. Therefore, it is necessary to support the decision maker by automatic situation recognition. We present the main problems in automatic situation recognition and state that the first challenge in automatic situation recognition is to find a suitable formalization of a situation. Based on various definitions of the term situation, we extract the requirements for a formalization of this term and outlined one formalized notation that is present in literature.

An important topic in future work will be to identify more formalizations of the term situation in literature. The first aim is to obtain a general, suitable, and useful formalization, which can be used for situation recognition. Further research may also concern matching the observed reality with predefined situations under uncertainty conditions.

Bibliography

[Cam]   Cambridge Dictionaries Online. http://dictionary.cambridge.org. Online; accessed 12-November-2009.

[EC08]   Mica. R. Endsley and Erik S. Connors. Situation awareness: State of the art. In *Power and Energy Society General Meeting - Conversion and Delivery of Electrical Energy in the 21st Century, 2008 IEEE*, pages 1–4, 2008.

[End95]   Mica. R. Endsley. Toward a Theory of Situation Awareness in Dynamic Systems. *Human Factors: The Journal of the Human Factors and Ergonomics Society*, 37(1):32–64, 1995.

[JBL07]   Gabriel Jakobson, John Buford, and Lundy Lewis. Situation Management: Basic Concepts and Approaches. In *Information Fusion and Geographic Information Systems*, pages 18–33, 2007.

[Lam01]   Dale A. Lambert. Situations for Situation Awareness. In *Proceedings of the 4th International Conference on Information Fusion (Fusion 2001)*, pages 1–7, 2001.

[Mer]   Merriam-Webster Online Dictionary. http://www.merriam-webster.com. Online; accessed 12-November-2009.

[NRJ+08] Lars Niklasson, Maria Riveiro, Frederik Johansson, Anders Dahlbom, Göran Falkman, Tom Ziemke, Christoffer Brax, Thomas Kronhamn, Martin Smedberg, Håkan Warston, and Per M. Gustavsson. Extending the scope of situation analysis. In *Proceedings of the 11th International Conference on Information Fusion (Fusion 2008)*, pages 1–8, 2008.

[OWL]   OWL Web Ontology Language. http://www.w3.org/TR/owl-features/. Online; accessed 13-November-2009.

[SB04]   Alan N. Steinberg and Christopher L. Bowman. Rethinking the JDL Data Fusion Levels. In *Proceedings of the Military Sensing Symposia (MSS) National Symposium on Sensor and Data Fusion (NSSDF)*, 2004.

[SBW99]   Alan N. Steinberg, Christopher L. Bowman, and Franklin E. Whit. Revisions to the JDL data fusion model. In *Sensor Fusion: Architectures, Algorithms, and Applications III, Proceedings of SPIE*, volume 3719, pages 430–441, 1999.

[UML]   UML Unified Modeling Language. http://www.uml.org/. Online; accessed 13-November-2009.

[Wor]   WordWebOnline. http://www.wordwebonline.com. Online; accessed 12-November-2009.

Deep Sea Navigation using SLAM

Philipp Woock

Vision and Fusion Laboratory
Institute for Anthropomatics
Karlsruhe Institute of Technology (KIT), Germany
woock@ies.uni-karlsruhe.de

Technical Report IES-2009-15

Abstract: Navigating an autonomous underwater vehicle (AUV) is a difficult task. Dead-reckoning navigation is subject to unbounded error due to sensor inaccuracy and is inapplicable for mission durations longer than a few minutes. To bound the estimation errors a global referencing method has to be used. SLAM (Simultaneous Localization And Mapping) is such a method. It uses repeated recognition of significant features of the environment to reduce the estimation error. Devices for environment sensing that are used in most land applications like cameras, laser scanners or GNSS signals cannot be used under water: GNSS signals are attenuated very strongly in water and light propagation suffers mainly from turbid water. In more than a few hundred meters water depth there is also no sunlight. Sonic waves suffer much less from these problems and that is the reason why sonar sensors are the prevalent sensor type used under water. A main difficulty is to extract three-dimensional information from side-scan images to perform SLAM. An overview of existing approaches to underwater SLAM using sonar data is given in this paper. A short outlook to the system that will be used in the TIETeK project is also presented.

1 Introduction

Dead-reckoning navigation in vehicles is subject to unbounded error due to accumulation of sensor inaccuracies. The most common solution to bound the estimation errors is to use some global referencing, e.g., GNSS (global navigation satellite system) signals. Under water GNSS (or similar) signals are unavailable and therefore other means to bound the estimation error are necessary. SLAM (Simultaneous Localization And Mapping, sometimes also termed Concurrent Mapping and Localization, CML [RRPL04]) is a method that uses significant features of the environment to reduce that error and to additionally build a map of the environment which allows self-localization within that map.

The difficulties in underwater SLAM are mainly due to the fact that cameras do not provide valuable information in most cases as there is no sunlight and small particles in the water scatter light and therefore limit the range of the area that could be lighted. However most research on SLAM is done on land using cameras or laser scanners. Due to the aforementioned reasons sonar sensors are used in the vast majority of underwater applications. There are different kinds of sonar sensors. Multi-beam sonar sensors are able to directly give distance information while side-scan sonars only provide an echo amplitude level varying over time.

Furthermore, SLAM relies on features in the environment that can be repeatedly observed and can unambiguously be associated to already known features. Seafloor has naturally a structure that is mostly fractal [BL97] what makes it rather difficult to distinguish different features that have a very similar appearance.

In Section 2, an overview of the different sensors used in deep sea environments is given. Section 3 shows the difficulties and ambiguities of interpreting sonar echo returns. Methods for extracting 3D information from side-scan sonar data are outlined and some solutions from literature to that problem are described in Section 4. Section 5 shows approaches to SLAM in underwater context. In Section 6 the plans for the TIETeK project and its realization are shown. Section 7 gives a short summary of the paper.

2 Sensors for Underwater Navigation and Localization

Deep sea navigation and mapping is more difficult than land or air navigation. The two main challenges are the lack of a GNSS under water and being unable to use cameras for image acquisition. An exhaustive review of the underwater acoustic image generation process is given by Murino and Trucco in [MT00]. Here only the most important sensors for underwater navigation are presented.

2.1 Dead reckoning

Using only inertial sensors like accelerometers, gyroscopes, magnetometers, and depth sensors an estimate about the motion performed by the AUV (autonomous underwater vehicle) can be given. Over the time period of a mission the accumulation of the sensor noise leads to significant errors. Therefore, inertial sensors alone do not allow sufficiently precise estimation of ego-motion. They need to be supported by complementary sensors.

2.2   Cameras

While it is technically possible to use cameras in deep sea applications, their practical use is small: As there is no sunlight in deep sea, passive cameras are useless and active lighting is necessary. Lighting is possible only for short distances because particles in the seawater scatter the light back to the camera – comparable to high beam headlights in a snowstorm. There is an interesting approach to alleviate that problem: a technique called gated viewing is able to overcome the scattering on particles by opening the camera shutter only for light that traveled over a certain distance [And05].

2.3   Long Baseline (LBL)

The lack of a GNSS can be overcome by setting up a so-called LBL array, where additional transducers have to be placed on the seafloor at known positions. They regularly send out a sonar beacon. From the delay of the signals an AUV can localize itself in the area within the transducers by means of trilateration. This approach is quite accurate but rather inflexible, complex and relatively costly.

2.4   GNSS Aided Ultrashort Baseline

In an ultrashort baseline (USBL) configuration a surface vessel sends an acoustic beacon to the AUV and the AUV sends an answer. From the angle of the incoming signal and the time delay, the relative position of the AUV to the surface vessel can be calculated.

Together with accurate GNSS (e.g., DGPS) information one gets global referencing of the AUV position. That information is then sent via an acoustic link down to the AUV. As the acoustic signals travel thrice the distance to the AUV ($2\times$ beacon, $1\times$ data), the position measurement arrives with some seconds of delay that has to be considered in the fusion step. A more detailed description is given in [MGJ01].

The usable range of the sound pulse restricts the area where one can communicate with the AUV. The term *inverted* USBL is used when instead of the surface vessel the AUV measures angle and distance to get the relative position to the ship.

 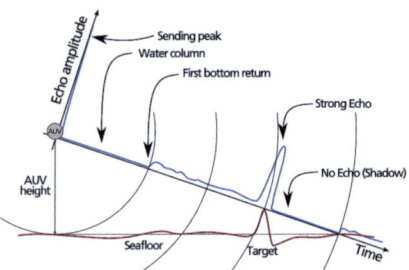

Figure 2.1: Side scan sonar beams (schematically).

Figure 2.2: Side scan sonar echo formation (frontal view).

2.5   Sonar Sensors

Sonar sensors cover a long range as sound waves are attenuated only very lightly in water. The sonar wavelengths allow resolutions down to centimeters. On the downside, sonar sensors are prone to exhibit speckle noise due to the use of coherent waves [Wes06]. In spite of the speckle noise sonar-based sensors are the de facto standard for underwater applications. Different kinds of sonar sensors exist, the most common are side-scan sonars and multi-beam sonars.

2.5.1   Side-scan Sonars

Side-scan (or side-looking) sonars have a very narrow beam ($\approx 1\,°$) in the horizontal plane perpendicular to the traveling direction of the AUV and a wide beam ($\approx 50\,°$) in the vertical plane (see Figure 2.1). The side-scan sonar typically has only one transducer beam per side. It sends out a so-called chirp and records the amplitude of the echo return over time. The sonar echo formation process is depicted in Figure 2.2. That information only yields a single scan line that is highly ambiguous. There is no way to directly extract the sea bottom relief from a particular echo as it is an ill-posed inverse problem.

Methods that try to recover the true relief from images belong to the family of shape-from-shading methods. Some that are used with side-scan sonar imagery are described in more detail in Section 4.

2.5.2 Multi-beam Sonars

A multi-beam sonar is the sonar equivalent of a LIDAR system. Usually it uses a fan of single pencil beams and has a separate transducer for each beam. That way it can immediately return a distance information per beam. Compared to the side-scan sonar, the spatial resolution is lower as for each 'pixel' a separate transducer is needed. That is also the reason why multi-beam sonars are usually bulkier and need more power. On the other hand, data interpretation is easier compared to side-scan data as multi-beam sensors directly provide 3D information about the environment whereas the 3D information from side-scan sonar images has to be extracted first and is ambiguous. Fairfield [FKW05] investigated different sonar geometries with respect to the suitability for underwater SLAM applications concluding that a configuration with three mutually orthogonal great circles works best. This configuration yields only relatively sparse 3D information but big areas of the sensor coverage are overlapping that way.

3 Ambiguity of Side-scan Sonar Returns

Side-scan sonar echo returns contain very much information additional to information about the shape of the seabed. Extracting the shape information is an ill-posed inverse problem and can only be solved through regularization.

That is probably the reason why most studies that were conducted did not focus on quantitative results but rather concentrate on giving qualitative correct results or classifying the seabed into regions of different types like sand ripples, rocks or flat silt areas.

What increases the complexity futher is the illumination/ensonification direction of the side-scan sonar [BCW99]. The sonar beam hits the ground at a low angle of incidence for the most part of the ensonified area and that same area will have a very different appearance when being viewed from another direction.

All reconstruction approaches do not consider dynamic objects like, e.g., fish and assume the seafloor to be completely static.

3.1 Challenges in Extracting Elevation Information

To be able to reconstruct 3D shape from side-scan images one has to regularize the problem first. The amplitude of the echo is influenced by many effects, where the most important are:

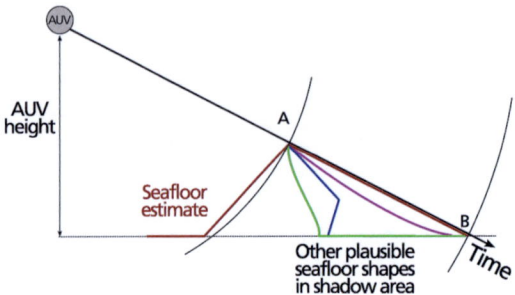

Figure 3.1: Many different geometries would yield the same echo image.

- angle of the seafloor relative to the source,

- distance to the source,

- sediment absorption characteristics,

- surface scattering properties,

- absorption and dispersion of sound in water,

- water currents,

- varying sound speed in different depths, temperatures as well as areas of different salinity,

- multipath propagation, and

- sonar beam form.

For regularization one has to make assumptions about these aspects. Assumptions that are common in literature are Lambertian surface scattering (i.e., a surface that is rough and isotropic and reflects energy equally in all directions) and the flat seabed assumption. Additional constraints can be given in the form of surface smoothness requirements (i.e., continuous, differentiable). Influences of sediment type, absorption and currents are neglected in most cases. Multipath propagation is only of minor importance because sonar uses time-gated pulses. The sonar beam form is either known in advance or can be estimated in parallel [CPL07].

Naturally, there is no information about shape in shadowed areas of side-scan images. Several different shapes could generate the same echo (see Figure 3.1). The side-scan imaging process also introduces geometric deformations especially in short distances to the sensor: foreshortening and layover [Wes06]. Foreshortening

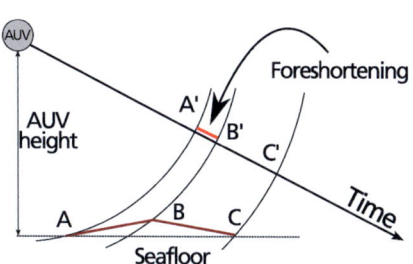

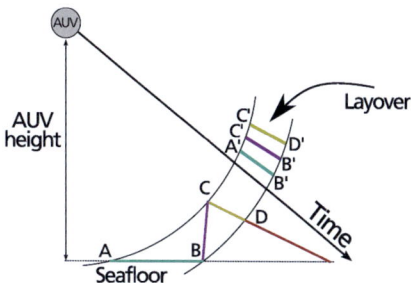

Figure 3.2: Long slopes may appear shortened in the echo image.

Figure 3.3: Echoes from different parts of the ground may arrive simultaneously at the sensor.

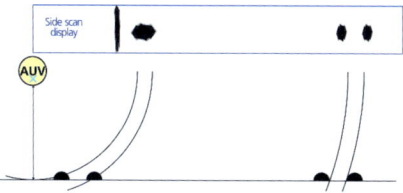

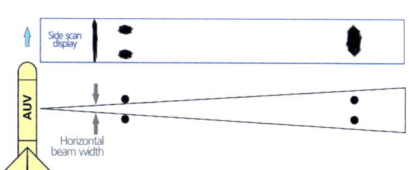

Figure 3.4: Change of side-scan resolution across-track.

Figure 3.5: Change of side-scan resolution along-track.

describes the effect that a slope towards the sensor is shortened in the sonar image. Layover describes the effect that echoes from points higher above the ground may arrive simultaneously with other echos and the echos could overlap. This is described in Figures 3.2 and 3.3.

Related to foreshortening is the observation that side-scan sonars exhibit changing spatial resolution across-track. Along-track the resolution is also varying due to the beam widening as the range increases (see Figures 3.4 and 3.5 adapted from [Maz85]). The mentioned effects stem from the sensor principle and cannot be avoided in general.

Despite the mentioned drawbacks and ambiguities side-scan sonars are used very often as the simple construction makes them comparably cheap. The output can also be easily visualized and is often interpreted by humans. That makes side-scan sonars probably the most prevalent sensor used in deep sea applications.

3.2 Simulator for Side-scan Imagery

J. Bell developed a sophisticated simulator for side-scan imagery based on ray-tracing that considers a stratified water column, sonar beam width, sonar beam directivity, multipath propagation, transmission losses, and ego-motion [BL97]. Most of the ambiguities shown in Section 3.1 have been taken into account. The resulting images were not only visually compared to real sonar images but the image statistics of the simulated images were also checked against real sonar images. It allows to compare shape reconstruction algorithms quantitatively with ground truth. A good simulation tool can also be seen as a formulation of the forward problem that needs to be inverted.

4 Elevation Information from Side-scan Data

To be able to make full use of the sensor measurements for SLAM, it is desirable to obtain a 3D representation from the 2D sonar measurements. A few methods to accomplish that are presented in this section.

4.1 Estimating Elevation from Shadows

Reed et al. [RPB04] use co-operative statistical snakes to detect highlight regions with neighbouring shadow regions that are facing away from the sensor. Assuming an otherwise flat seabed reconstructing object elevation information from the shadow lengths with the help of the theorem on intersecting lines is a simple and natural approach. Some methods work on two-dimensional images. Those have to be created via registering the single scans lines first. The easiest approach is to just stack the scan lines. More sophisticated approaches would pre-process the scan lines considering geometrical configuration as well as vehicle motion prior to stacking.

4.2 Propagation Shape-from-Shading (SfS)

Propagation SfS was pioneered by Langer and Hebert [LH91] and modified with a different scattering model by Dura, Bell and Lane [DBL04]. The seafloor reconstruction uses one scan line at a time. The reconstruction is starting from directly beneath the sensor where a flat seabed is assumed. The vertical distance from the sensor to the seafloor is either known or can be estimated from the sonar data. Starting from there, the inclination angle to the surface normal is propagated towards the outer end of the sensor coverage area depending on the reflectivity. Propagation SfS is quite robust against shadowing effects and gives good results on directional surfaces like sand ripples. Langer and Hebert suggest additional scan line preprocessing for noise reduction. They propose median filters and a graduated non-convexity (GNC) filter which is able to maintain discontinuities. Pre-filtering is necessary due to noise which is easily corrupting the reconstruction as errors add up towards the outer ends. As every sonar line is processed individually this approach lends itself well to online use. However the correct mutual registration of the processed scan lines depends on the ego-motion of the AUV which has to be estimated. Ego-motion estimation errors lead to errors in the 3D reconstruction of the seafloor surface.

4.3   Linear Shape-from-Shading

The Linear SfS method [DBL04] from Dura, Bell and Lane is based on the work from Bell et al. on side-scan image directionality effects [BCW99]. The approach is working in the frequency domain and uses the fact that the sonar image is a directional filtered version of the seabed height map. They provide a linear transform that relates the Fourier transform of the two-dimensional sonar images to the seabed height.

Linear SfS is not as robust as Propagation SfS when processing ripples, however, it is much more robust in the presence of noise and in processing isotropic seabeds. Processing two-dimensional sonar images makes it more difficult to use this method as an online method.

4.4   Hierarchical Recovering of Shape from Side-scan Data

In the works of Coiras, Petillot and Lane ([CPL07], [CPL05]) an elevation map is reconstructed from side-scan sonar images. They start at a coarse resolution using an expectation-maximization approach with gradient descent to iteratively refine the most probable shape that corresponds to the echo amplitude. They assume Lambertian surface scattering.

Their method is not designed as an online method. They work with two-dimensional side-scan images. This has the advantage of incorporating parameter dependencies across scan lines but needs scan line registration first.

5 SLAM on Sonar Data

SLAM is a method to reduce and bound uncertainty in vehicle localization and the resulting environment map through multiple re-observation of salient features and incorporating prior knowledge via a motion model. For the method to succeed it is essential that a certain feature can be recognized with high certainty and is not mistaken for another one. When the algorithm is able to identify landmarks as already visited ones the accumulated errors from inertial navigation can be significantly reduced.

Side-scan sonar images, however, do not provide 3D information directly. The sensor output after registering the scan lines is 2D. Although 3D information is not strictly necessary to perform SLAM, the different appearance of features when ensonified from different angles makes it nearly impossible to recognize landmarks from the 2D image alone. Therefore, it is clearly beneficial to be make use of the three-dimensional reconstruction from the methods described in Section 4.

5.1 SLAM on Side-scan Data

An approach using side-scan sonar data for SLAM is introduced in [RRPL04]. The localization is done only in 2D with three parameters (2D position and yaw angle, $[x, y, \phi]$). Not only a side-scan sonar has been investigated but also a forward-looking sonar that is able to make more frequent re-observations of landmarks. A comparison with dead reckoning alone shows that the drift error in the estimation that makes additional use of the side-scan sonar is half of the pure dead reckoning estimation error. The landmark matching however was done offline by hand yielding perfect matches and no mismatches. All landmarks were observed twice or thrice. They use EKF-SLAM, which is unsuitable for large numbers of landmarks and works only correctly when no mismatches are present. The focus of the paper, however, lies more on the offline post-processing using a Rauch-Tung-Striebel (RTS) smoother [Sär08] and they did not compare their SLAM algorithm without the RTS smoother. The authors emphasize the great value of smoothing as a post-processing step.

5.2 3D SLAM on Sonar Data

Fairfield et al. [FKW07] use multi-beam sonar information to create a map of the environment. The sonar sensors give sparse 3D information about the shape of the surroundings. Their SLAM method is based on Rao-Blackwellized particle filters (RBPFs) [MT07]. Additionally, they use a sophisticated data structure called Deferred Reference Counting Octrees (DRCO) to keep the memory requirements low as each particle has to carry the full evidence grid. They show an adaptive method where they use only as many particles as is feasible for real-time operation. They are able stay well below 10 m of localization error even after about 10000 SLAM iterations. This is a very promising approach that shows how to combine such conflicting requirements as real-time operation and using as many particles as possible at the same time.

6   Outlook – The TIETeK Project

In the TIETeK (Tiefsee-Inspektions- und Explorations-Technologiekonzept) project an AUV is developed that is able to autonomously map and explore the bottom of the deep sea. As water pressure is very high in the deep sea, most parts of the AUV should be built in a pressure independent manner to withstand depths of about 6000 m. However, emphasis is also on creating a comparatively cheap, highly configurable vehicle that is able to use different sensors depending on the task at hand.

The main sensor will be a high resolution side-scan sonar accompanied by IMUs (inertial measurement unit), DVL (doppler velocity log) and depth sensors. Additionally, SLAM will be used to support navigation and to facilitate exploration. The SLAM procedure to be developed should also work with multi-beam sonar data.

6.1   Project Workflow

The first step will be to extract seafloor elevation information from the side-scan sonar data. Vehicle movement at acquisition time has to be taken into account to interpret the echo correctly.

Next, it is important to find salient features within the relief that can be re-observed with high reliability. This is a very challenging task as the appearance of the features will change significantly when the viewing direction changes. The relief of, e.g., sand ripples may be nearly unobservable for the side-scan sonar when viewed from certain angles. In case the approach is unfeasible due to landmark extraction and association being too ambiguous, a grid-based approach using 2.5D elevation maps will be evaluated.

Thirdly, the SLAM method will be employed to obtain accurate navigation and map information. It is crucial to keep the map sizes low and use the computing resources efficiently as the algorithm needs to run in real time on COTS (commercial off-the-shelf) hardware inside the AUV.

The map and the improved ego-motion information from the SLAM algorithm will be used to support vehicle navigation and is the basis for explorative actions taken autonomously by the vehicle. In an additional post-processing step, maps of higher quality than the online maps will be built.

7   Conclusion

The side-scan sonar echo return is highly ambiguous which makes shape extraction from that signal a challenging task. Additionally, SLAM in underwater applications is far from being as well-understood as in airborne or land applications. As ground truth is basically unavailable, quantitative evaluation is extremely difficult. That is the reason why an underwater simulation environment is of great help.

SLAM has been used only very sparsely in underwater applications yet. Once computational power becomes cheaper, more real-time solutions to underwater SLAM will surely emerge.

Bibliography

[And05]   Adam Andersson. Range Gated Viewing with Underwater Camera. Technical report, Linköping University, Department of Electrical Engineering, 2005.

[BCW99]   Judith M. Bell, Mike J. Chantler, and T. Wittig. Sidescan sonar: a directional filter of seabed texture? *IEE Proceedings -Radar, Sonar and Navigation*, 146(1):65–72, February 1999.

[BL97]   Judith M. Bell and L. M. Linnett. Simulation and analysis of synthetic sidescan sonar images. *IEE Proceedings -Radar, Sonar and Navigation*, 144(4):219–226, August 1997.

[CPL05]   Enrique Coiras, Yvan Petillot, and David M. Lane. An Expectation-Maximization Framework for the Estimation of Bathymetry from Side-scan Sonar Images. In *Proc. Oceans 2005 - Europe*, volume 1, pages 261–264, June 20–23, 2005.

[CPL07]   Enrique Coiras, Yvan Petillot, and David M. Lane. Multiresolution 3-D Reconstruction From Side-Scan Sonar Images. *IEEE Transactions on Image Processing*, 16(2):382–390, February 2007. Heriot-Watt University Edinburgh.

[DBL04]   Esther Durá, Judith M. Bell, and David M. Lane. Reconstruction of textured seafloors from side-scan sonar images. *IEE Proceedings – Radar, Sonar and Navigation*, 151(2):114–126, April 2004.

[FKW05]   Nathaniel Fairfield, George A. Kantor, and David Wettergreen. Three Dimensional Evi-
          dence Grids for SLAM in Complex Underwater Environments. In *Proceedings of the 14th
          International Symposium of Unmanned Untethered Submersible Technology (UUST)*, Lee,
          New Hampshire, August 2005. AUSI.

[FKW07]   Nathaniel Fairfield, George A. Kantor, and David Wettergreen. Real-Time SLAM with
          Octree Evidence Grids for Exploration in Underwater Tunnels. *Journal of Field Robotics*,
          2007.

[LH91]   Dirk Langer and Martial Hebert. Building Qualitative Elevation Maps From Side Scan
          Sonar Data For Autonomous Underwater Navigation. In *Proc. IEEE International
          Conference on Robotics and Automation*, pages 2478–2483, April 9–11, 1991.

[Maz85]   Charles Mazel. *Side Scan Sonar Training Manual*. Salem, Klein Associates, 1985.

[MGJ01]   Magne Mandt, Kenneth Gade, and Bjørn Jalving. Integrating DGPS-USBL position mea-
          surements with inertial navigation in the HUGIN 3000 AUV. Technical report, Forsvarets
          Forskningsinstitutt (Norwegian Defence Research Establishment), 2001.

[MT00]   Vittorio Murino and Andrea Trucco. Three-dimensional Image Generation and Processing
          in Underwater Acoustic Vision. *Proceedings of the IEEE*, 88(12):1903–1948, December
          2000.

[MT07]   Michael Montemerlo and Sebastian Thrun. *FastSLAM: A Scalable Method for the Simul-
          taneous Localization and Mapping Problem in Robotics*. (Springer Tracts in Advanced
          Robotics). Springer-Verlag New York, Inc., Secaucus, NJ, USA, 2007.

[RPB04]   Scott Reed, Yvan Petillot, and Judith M. Bell. Automated approach to classification
          of mine-like objects in sidescan sonar using highlight and shadow information. *IEE
          Proceedings – Radar, Sonar and Navigation*, 151(1):48–56, February 2004.

[RRPL04] Ioseba Tena Ruiz, Sébastien de Raucourt, Yvan Petillot, and David M. Lane. Concurrent
          Mapping and Localization Using Sidescan Sonar. *IEEE Journal of Oceanic Engineering*,
          29(2):442–456, April 2004.

[Sär08]   Simo Särkkä. Unscented Rauch-Tung-Striebel Smoother. *IEEE Transactions on Automatic
          Control*, 53(3):845, 2008.

[Wes06]   Birgit Wessel. *Automatische Extraktion von Straßen aus SAR-Bilddaten*. PhD the-
          sis, Fakultät für Bauingenieur- und Vermessungswesen, Technische Universität München,
          2006.

Object-Oriented World Modelling
for Autonomous Systems

Andrey Belkin

Vision and Fusion Laboratory
Institute for Anthropomatics
Karlsruhe Institute of Technology (KIT), Germany
belkin@kit.edu

Technical Report IES-2009-16

Abstract: Modern autonomous systems are challenged by a necessity of the permanent situation awareness: perception, comprehension, and prediction of the surrounding environment. A basis for such awareness is a reliable world modelling that serves as an efficiently structured memory.

This contribution proposes several new approaches in the world modelling. The Progressive Mapping represents a dynamical description of real world elements with mapping sets of objects and attributes. The prior knowledge about object types and relations is introduced as a collection of semantic networks of classes, while dynamic relations within the world model are represented by semantic networks of objects. Also, current contribution presents a processing of degree-of-belief distributions and a possibility of calculation of memory limits.

1 Introduction

An autonomous system operation requires constant situation awareness (SA). The most acknowledged definition of SA was given by Endsley [End95]:

> "the perception of elements in the environment within a volume of time and space, the comprehension of their meaning, and the projection of their status in the near future"

The foundation for such awareness is a world modelling, which describes the surrounding environment and serves as an information hub for all subsystems. The information can be provided by sensors or by prior knowledge storage. Each incoming information piece contains some amount of uncertainty that can be characterized by a degree-of-belief (DoB) distribution and can be merged into existing models by means of Bayesian fusion.

Modern world modelling systems for autonomous systems are usually limited to a concrete set of tasks. For example, in the case of path planning, exploration and localization tasks, the modeling system is often represented by SLAM or other geometry and topology systems. For another example, the autonomous receptionist or medical assistant robot is classifying surrounding objects and situations for reactive decision taking. In the most common case, the world modelling system has to represent all objects and relation of the surrounding environment and to model them in a way of a digital sandbox. This allows for reactive as well as proactive operation, which are vital for many advanced applications (e.g., autonomous cars or humanoid robots).

A world modelling subsystem presented in this contribution accumulates information, builds relevant models of the real world, and provides information to other subsystems. The modelling can process information streams in a form of Degree of Belief distributions with parameterized uncertainties and merge distributions with Bayesian fusion. An adequate and efficient environment representation requires modelling of the environment elements and as well their relations. Each element can be described as an object and its relations as connections in semantic networks. It is important also to specify semantic of each object by introducing information from a prior knowledge. The modelling subsystem serves also as an information hub for all subsystems from lower levels (hardware response) to the highest one (planning, context recognition, etc).

The presented material is structured as follows: Section 2 describes the structure of a prior knowledge, Section 3 deals with dynamic modeling, Section 4 introduces the idea of probabilistic matching of dynamic objects to prior knowledge, Section 5 presents the experimental set up and test results. Finally, a short summary is given in Section 6.

Modelling domains   The description of the environment is performed by modelling its elements and their relations. It is convenient to design the modelling system within the object-oriented methodology, where the real world elements are represented by classes and particular things by class instances (objects). For clear terminology, it is important to distinguish domains of environment and model realms: the Dynamic World (real things and relations), Dynamic Models (objects and networks), and Prior Knowledge (concepts of classes and relations, prior records) (Figure 1.1).

Real world	World modeling	
Dynamic World	**Dynamic Models**	**Prior Knowledge**
Dynamic elements things; relations	**Dynamic instances** object and attribute instances; semantic networks of instances	**Class concepts** object, attribute, and relation types
		Relation concepts semantic networks of class concepts
		Prior records specific elements

Figure 1.1: Modelling domains.

The Real world realm is represented by the Dynamic World domain. It is populated by environment elements, which can be perceived by sensors or estimated by cognition processes.

The World modelling realm covers the Prior Knowledge and Dynamic Models domains. The Prior Knowledge domain (Section 2) contains Class concepts (known types of real world elements), Relation concepts (relations between classes), and Prior records (information about specific environment elements). The Dynamic Models (Section 3) domain contains semantic networks of objects (Figure 1.2).

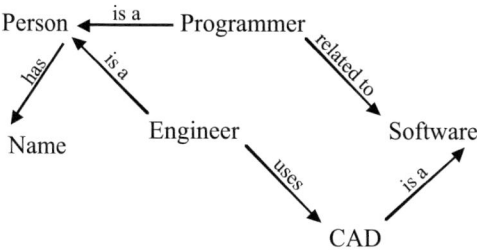

Figure 1.2: Example of a semantic network.

2 Prior Knowledge

The prior knowledge domain defines the class and relation types known to the modelling subsystem, relations between concepts, and additional information about specific objects.

Class concepts   The Class concepts define object, attribute, and relation types and semantic.

Relation concepts   Relations specify possible connections between objects and are defined as semantic networks of Class concepts. Most of the previous researches on knowledge representation for autonomous systems are focused on a narrow set of tasks, using one or two semantic networks (e.g., geometrical and functional primitives [RDR95] or spatial hierarchies with additional attributes (color, weight) [Fri98], [Rie97], [Rog03]). However, an autonomous system requires different relations (e.g., "part of", "is a") of correlated classes or objects. Thus, multiple semantic networks over the same classes or objects are vital (Figure 2.1), which allows for multi-dimensional relations processing.

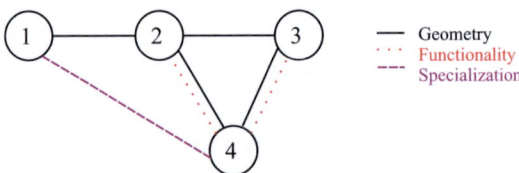

Figure 2.1: Multiple semantic networks.

Levels of abstraction   One of the relations defined within the relation concepts is the specialization, i.e. a hierarchy of classes with the "is a" connection (Figure 1.2). Specialized classes have more attributes than the more abstract parent class. Specializations can be arbitrary assigned to some abstraction levels by known attributes. The hierarchy can be represented as a pyramid of abstraction levels (Figure 2.2) with the blank class at the top, meaning the existence of "something". Each object of a world model can be processed on any abstraction level [GHB08] above the reached one, thus containing different granularity of information. Dynamic objects for world modelling can be instantiated from the Class concepts of the hierarchy of abstraction pyramid [GHB08].

The concept of abstraction hierarchies is motivated by several ideas. At the very

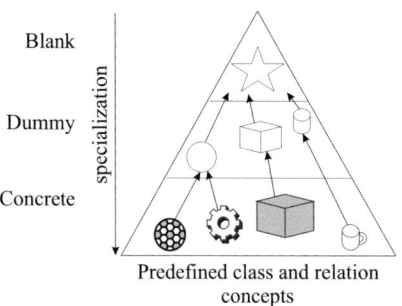

Blank

Dummy

Concrete

specialization

Predefined class and relation
concepts

Figure 2.2: Classification abstraction pyramid.

beginning, the autonomous system knows little about the environment and perceives only things around as much as sensors allow. As time passes, it gathers more information about the surrounding world and updates the model objects, lowering their abstraction level in the pyramid. The shift to lower levels occurs, for example, by specialization of the object from a common structure (e.g., "box") to some specialized structure (e.g., "postal package"). If some inconsistencies are found in the model (e.g., "postal package" starts to fly) the object is raised to the upper abstract levels of the pyramid hierarchy, which corresponds to removing wrong specializations.

Another reason for processing objects on different abstraction levels is context dependency. The same object can be viewed differently depending on the context: a bookcase is considered an obstacle during a path planning (leaving many attributes and contained books out of scope) or a storage for books by text finding.

In spite of advantages of categorization of objects according to prior knowledge, the classification mechanism is affected by several problems:

1. Multiple hierarchies – it is not clear how to organize a specialization hierarchy if the system receives different sequences of data, like in one case "shape" before "temperature" (visible distant thing), in another case "temperature" before "shape" (large complex structure in the proximity). Which attribute should be on a lower level of abstraction is not obvious in this case;

2. Fixed construct limitations – the classification approach is, in principle, rigid and limited comparing to symbolic description [Ahl02]. This means, it is possible to classify objects only among predefined categories and on the basis of expected attributes. An arbitrary unexpected situation cannot be processed properly;

3. Quantity complexity – a set of classes can be enormously large for representing any complex real-life environment. Large information sets are hard to develop and maintain for programmers and are also memory and CPU consuming. Moreover, large sets lead to increased miss-matching due to a large number of objects of similar structure and different semantic.

Due to the first two problems, the classification approach represents an engineering workaround limited in its narrow scope of given tasks. A more flexible approach has to be used to advance objects through hierarchy levels and to select matching attributes for different tasks. This approach is the Progressive Mapping (Section 3.3) that allows flexible selection of attribute sets for each given task or matching to prior knowledge (Section 4.1).

Prior records Prior records contain information about specific things and relations of the environment (e.g., information about a specific person or location).

Prior knowledge storage The prior knowledge about the real world can be stored as semantic networks at back-end layer. The idea of back-end comes from the consideration that prior knowledge database should represent all relevant knowledge about the real world, thus, it can be too complex for a real-time dynamic modelling.
The size of the prior knowledge collection is limited by the combinatorial complexity of large multidimensional data sets. To overcome this problem (the third problem in Section 2), a modular thematic architecture is proposed. Each module contains information relevant to a current scene (e.g., kitchen or living room) or context (e.g., party or siesta). The back-end system can load and unload modules on demand by cognition subsystem.

3   Dynamic Models

The Dynamic Models domain contains semantic networks with objects and their relations, which are found in the surrounding environment.

3.1   Uncertainty

Dynamical modelling implies modelling object attributes, which are in the ideal case, single values. However, sensor data contain uncertainties due to acceptance

Table 3.1: Attribute modelling with uncertainty.

Representation	Type (t)	Mass (m) [g]
Fixed value	Netbook	1000
Fixed value with uncertainty	Netbook (48%)	$1000 \pm \sigma$ ($\sigma = 32$)
Marginal DoB distribution	Netbook (48%) Ultraportable laptop (40%) Thin laptop (12%)	$0.48 \cdot N(1000, 32)$ $+ 0.4 \cdot N(1200, 35)$ $+ 0.12 \cdot N(1600, 45)$
Pair DoB distribution		*P(s, m)*
...		...
Joint DoB distribution		*P(s, m, ..., k)*

problems or environment noise. The uncertainty can be specified, for example, via confidence levels for discrete values and the standard deviation for continuous values. Though, the more informative representation is a Degree of Belief (DoB) distribution P (Table 3.1). The DoB of objects with different attributes can be simplified to marginal distributions for each of the attribute or given as a joint DoB distribution of correlated parameters.

The lower the level of the representation is, the more information about the attribute it contains. It is always possible to process information at any level above but not below. Although the joint DoB is preferable as the most complete description, it is not used in this contribution due to fast growing (e.g., exponential) complexity.

The Degree of Belief considered in the current contribution is a distribution $P(s)$ over one attribute parameter s (Table 3.1). Each attribute of the modelling object is given by a DoB distribution P. The incoming information I_1 is fused with existing information I_0:

$$P(s|I_0) \overset{I_1}{\to} P(s|I_0, I_1).$$

The entropy of the DoB distribution is:

$$H(s) = -\sum_s P(s) \log(P(s)).$$

The incoming information narrows the distribution peak over a given value, thus, reducing the entropy. The change in the quality of information (mutual information) can be calculated numerically as a change of the entropy from the initial state to the state with information I_1:

$$MI(s; I_1) = H(s|I_0) - H(s|I_0, I_1).$$

3.2   Object Aging

Elements of the real world are not persistent: an apple on a table is not meant to be on its place for all time. So, each object in the model should be reconfirmed after some amount of time or stated to exist with some decreased DoB value (object aging). The object aging represents awareness about changes in the real world and a need to perceive them. Each modeled object contains a DoB of existence [GHB08]. If its value exceeds some threshold D_c, then the object is counted to exist in the model at least as a blank one. If it decreases below some level D_d, then the object is deleted from the world model.

The object's life cycle is given in [GHB08] as a constantly falling DoB of existence (e.g., by exponential decrease with aging factor F_{aging}) with risings on sensory reconfirmations (Figure 3.1(a)). The reconfirmation threshold D_r assures that the system is signaled about sensory validation need. The validation itself can occur during some allowed time period determined by $D_r - D_d$ and clock frequency.

Similar to object aging, which decreases the existence DoB value, an attribute aging can disperse the attribute's DoB distribution. For example, if a DoB of the "temperature" attribute is peaking sharply at 21°C, it becomes flatter and wider as time passes, reflecting the increased uncertainty about the current temperature (Figure 3.1(b)).

The concept of aging helps also by learning corrections. For example, if a system has noticed a car driving over water (actually, over a large puddle), it can classify the car as an amphibian (peaking the DoB distribution over the "amphibian" type). With passing time, the system perceives that this object drives only over ground

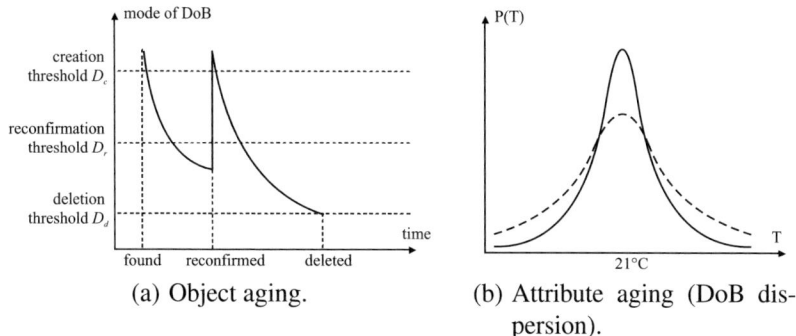

(a) Object aging.

(b) Attribute aging (DoB dispersion).

Figure 3.1: DoB of existence (a) and attribute (b)

(increasing DoB peak over the "car" type), so it "forgets" about the water floating possibility (similar as a human being does).

The aging factor F_{aging} can be different for different classes. For example, a table is more persistent than a cookie. So, an aging correction, called "class correction" C_{class} can be applied to the aging factor F_0. A context (e.g., party or siesta) and other world parameters can also alter the aging, introducing a set of corrections $C_{context}, \ldots, C_N$ to F_0:

$$F_{aging} = F_0 + C_{class} + C_{context} + \cdots + C_N.$$

Since objects are deleted after reaching the D_d, the aging factor and a set of corrections determine memory time limits (i.e. for how long can the system contain objects) and enable numerical estimation of memory usage at an arbitrary time point.

3.3 Progressive Mapping

The dynamical models represent environment elements as objects and their relations. The incoming sensory information, the cognition results, and the object aging refresh the dynamic state of the model. Objects can be instantiated from classes of the Class concepts domain and reinstantiated by derived specialization classes each time new information arrives [GHB08]. This approach, though, is not optimal for dynamic states due to problems mentioned in Section 2. Instead, this contribution proposes a dynamic description of objects – an on the fly assignment of attributes.

The dynamic description approach developed in this contribution is called *Progressive Mapping* (Proming). The incoming information (even unclassified) are fused into the existing model by the means of Bayesian fusion. The atomic level of information is an attribute, which describes an arbitrary parameter (e.g., position or color) of an environment element in a form of a DoB distribution. Like real world attribute, each modelling attribute can have multiple values (e.g., a ball can be white-black colored), so, peaking over multiple values in the DoB distribution. Objects contain a set of attributes, which describe physical properties, semantic meaning, or other information. Objects of one part of the environment (e.g., room or area) are grouped into a scene. The visual scheme for such an architecture is presented in Figure 3.2.

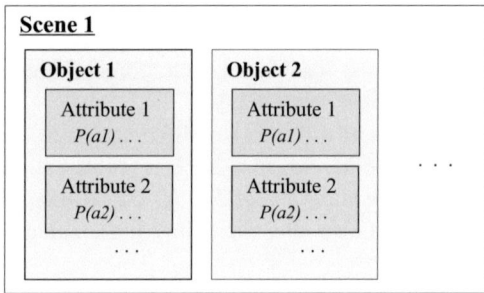

Figure 3.2: World modelling architecture.

Each information piece contains intrinsic properties, like name (e.g., "temperature", "color" for attributes; "Andrey", "coffee machine" for objects), DoB distribution and some others.

At the beginning, each object is created as an empty container. The incoming data is fused into existing maps with consistency and meaning checks between new and existing information. The progression of information maps over the time is shown in Figure 3.3. The granularity of Proming levels is so small that it is not reasonable to distinguish them. The abstraction pyramid becomes quasi gradual as shown in Figure 3.4.

The Progressive Mapping mechanism eliminates the first two problems of the direct classification approach (Section 2). Namely, instead of static class specializations, flexible progressive data structures are employed.

Although, the Progressive Mapping delivers flexibility of a dynamic description, it has problems with prior knowledge representation. A solution to this issue can be achieved by a hybrid approach: the dynamical world model is represented by Proming, which is linked to Prior Knowledge domain (Figure 3.4).

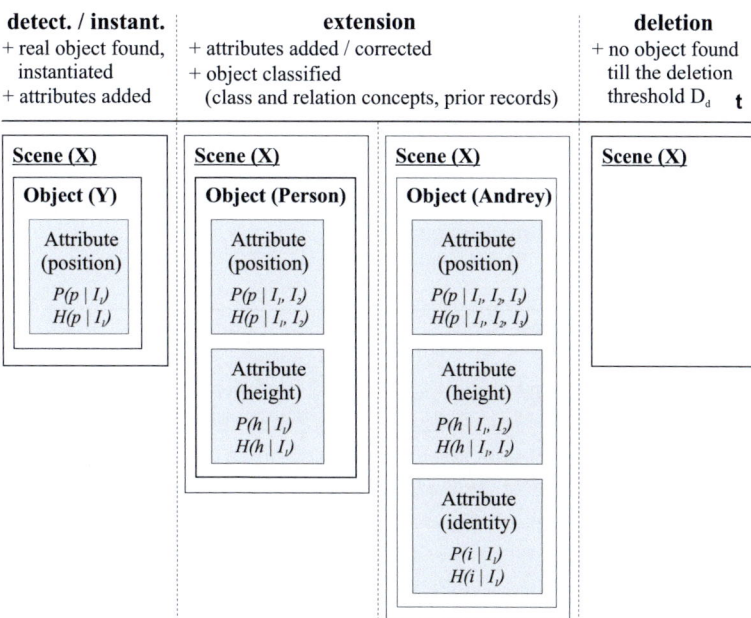

Figure 3.3: Progression of a scene map over the time with a typical life cycle of an object.

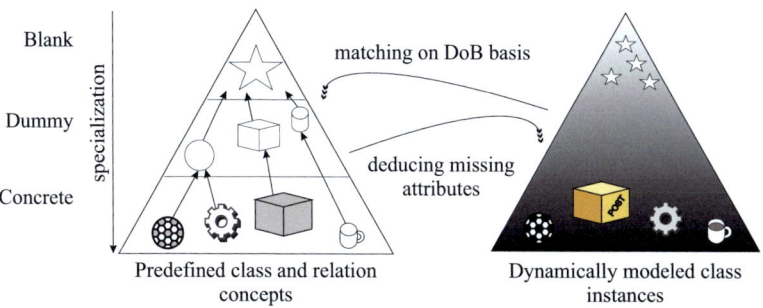

Figure 3.4: Classification (left) and Proming (right) pyramids.

4   Domains Interchange

For correct cognition and semantic processing of environment elements it is vital
to synchronize the dynamic models with the prior knowledge.
Inspite that the Classification pyramid implies the classical object-oriented approach, the modelling objects are not instantiated from these classes directly. The
Proming is based on container objects, which can be assigned to specific classes
by a matching process described in Section 4.1. The container objects concept lays
aside the object-oriented methodology.

4.1   Class Matching

One of the most important things in the world modelling is the connection of dynamical model and prior knowledge. At this point, model objects with a set of
perceived attributes are recognized as objects of known classes (class matching) or
known class instances (prior record matching). During matching, a set of object attributes is compared to class attributes in the classification pyramid on a probability
and semantic basis. An attributes deviation vector $\sigma(a_1, a_2, \ldots, a_N)$ determines
the confidence level of the matching to some known Class concept. The class
matching advances objects through the pyramid as soon as object attributes match
a predefined class and constantly links the object to prior knowledge (Figure 3.4).
For example, if an object is classified as a cup, then the system automatically receives information that the object can be used to carry liquid, has a stable surface
on the bottom, and can be found in a kitchen. The matching process can go recursively to lower levels as long as the attributes and semantic deviation is less than
some limit $\sigma_{matching}$.
A deduction of missing attributes can also be made upon class matching. For example, if an autonomous system detects a ball of about 22 cm diameter and of a
distinct black-white pattern of truncated icosahedron, then it can try to match the
prior knowledge and classify the ball type as $P(t)$. The type distribution can, for
example, peak over the "football" $P(t = F)$ and, due to perception uncertainty,
a volleyball $P(t = V)$. The missing DoB distribution for the attribute "weight"
$P(w)$ can be estimated from the DoB for the type $P(t)$ and the prior knowledge
about the weight attribute given the class type $P(w|t = X)$:

$$P(w) = \sum_X P(w|t = X)P(t = X).$$

A similar process of matching and deduction can also be useful for other tasks, like context (e.g., party or siesta) recognition.

The abstraction pyramid allows a classification mechanism, where each modeled object is assigned to some abstraction level. A model object is progressing over the time (receiving more attributes and values) and can be at any moment matched to Class concepts of the abstraction pyramid. A deduction of missing attributes can also be made upon class matching.

Objects of a world model can be viewed and processed on all levels from the classified to the top (Figure 3.4). For example, a football can be processed on the levels of football, ball, point cloud, bounding box, centroid, and blank object.

The prior knowledge back-end represents not only the classification pyramids for object specializations but also semantic meanings to possible attributes and relations. This helps finding inconsistencies, like the measured temperature is below 0 K or a door has two rotation axis.

4.2   Dynamical Prior Records

Prior records are predefined or can be created dynamically by an autonomous system during the perception and cognition processes. Since the dynamical information is affected by object and attribute aging, it can be lost after some time. There are situations when such a direct deletion of objects is not optimal. For example, a cup is moved from a table into a dishwashing machine. After several hours the cup should be recognized during the dishwasher unloading process. For this case, the deletion of the object can be performed in two steps. Firstly, the object is shifted from the world model to dynamical prior records. This reduces the model, saves processing time and system resources, and at the same time preserves the object. After a while, unused objects of the prior records are ultimately removed (e.g., a person was a visitor for a single time) similar to object aging mechanism (Section 3.2).

The prior records can be organized in the same manner as class and relation concept domains. The matching of detected objects and those from the prior records is similar to class matching (Section 4.1).

5   Experimental Tests

The practical realization of the current contribution is performed within the Deutsche Forschungsgemeinschaft (DFG) Sonderforschungsbereich (SFB) 588 "Humanoid Robots – Learning and Cooperating Multimodal Robots" project (Figure 5.1). The world model contains environment knowledge in form of objects and relations and serves as an information hub for all subsystems of the robot.

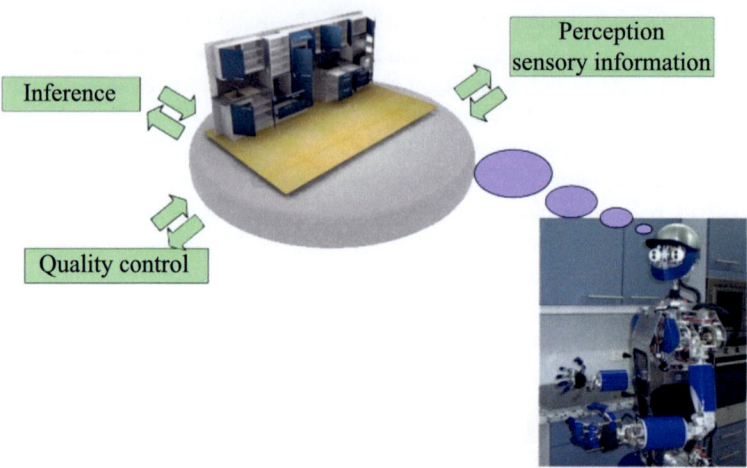

Figure 5.1: SFB 588 world modelling (Armar-III robot) [M2].

Also, a reduced world modelling was implemented in Network Enabled Surveillance and Tracking (NEST) project, developed at the Fraunhofer-Institute for Information and Data Processing IITB. *"The model represents relevant information extracted from a large number of sensors of a surveillance system, fused into a single comprehensive, dynamic model of the monitored area"* [EGB08].
The world model in SFB 588 is realized in a modular cross-platform (i.e., Windows or Linux) architecture. The Core subsystem is responsible for dynamic models and the Back-End for the prior knowledge (Figure 5.2).

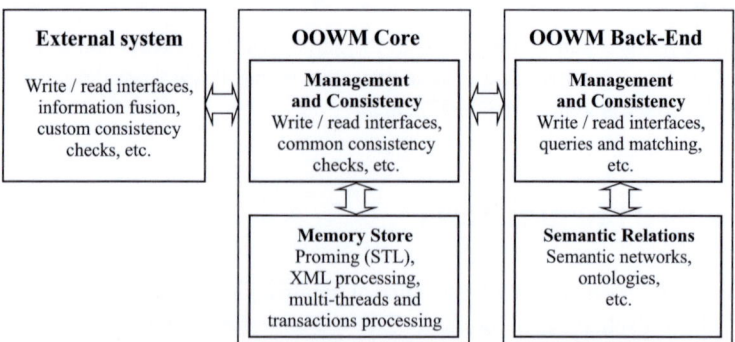

Figure 5.2: Object-oriented world modelling architecture.

The communication interface to the External system is realized via XML data exchange. The XML coupling allows serialization capability for persistent storage, network interchange, or snapshots recording.

The OOWM Core front-end consists of the Memory Store and Management and Consistency modules. The Memory Store module contains semantic networks of objects with attributes of arbitrary type. It provides robust processing and clone storage independent of external objects in a multi-threaded and transaction safe manner. The Core Management and Consistency module provides interfaces for external subsystems and performs basic consistency checks (e.g., a cup is reported to be two cups with overlapping spatial disposition). It also communicates with the Back-End subsystem.

The OOWM Back-End subsystem consists of two parts: the Semantic Relations and Management and Consistency modules. The Semantic Relations retain semantic networks of prior knowledge and attributes schema. The Back-End Management and Consistency module communicates with the Core subsystem, delivers information per queries (matching), and performs basic consistency checks (e.g., checks on type miss-match).

6 Conclusion

This contribution presents an object-oriented world modeling for autonomous systems based on hybrid Progressive Mapping and classification approach. The world modeling provides a foundation for a permanent situation awareness and serves as an information storage and hub for all subsystems. The Progressive Mapping allows a much more flexible dynamic description of environment elements compared to a direct classification approach. Dynamic relations and prior knowledge are represented by multiple semantic networks. All object attributes as well as the object existence are defined as probability distributions in a form of Degree of Beliefs, which gives the advantage for information processing by means of Bayesian fusion. The class matching approach enables matching of prior knowledge and the model objects on a probabilistic basis. A mechanism for constant information reconfirmation is given by objects and attributes aging. The aging is represented by a set of factors affecting the DoB distributions, which allows estimation of object time limits and memory usage at an arbitrary moment. The overall architecture presented in the current contribution is developed within the DFG SFB 588 "Humanoid Robots – Learning and Cooperating Multimodal Robots" project and can be used as a high-level memory model for any autonomous or surveillance system.

7 Acknowledgement

This work has been supported by the German Science Foundation (DFG) within the Sonderforschungsbereich (SFB) 588 "Humanoid Robots".

Bibliography

[Ahl02] Ulrike Ahlrichs. *Wissensbasierte Szenenexploration auf der Basis erlernter Analysestrategien.* PhD thesis, University Erlangen-Nürnberg, 2002.

[EGB08] Thomas Emter, Ioana Gheţa, and Jürgen Beyerer. Object Oriented Environment Model for Video Surveillance Systems. In *Future security: 3rd Security Research Conference*, 2008.

[End95] Mica Endsley. Toward a theory of situation awareness in dynamic systems. *Human Factors*, 37(1):32–64, 1995.

[Fri98] Holger Friedrich. *Interaktive Programmierung von Manipulationssequenzen.* PhD thesis, Universität Karlsruhe (TH), 1998.

[GHB08] Ioana Gheţa, Michael Heizmann, and Jürgen Beyerer. Object Oriented Environment Model for Autonomous Systems. In *SWIFT 2008 - Skövde Workshop on Information Fusion*, 2008.

[M2] SFB 588, Projekt M2 "Objektorientierte Umweltmodellierung für humanoide Roboter" http://www.ies.uni-karlsruhe.de/forschung_sfb588m2_umweltmodellierung.php.

[RDR95] Ehud Rivlin, Sven Dickinson, and Azriel Rosenfeld. Recognition by functional parts. *Computer Vision and Image Understanding*, September, 1995.

[Rie97] Markus Riepp. Wissensbasierte Parametrisierung von Operatorsequenzen. Master's thesis, Universität Karlsruhe (TH), 1997.

[Rog03] Oliver Rogalla. *Abbildung von Benutzerdemonstrationen auf variable Roboterkonfigurationen.* PhD thesis, Universität Karlsruhe (TH), 2003.